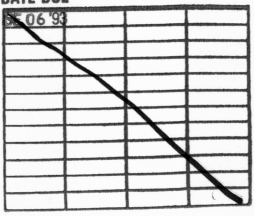

PITT SERIES IN
Policy and Institutional Studies

The SPEAKER
and the Budget

Leadership in the

Post-Reform House

of Representatives

Daniel J. Palazzolo

University of Pittsburgh Press

Pittsburgh and London

Published by the University of Pittsburgh Press, Pittsburgh, Pa. 15260
Copyright © 1992, University of Pittsburgh Press
All rights reserved
Manufactured in the United States of America
Printed on acid-free paper

Library of Congress Cataloging-in-Publication Data

Palazzolo, Daniel J., 1961–
    The speaker and the budget : leadership in the post-reform House
of Representatives / Daniel J. Palazzolo.
      p. cm. — (Pitt series in policy and institutional studies)
    Includes bibliographical references and index.
    ISBN 0-8229-3715-8
    1. United States. Congress. House—Speaker. 2. Budget—
Political aspects—United States. 3. United States—Politics and
government—1945–1989. I. Title. II. Series.
JK1411.P35   1992
353.0072'221—dc20   92-11903
                                                       CIP

A CIP catalogue record for this book is available from the British Library.
Eurospan, London

To my parents

Contents

Acknowledgments   *ix*

1. Problems and Opportunities: The Origins of
   Leadership   3

2. The Reforms of the 1970s   25

3. From Nurturer to Process Manager:
   The Speaker's Roles, 1975–80   46

4. The Speaker Under Stress: Budget Politics in 1981   90

5. Speaker O'Neill: Opposition Party Leader and
   Process Manager, 1982–86   128

6. Speaker Wright: Activist Leadership in the
   Hundredth Congress   172

7. Leadership in the Post-Reform House:
   Patterns and Paradoxes   209

Notes   225

Index   255

Acknowledgments

I am very grateful for the institutional, intellectual, and moral support I have received in researching and writing this book. The many people who have helped me deserve more thanks than I can possibly give, but permit me to share a small part of my gratitude.

This project began in 1988 as a dissertation on the Speaker's role in the budget process under the direction of Charles O. Jones at the University of Virginia. Chuck figured most prominently in the innovation and development of the dissertation and the book. I have benefited tremendously from his wisdom, time, and encouragement; we should all be so lucky to work with such a knowledgeable scholar, patient advisor, and caring friend. I am also indebted to James Ceaser, whose persistence, enthusiasm, and good humor helped me through the most difficult parts of the dissertation, and whose suggestions for key transitions in the book have survived numerous rounds of editing. Randall Strahan and John Gilmour carefully reviewed the entire manuscript and made many thoughtful suggestions that have been incorporated into the text. Several other political scientists commented on parts of the manuscript, including Martha Derthick, John Whelan, Tom Morris, Ronald Peters, and Steve Van Beek. In addition, Tom Sheehy, Oscarlyn Brown, and Pat Thiel provided timely technical assistance at various stages of the project. I also thank Bert Rockman, Frank Moone, and Kathy McLaughlin at the University of Pittsburgh Press, who facilitated the production of the book, Pipp Letsky, who edited the manuscript, and Jane Flanders, who indexed it.

Several institutions deserve special recognition for their support. The Lynde and Harry Bradley Foundation, the Everett McKinley Dirksen Congressional Center, the Robert H. Horwitz Memorial Trust, and the University of Richmond Summer Research Grant Program all contributed generous funds that allowed me to concentrate my efforts on research and writing. The Brookings Institution granted me special guest privileges, including a desk and a telephone, while I was in Washington. And I am obliged to the members of Congress and staff personnel who took time to speak with me during my stay at Brookings and thereafter.

Finally, I wish to convey the deepest appreciation to my family. Special thanks goes to Jennifer, who has been with me every step of the way, first as my girlfriend, then as my fiance, and now as my wife. Her computer expertise and editorial skill are surpassed only by her love and patience. Above all, I wish to acknowledge the contribution of my parents. While others have educated me in the ways of researching and writing, they have taught me the values that I apply to my life and work. I owe them the dedication of my first book and much, much more.

Of course, the time, effort, resources, and thoughtful contributions of others have only enhanced the quality of this book. I am responsible for any remaining errors, omissions, or shortcomings.

The SPEAKER
and the Budget

1

Problems and Opportunities:

The Origins of Leadership

One can hardly understate the importance of budget policy in congressional politics. The federal budget has occupied center stage in public policy-making since the extensive reforms passed by Congress in the 1970s. Meanwhile, despite Congress's reputation as a "leaderless" institution, leadership in the House of Representatives became more centralized than at any time since the revolt against Speaker Cannon in 1910.[1] The Speaker of the House, in particular, emerged as a more active and central player in congressional politics. These developments, taken together, should stir our curiosity beyond the popular belief that Congress is "leaderless." For surely congressional leaders serve important functions, and it is important to consider more systematically how those functions have been affected by budget politics, and what role leadership plays in the budget process.

The budget process, established by the Congressional Budget and Impoundment Control Act of 1974 (Budget Act) and reformed by the Balanced Budget and Deficit Control Act of 1985 (Gramm-Rudman-Hollings [GRH]), has been at once a major institutional development and a major source of problems for Congress. The process was designed to improve congressional policy-making and strengthen Congress's position vis-à-vis the president. The Budget Act gave Congress the potential to generate its own budgetary information, coordinate spending and revenue bills, and establish its own fiscal policy and national priorities.

Yet, despite these gains, critics charge that the process has been riddled with problems. The budget process has failed to control federal spending and coordinate a fragmented committee system; Congress regularly misses procedural deadlines; omnibus appropriations bills are passed at the end of the session and contain extraneous riders to serve the particular interests of members; the process seems forever deadlocked as leaders of the two parties quarrel over national priorities; and, we are told, members lack the political will necessary to reduce the massive federal deficit.[2]

What have the potential of the Budget Act and the problems associated with the budget process meant for congressional leadership? The criticisms we hear about the malfunctions of the budget process, combined with expectations that Congress should formulate and enforce its own budget, have prompted the Speaker to play a critical role in budget decisions. The Speaker's rise in the post-reform House is based on the premise that leadership entails responding to institutional and party-related problems and taking advantage of opportunities to advance party objectives. Problems and opportunities in budget policy-making create demands on the House and the majority party and facilitate roles that only the Speaker can perform by virtue of his position as leader of the House and of the majority party.

Thus the Speaker's role in the budget process during the post-reform era is a story of how the House adapted, and how its principal leader responded, to the growing pains of a representative institution attempting to make budget policy. The story involves at least three central questions. First, what institutional, political, and policy-related conditions create the problems and opportunities in budget-making that require the Speaker's attention? Second, what roles has the Speaker played in response to those problems and opportunities? Finally, how have different Speakers performed those roles? In this chapter I begin consideration of these questions by introducing the theoretical premises and critical components of this study.

Congressional Leadership Reconsidered

I begin with three central premises about congressional leadership that distinguish this study from others. The first premise is that leadership is a dynamic process: leadership roles change according to the problems or opportunities of the day. To be sure, the Speaker is always involved in the traditional tasks of party leadership—maintaining party harmony and building coalitions.[3] But the Speaker's roles are not restricted to those two functions, nor are they always the most important functions he performs. In the early part of the post-reform period the Speaker concentrated mostly on coalition-building and party-maintenance tasks. As the period progressed, however, he began to take on policy-oriented functions: helping to define the majority party's national priorities, for example, and negotiating settlements with the president and Senate leaders of the opposite party. Understanding congressional leadership demands a description of how, and an explanation of why, the Speaker's functions change over time.

The second premise is that explaining leadership involves assessing the effects of both the context (the conditions that shape House politics) and the individual qualities of leaders. The question of whether leadership style is a function of conditions or of individual factors is a source of debate in many studies of congressional leadership. At one extreme, journalists and politicians describe politics in general—and leadership in particular—in terms of personalities.[4] Their observations are based mostly on anecdotes and first-hand experiences or information. The strengths of these studies rest on fascinating inside accounts of personal relationships and behind-the-scenes politicking. But these studies are criticized for neglecting the broader political, institutional, and policy-agenda factors that structure political behavior. These writers might be accused of suffering from a sort of Potomac syndrome—the closer one gets to Washington, the more personalities seem to matter in explaining how politics works.

At the other end of the spectrum, some political scientists stress the importance of contextual factors, to the neglect of personal variables.[5] The contextualist view argues that leadership is shaped by conditions largely beyond a leader's control. Thus, leaders have very little autonomy to develop their own styles or pursue their own goals. This view comes closest to advancing the objectives of behavioral political science. Ideally, political scientists seek to conceptualize and measure variables as precisely as possible, develop models that identify relationships between variables, and verify relationships with the hope of discovering generalizations that might help to explain or predict political behavior. Yet, rigorous as the approach might be, a purely contextualist analysis of leadership ignores relevant individual qualities by judging them to be either immeasurable or unimportant.[6]

Between these two perspectives are political science studies of leadership that combine conditions with individual variables.[7] These studies incorporate a wide array of factors, some of which can be measured more precisely than others. They assume that leadership is too complex to be explained solely in terms of either contextual or individual variables. Ronald Peters makes this case in his study of the speakership in historical perspective. "An approach to interpreting the speakership that leans wholly on institutional factors will fail to grasp the complex interplay of institutional alignments, policy positions, and personal factors involved in the process of governance."[8]

I do not pretend this book will settle the debate over which factors—contextual or individual—explain "more" or "less" about leadership style, but I hope this discussion will be a valuable contribution. My study concurs most with those that stress the importance of both individual and contextual factors. But it elaborates on that perspective by identifying the individual factors important to leadership style and specifying how those individual factors interact with contextual variables.

Conditions structure problems and opportunities, establish the limitations to congressional leadership, generally define the Speaker's roles in the budget process, and help to explain why the Speaker has emerged as a more powerful leader in the post-reform House. But once leadership roles are defined in terms of the functions the Speaker is expected to execute, both conditions and individual factors affect how different Speakers play their roles. Thus, leaders have more discretion in developing leadership style than the purely contextualist view would permit. We should seek to identify both the conditions under which the Speaker's roles change and the individual factors that affect how those roles are performed.

The third premise I develop here is that, although congressional leaders must respond to the political goals and policy preferences of individual members, leadership is an interactive process, involving the preferences of both leaders and followers. Consistent with the notion that conditions determine leadership style, scholars have argued that leaders must be responsive to the goals of individual members.[9] Leadership in the House is particularly sensitive to member goals and expectations, since national parties are weak, members are generally autonomous, and leaders lack power to coerce members to comply with their wishes.

Yet an approach that focuses only on member preferences fails to account for the preferences of leaders and the variety of relationships that might occur between leaders and members. There are at least four scenarios in which the relationship between a leader and members cannot be defined solely in terms of member expectations. First, a leader may express disagreement with the members' preferences but set personal preferences aside to serve a broader institutional or party role.[10] Second, member preferences may be unclear, in which case the leader lacks sufficient information to respond to members. Third, a leader defines preferences ahead of members and then attempts to build support for them. Fourth, the leader deliberately ignores the preferences of members, and the members respond by withdrawing support from the leader. If the leader continues to ignore the members, they might eventually enact reforms to limit the leader's powers.[11]

Though this study supports the proposition that leaders generally respond to member expectations, the four scenarios outlined above are also present. As the book develops, I shall describe each case and elaborate on the implications for the Speaker's role in the budget process. For now I propose that, although any congressional leader must surely be responsive to member expectations, the Speaker's preferences should also be considered, for the relationships between leaders and members are too varied and complex to be defined solely in terms of the members' goals.

The Speaker and the Budget Process

With these three guiding premises in mind, we may begin to explore how the Speaker's roles in the budget process developed and how they are performed. Here four key elements need to be introduced: (1) the basic stages of the budget process, (2) the Speaker's formal position in the House, (3) the conditions under which problems and opportunities emerge, and (4) the different qualities of individual leaders. Let me briefly define each of these factors and consider their relationships with each other.

THE BUDGET PROCESS. A more comprehensive discussion of the formal budget process and how it came into being is reserved for the next chapter. For now, I simply aim to identify the basic aspects of the process so we might consider some problems and opportunities the Speaker is expected to address.

Prior to the Budget Act of 1974, budgeting was primarily an executive task. The Budget and Accounting Act of 1921 gave the president the resources to draft the federal budget, through which he could develop a fiscal policy and define national priorities. Congress retained its constitutional prerogative to authorize and appropriate funds and collect revenues. But spending and revenue bills were dealt with individually in the authorization, appropriations, and revenue committees. Congress lacked the formal procedures and institutional arrangements to account for spending, revenue, and deficit or surplus totals, to establish its own budget priorities, and to coordinate separate policy decisions into a coherent budget plan. One attempt was made to strengthen Congress's budget-making capacity prior to the Budget Act of 1974. The Legislative Reorganization Act of 1946 created a Joint Committee on the Budget consisting of members from the House Ways and Means Committee and the Senate Finance Committee, which was intended to construct a budget to rival that of the president. But this experiment failed after only two years.[12]

The Budget Act of 1974 attempted to address these shortcomings by allowing Congress to draft, approve, and enforce its own annual budget guidelines. The act created two budget committees (one in each chamber), the Congressional Budget Office (CBO) to provide information and analysis for the congressional budget, and a timetable for enacting budget decisions (see table 1). The budget committee in each chamber is responsible for drafting a first budget resolution (which sets targets for total budget outlays, total budget authority, federal revenue, and federal debt) and for recommending spending estimates for program functions (which essentially represent budget priorities).[13]

Once enacted by both chambers, the first budget resolution sets the guidelines for legislative action on separate authorization, appropriations, and tax bills. Originally, by September 15 Congress was required to pass a second resolution, which substituted ceilings in place of the targets adopted by the first resolution. Reconciliation procedures could be implemented if the separate spending and revenue decisions enacted by Congress did not coincide with the aggregate ceilings of the second budget resolution (total outlays, revenues, and the deficit).[14] Using reconciliation, the House votes to instruct certain committees to cut spending or raise revenues in order to meet the ceilings of the second budget resolution.

Today the formal budget process rarely works as it was designed under the Budget Act of 1974. In fact, new procedures for budget-making have been introduced almost every year since 1980.[15] One of the most prominent innovations is the use of reconciliation along with the first resolution. Instead of applying reconciliation procedures to the second budget resolution, as specified by the Budget Act, Congress has used reconciliation with the first resolution in order to control entitlement spending. Another major development was the Gramm-Rudman-Hollings Deficit Reduction Law (GRH), which revised the Budget Act's timetable (see table 1) and created a six-year schedule of annual deficit ceilings, which was originally designed to balance the budget by fiscal year 1991. (GRH itself was revised in 1986 and 1987.) A sequestration process was also included to enforce the deficit ceilings. With sequestration, automatic cuts are levied if the budget deficit exceeds the statutory deficit ceilings set by GRH for any given fiscal year. I will assess the effects of these changes, and others, as I define the Speaker's roles in the budget process, later in this chapter, and as I develop those roles throughout the book.

THE SPEAKER OF THE HOUSE. The Speaker of the House is a multifaceted leadership position that is charged with important institutional and party-related functions and endowed with numerous resources. Throughout history, the Speaker has held three formal positions in the House: presiding officer, leader of the majority party, and elected representative of a House district.[16]

For each of these positions the Speaker is elected by, and therefore represents, a different constituency. As presiding officer, the Speaker represents the House and attempts to facilitate the legislative process and conduct parliamentary procedures in a fair, impartial, and reasonably efficient manner. The Speaker's formal legislative powers and his relationship with the Rules Committee are critical to serving these ends. As

TABLE 1

Timetable for the 1974 Budget Act and Revised by the Gramm-Rudman-Hollings (GRH) Law

Action	Budget Act	GRH Law
President submits budget	End of January	First Monday after Jan. 3
Congressional Budget Office (CBO) reports to budget committees	April 1	Feb. 15
Committees report to the HBC	March 15	Feb. 25
Congress approves first resolution	May 15	April 15
Congress approves second resolution	Sept. 15	—
Congress completes reconciliation	Sept. 25	June 15
CBO and Office of Management and Budget (OMB) analyze economic indicators and laws affecting spending and revenue	—	Aug. 15
CBO and OMB report to General Accounting Office (GAO) on deficit and automatic cuts for sequester order	—	Aug. 20
GAO forwards deficit and sequester order to president	—	Aug. 25
President issues sequester order	—	Sept. 1
Sequester order takes effect	—	Oct. 1
Fiscal year begins	Oct. 1	Oct. 1
CBO and OMB issue revised reports to reflect congressional action	—	Oct. 5
GAO issues revised report to president	—	Oct. 10
Final sequester order based on revised report comes into effect	—	Oct. 15
GAO issues compliance report on sequester order	—	Nov. 15

Source: Compiled by author from Elizabeth Wehr, "Congress Enacts Far-reaching Budget Measure," *Congressional Quarterly Weekly Report*, December 14, 1985, p. 2608.

representative, the Speaker responds to his constituents' needs and expresses his own preferences in deliberations over national priorities.

As leader of the House majority party, the Speaker helps to build party coalitions, mediate intra-party conflict, collect and distribute information, and advance the president's legislative priorities if the president is of the same party. If the president is of the opposite party, the Speaker is the most prominent national leader of his party.[17] In this situation, the Speaker represents and protects the interests of party members and promotes the party's legislative agenda. The party whip system, the Steering and Policy Committee, and staff personnel help the Speaker perform party-related tasks.

Although the Speaker has always been an important political and organizational leader in the House, his power has generally been modest except for a brief period at the turn of the twentieth century. From about 1890 to 1910, the "czar" Speakers exercised strong, centralized party leadership: they wielded almost exclusive power over committee appointments, floor deliberation, and scheduling legislation. But the reign of the czars ended in 1910 when a group of progressive Republicans coalesced with the Democratic minority party to reduce Speaker Joe Cannon's powers.[18] The Speaker was removed from the Rules Committee; the committee was enlarged from five to fifteen members; and Rules Committee assignments were decided by a majority vote of the House rather than appointed by the Speaker.

When the Democrats won a majority in the 1910 elections, they continued to strip the Speaker's powers. They transferred power over committee appointments from the Speaker to the newly created Committee on Committees, which was comprised of Democrats on the Ways and Means Committee. For a brief period, party government persisted with the Democrats' policy aims decided by a disciplined party caucus.[19] Under this system, the centralized rule exercised by the czar Speakers was replaced by "collegial" leadership, or leadership by "commission"—a group of party leaders (the Speaker, floor leader, chairman of the Rules Committee, chairman of the Appropriations Committee, and chairman and members of the Ways and Means Committee), working together to draft a legislative program and guide it through the House.[20]

By 1917, government by party caucus gave way to a long period of entrenched committee government, which lasted at least until the reform of the Rules Committee in 1961. During this period, policy formulation was dispersed throughout a fragmented committee system, and powerful committee chairmen held sway over their particular policy areas. In contrast with the Republican Speakers at the turn of the century, who ruled through discipline and coercion, Speakers of the strong-committee era relied mostly on persuasion. One finds innumerable cases of Speakers meeting informally with committee chairmen to compromise, bargain, and discuss legislative strategy. But the Speaker played almost no part in formulating the details of legislation. With regard to party leadership, the Speaker acted mostly as a middleman who maintained a neutral ideological position so as to mediate differences between members.[21] Overall, the Speaker dealt mostly with procedural tasks, floor management, and coalition building.

How and why did this portrait of the pre-reform Speaker change in the post-reform era? As noted in the following chapter, the reform movement brought renewed interest in strengthening the Speaker's powers. He was given the authority to refer bills to more than one committee (so-called multiple referral) and to nominate appointees to the Rules Committee, and he was made chairman of the newly created Steering and Policy Committee. In order to assess the effects of these formal powers on the Speaker's role in the budget process, we need to account for the conditions that shaped the post-reform era and the individuals who occupied the Speaker's office.

CONTEXTUAL AND INDIVIDUAL FACTORS. As noted above, this study combines contextual and individual factors to explain the development and performance of the Speaker's leadership roles in the post-reform House. It is important, first of all, to distinguish between policy conditions, political conditions, and institutional conditions. Conditions should also be classified as fluid or stable, to indicate which conditions induce

changes in the Speaker's role and which conditions remain relatively constant over time (see table 2). More precisely, stable
conditions are the semi-permanent arrangements that constitute the enduring limitations to House leadership. These limitations are loosened only by constitutional amendment, major
institutional reform, or a significant shift in the policy agenda.
Thus, the constitutional design of representation and associated norms encourage members to address their constituents'
needs—an activity that might limit the Speaker's ability to
build and maintain party unity. Fluid conditions are of shorter
duration: they refer to elements that can change from one Congress to the next, or even from one year to the next.

In addition to conditions, three individual factors improve
our assessment of leadership: the Speaker's policy expertise,

TABLE 2
Fluid and Stable Political, Policy, and Institutional Conditions

Political Conditions	
Fluid	*Stable*
Partisan control of Congress and the presidency	Representation norm
Majority party unity	Weak parties
Minority party unity	
Presidential leadership and popularity	

Policy Conditions	
Fluid	*Stable*
State of the economy	Incremental policy change
Size of deficit	
National priorities	

Institutional Conditions	
Fluid	*Stable*
Budgetary procedures	Bicameralism
Reconciliation	President's formal powers
	Separation of powers
	Single-member districts
	Fragmented committee system

his conception of leadership, and his policy preferences. Policy expertise reflects a leader's familiarity with budget policy-making and determines the extent to which a Speaker is involved in policy-related tasks. Leaders with policy expertise are more inclined to manage policy-related tasks personally, while leaders with limited expertise need to delegate tasks to other members or to staff personnel. Conception of leadership is a leader's own view of how to perform his roles, how the powers of the Speaker's office should be used, and for what purposes. Policy preferences constitute the leader's budget priorities. Policy preferences are important to consider in assessing the Speaker's relationships with other actors in performing policy-oriented tasks.[22]

Thus the development and the performance of leadership roles are best explained within a framework that allows for the interaction between stable conditions (which define limitations to leadership), fluid conditions (which produce short-term problems and opportunities for leadership and create changes in the Speaker's roles), and individual qualities. A principal aim of this study is to explain how the Speaker's roles reflect the problems and opportunities defined by varying conditions, and how the qualities of different Speakers affect the manner in which those roles are performed.

The Speaker's Multiple Roles

Now that we have clarified the theoretical premises and basic concepts of this study, we can apply them directly to the Speaker's roles in the budget process. The first step is to describe the Speaker's multiple roles. What have been the Speaker's roles in the budget process? What have been the functions associated with each role? How do the Speaker's roles in the budget process correspond with his roles of presiding officer and party leader? Relying on the framework of conditions set out in table 2, a second objective is to explain how those roles develop over time. Under what conditions do the Speaker's

roles change? How are those roles limited by enduring constraints on leadership? A third objective is to explore the relationships between roles. Under what conditions are the roles
compatible or in conflict with each other? How does the
Speaker resolve conflicts between roles? Finally, we need to
address the question of how leadership style is shaped by
conditions and individual qualities. Let us begin by defining
the Speaker's roles and explaining how they have changed
over time.

The Speaker has played one or more of three constructive
roles in response to problems and opportunities in the budget
process: nurturer, process manager, and opposition party
leader. Each role is characterized by certain leadership functions or tasks, which correspond with the particular problems
or opportunities posed by prevailing conditions. The nurturer
role was born immediately on the passage of the Budget Act,
when the House needed a recognizable leader to incorporate
the new budget process into the legislative calendar without
disrupting existing authorization and appropriations processes.
Speaker Carl Albert (D-Okla.) performed several tasks charac-
teristic of the nurturer role: he explained the new budget procedures to participants in the process, organized the committees for action, and moderated members' fears about
the uncertain potential of the Budget Act. These functions
coincided primarily with Albert's responsibilities as presiding
officer.

Before long, however, intra-party conflicts over budget priorities and the spending constraints posed by large deficits
demanded that the Speaker perform a more critical role in the
budget process. The Speaker emerged as a process manager—
a role played by Speakers Tip O'Neill (D-Mass.) and Jim
Wright (D-Texas). In this capacity, the Speaker reconciled
intra-party differences over budget priorities and mediated the
procedural and policy disputes that occurred as the House
tried to control federal spending. During the late 1970s the
House struggled to pass budget resolutions, and its capacity
to meet the basic guidelines of the Budget Act was called

into question. The Speaker actively pursued coalition-building strategies to pass first budget resolutions, partly as an extension of his role as party leader and partly as an effort to maintain the budget process. Thus, the Speaker's role as process manager reflected his general responsibilities as both presiding officer and party leader. For if the House failed to pass a first budget resolution each year, it would mean the party had failed to agree on a set of priorities and the House had failed in its attempt to make budget policy.

The Speaker's role as process manager also involves mediating conflicts between committees over policy jurisdictions (so-called turf battles). For example, the Appropriations Committee often challenges the Budget Committee's authority to recommend spending levels for specific programs, as it attempts to estimate total amounts for budget functions in the first budget resolution. In other cases, spending cuts that come with reconciliation produce jurisdictional conflicts, either between the House membership and the authorization committees or between the committees themselves. The Speaker tries to resolve these tensions in order to keep the process moving along.

With the period of divided government, large deficits, and intense partisanship during the 1980s, the Speaker's role expanded to include more than managerial tasks. Under these conditions, the Democratic Speakers also served as opposition party leaders. House Democrats needed the Speaker to protect and advance their interests, articulate the priorities of the party, and negotiate budget agreements with Senate leaders and the president. Because of his unique position as opposition party leader during periods of divided government, the Speaker is called upon to respond to these needs.

RELATIONSHIPS BETWEEN ROLES. It is important to describe how the Speaker's roles in the budget process changed over time, and also to describe the relationships between different roles. The Speaker's performance in any role depends in part on how his roles correspond with one another and the extent to which a Speaker's roles concur with his preferences. The Speaker essentially represents three different constituencies (the House, the majority party, and his district), and his roles in the budget process largely stem from his responsibilities as leader of the House and the majority party. Speakers also have their own policy preferences, which may stem from constituency interests or a Speaker's vision of what the party's priorities should be. As a consequence of multiple commitments, the Speaker is often confronted with role conflicts: when one role conflicts with another, or when the Speaker is expected to carry out a role that conflicts with his personal preferences.[23] Role conflicts occur because, in addition to trying to advance his own preferences, the Speaker is often expected to represent the diverse preferences of his various constituents—the House, the majority party, and his district.

Role conflicts can take a variety of forms, but they leave the Speaker to reconcile the tension between his personal preferences and the functions he is expected to perform in the interests of the House or his party. It is important to identify the conditions under which role conflicts occur, which role takes precedence for the Speaker, and the consequences for the budget process. Let me give a broad overview of what to expect, as we consider the relationships between the Speaker's roles in the budget process.

As the post-reform period developed and the Speaker's roles expanded, role conflicts became more complicated. Up until the Reagan presidency, the Speaker's roles hardly conflicted with each other. The Speaker's position as party leader coincided with the roles of nurturer and process manager. Helping to build coalitions to pass budget resolutions, for example, was favorable to the party and the maintenance of the budget process. Speaker O'Neill's only role conflicts occurred when he disagreed with the policy preferences endorsed by a majority of House Democrats. But the conflicts were not difficult to resolve: once President Carter and a majority of House Democrats agreed upon a set of budget priorities, Speaker O'Neill had to go along.

The most difficult role conflicts occurred during the Reagan presidency, when the Speaker emerged as the opposition leader for the Democrats. During this period, the Speaker's role as process manager often conflicted with the role of party leader. In the most acute case, Speaker O'Neill was expected to help carry out reconciliation instructions approved by a House coalition of Republicans and conservative Democrats that would cut spending for many traditional Democratic programs. Despite his obligation to carry out the will of the House to enforce reconciliation, O'Neill wished to salvage those Democratic programs and was joined by a majority of his party who voted against the spending cuts. In numerous other cases throughout the remainder of Reagan's presidency, the Speaker had to choose between protecting his party's interests and facilitating the budget process. Though the Speaker often tried to reconcile the conflicts between process and policy interests, he normally subordinated formal procedures to the party's policy objectives.

One of the most profound effects of the conflicts between the roles of process manager and opposition party leader is the primacy of partisan and policy interests over the maintenance of an orderly process. As the budget process incurred problems the Speaker was called upon to deal with, he was also expected by House Democrats to ignore the stability of formal and impartial procedures in favor of the party's interests. When confronted with a conflict between the roles of process manager and opposition party leader, both O'Neill and Wright realized their commitment to the Democratic party over and above the maintenance of an orderly process.

Opportunities for Policy Leadership

As the post-reform period developed in the 1980s, opportunities emerged for the Speaker to participate in defining the majority party's budget priorities. These opportunities are partly rooted in the procedural changes enacted by the Budget Act,

but they stem mostly from short-term political and policy-related conditions. Once the conditions for policy leadership are favorable, individual qualities affect a Speaker's response to those conditions. An activist leader with policy expertise is most likely to take advantage of opportunities to define the party's priorities. Yet, all Speakers are restricted by enduring constraints on policy leadership in the House. Leadership roles and styles are best understood through complex relationships in which individual factors merge with both stable and fluid conditions.

The advent of a first budget resolution, in combination with the new Steering and Policy Committee, ostensibly provided the Speaker with the opportunity and the resources to help initiate the majority party's budget priorities. Prior to the passage of the Budget Act, the president and committee chairmen were largely responsible for setting the policy agenda. But the first budget resolution is a planning instrument, a nonbinding statement of priorities and fiscal policy, that provided at least a potential vehicle for leaders to establish their party's priorities. As my next chapter illustrates, during the debate over the Budget Act several members observed that the budget resolution invited the Speaker to recommend policy priorities on behalf of the majority party.

Yet, while the Budget Act offered the Speaker the potential to advance party priorities, it also threatened the existing norms of policy deliberation and the decentralized power structure in the House. Any efforts to use the first budget resolution as an instrument for policy leadership would have to be reconciled with traditional institutional arrangements. The very nature of budgeting clashed with the existing committee system. As Allen Schick has pointed out, budgeting is almost naturally an integrative process: "[Budgeting involves] the pulling together of disparate interests and perspectives in a reasonably comprehensive and consistent decisional process. Budgeting demands attention to the relationship of the parts and the whole, to linkage of tax and spending policies, as well as priorities accorded the competing claims for public resources."[24]

The prevailing institutional characteristics of the House tend toward fragmentation, the very opposite of integration. Randall Ripley finds that "integration is characterized by a centralized organization and by the potential (although not the certainty) for planned coherence between individual policies," while fragmentation implies decentralized organization and a "lack of planned coherence (and only limited random coherence) between individual policies."[25] Furthermore, the House is essentially a representative body, and most of the other reforms passed during the 1970s further decentralized the committee system and expanded member participation. Hence, while budgeting is an integrative process, these disintegrative forces were likely to limit the Speaker's capacity to use the budget resolution to advance the party's policy objectives.

Nevertheless, alterations in short-term conditions can offset the centrifugal tendencies of congressional policy-making and mitigate the constraints on policy leadership. In fact, favorable conditions for policy leadership did emerge during the 1980s. Divided government made the Speaker the leading member of the opposition party. High levels of party unity reflected more homogenous preferences among House Democrats and improved the Speaker's ability to build support for the budget priorities recommended by the Budget Committee.[26] Finally, increases in the use of omnibus bills and a contracted policy agenda stemming from large deficits centralized decision-making power in the Speaker's hands.

How did the Speaker respond to conditions that enhanced opportunities for policy leadership? Conditions not only define opportunities for leadership but place constraints on the variety of leadership styles a Speaker can adopt. We should not expect the leadership styles of post-reform Speakers to differ radically, for in important ways the periods in which they led were defined by similar circumstances. The post-reform Speakers accommodated an open House in which power is distributed more equally among the membership than ever before and members expect to participate actively in the legislative process.[27] Yet within this broader context, fluid or short-term conditions offer more or less latitude for individual Speakers to pursue different styles. And even within the constraints posed by similar short-term conditions, different individual qualities also affect leadership style.

The importance of the individual leaders' different qualities is evident in the contrasting styles of O'Neill and Wright in the role of opposition party leader during the 1980s. O'Neill acted as a party spokesman: he delegated tasks to staff personnel, solicited opinions on budget priorities from majority party members, protected traditional party programs from pressure to reduce the deficit, and projected a general partisan philosophy of governing. Wright performed the role of opposition party leader as a policy activist: he worked directly with the Budget Committee, personally defined budget priorities prior to consulting with party members, initiated specific proposals, and aggressively pursued the enactment of those proposals. These differences cannot be explained by conditions alone. Different levels of policy expertise and different conceptions of leadership affected the way these two Speakers performed the same role.

Even at the height of Wright's speakership, however, representative norms and the fragmented power of the House loomed in the background of centralized policy leadership. While members of a unified majority party respect the Speaker's budget priorities, they seldom give him carte blanche privileges to direct the party. If a Speaker seeks to formulate budgetary priorities, he normally either competes or bargains with other members of the party, particularly those on the Budget Committee. Furthermore, the leader's initiatives must survive pressures from outside the House. As a testimony to the limitations to activist leadership in the House, we shall see that even Speaker Wright found it difficult to maintain support for his priorities as the budget resolution progressed beyond the House stages of the budget process. Thus, although fluid conditions and different qualities in the leader may enhance prospects for policy leadership, the enduring political and institutional demands of representation and lawmaking place limitations on activist policy leadership.

Summary

In summary, this book considers how and why the Speaker's role in the congressional budget process has evolved over time. It aims to identify the conditions under which the Speaker's role grew from supportive functions (entailing mostly procedural and mediating tasks within the House) to a wider role that incorporates policy-oriented tasks both inside and outside the House. This transformation included complex relationships between the Speaker and the constituencies that elected him, as well as conflicts among the Speaker's multiple roles. My analysis includes comprehensive descriptions of budget policy-making and assesses the effects of institutional, political, and policy-related factors on congressional leadership style. In so doing, I attempt to capture the interaction between changes in contextual variables and the individual qualities of particular Speakers who addressed the problems and opportunities associated with budgetary politics.

The book is organized chronologically. Chapter 2 concentrates on the institutional context of the post-reform era by surveying the major reforms of the 1970s. I pay particular attention to those aspects of budgetary reform that involve the Speaker. The remainder of the study consists of descriptive analyses of the Speaker's role since the reforms, and I rely on numerous sources: journal and newspaper accounts of events, government documents, data on roll call voting and budget figures, and interviews with members of Congress and staff personnel.[28] Chapter 3 traces the evolution of the Speaker's role from nurturer to process manager during the period from 1975 to 1980. Chapter 4 treats the critical first year of the Reagan administration (1981) when Reagan enacted his economic policy mandate by winning four major budget battles. Chapter 5 addresses Speaker O'Neill's roles as process manager and opposition party leader during the remainder of his speakership, from 1982 to 1986. In Chapter 6, I consider Speaker Wright's activist approach to the Speaker's roles of process manager and opposition party leader. Chapter 7 draws conclusions from the central findings of the book and assesses its contribution to the study of congressional leadership.

2

The Reforms of the 1970s

T*he reforms* of the 1970s dramatically altered the character of power relations in the House. The reform period spread over five years and affected four general areas: the committee system, campaign finance, war powers, and the budget process.[1] Not all of the changes we detect today were always clearly intended. To be sure, some reforms were clear and straightforward, such as those aimed at reducing the power of committee chairmen and enhancing member participation in the legislative process. But other reforms, including the Budget Act, were necessarily vague. Any clear intentions for the new budget process were obscured by the practical aim of accommodating enough interests to pass a budget reform bill. Once the chore of reconciling various political interests and ideological views was complete, no one could be certain of what budget reform would accomplish, or how the budget process would operate in practice.

Though the House had already approved several changes that broadened the Speaker's powers, the Speaker's role in the budget process was not defined by the Budget Act. During the debate over the Budget Act, several members suggested the Speaker should play a more authoritative role in the budget process. But these proposals gave the Speaker more authority than most members were willing to permit. Thus, the Speaker's role was also caught in the political tides of give-and-take. Nevertheless, the politics of the reform period are important: they convey the ambiguous intentions of the Budget Act, they specify the key elements of the formal budget process, and they create the institutional context from which the Speaker's roles eventually emerged.

Congressional Reform

Years of criticism about the inefficiency of Congress indicate that improvements were desperately needed in the prevailing institutional norms and organizational structure of the House. Conditions were poorly suited for congressional leaders to facilitate the two basic functions of a representative body, what Charles O. Jones refers to as "expression" and "integration."[2] Leaders could neither insure all members sufficient opportunities to express their opinions, nor integrate the fragmented parts of the legislature efficiently enough to pass timely solutions to public problems. Powerful committee chairmen ruled over their particular policy areas, frustrating the efforts of party leaders to advance legislation and discouraging junior members, especially liberal Democrats, from meaningful participation in policy deliberations.

Ultimately, resistance to change gave way to external pressures on the institution and internal demands from its members.[3] Externally, the Vietnam war and the Watergate scandal symbolized the already widely recognized imbalance of power between an imperial president and an impotent Congress. Internally, an emerging group of younger liberal members protested against the old guard (the powerful, mostly conservative chairmen) who benefited from the entrenched committee structure and the informal norms of apprenticeship and seniority.

Consequently, the reforms sought to improve conditions for expression and integration, but most of all they were intended to improve expression, through changes that enhanced opportunities for members to participate in the legislative process.

The Legislative Reorganization Act of 1970, for example, opened committee proceedings to the public and instituted the recorded teller vote, thus encouraging members to participate more often in floor debate and roll call voting.[4] Meanwhile, the Democratic caucus adopted many of the Hansen Committee proposals, thus taking aim at the seniority rule for committee assignments and restructuring the committee system. These reforms allowed full caucus voting on committee chair nominations; distributed subcommittee chair positions to more members; instituted the subcommittee bill of rights, which made subcommittees more independent of their full committees; expanded the Ways and Means Committee from twenty-five to thirty-seven members; checked the power of the Rules Committee to issue closed rules limiting floor amendments; and opened conference committee deliberations to the public. These reforms made Congress a more open and democratic institution: they allowed wider public access to institutional proceedings, enabled more members to participate in the policy process, and reduced the authority of committee chairmen.

While reforms designed to enhance expression sought to make Congress more responsive, reforms aimed at integration intended to make Congress a more responsible legislative body. The reforms attempted to restore congressional capacity to legislate more efficiently and redress the imbalance of power with the president. As Jones points out, "making laws requires drawing conclusions. Thus, integrative mechanisms, too, are required to meet the leadership condition."[5] Reforms aimed toward integration included enhancing the majority party's ability to act collectively, increasing the Speaker's powers, and establishing a formal budget process.

In 1973, House Democrats created a twenty-four-member Steering and Policy Committee for the purposes of organizing the majority party and advancing the party's legislative priorities. The Speaker was made chairman of the committee, which also consisted of the majority leader, the Democratic caucus chairman, twelve caucus-elected members representing geographic regions, and nine members appointed by the

Speaker. The following year, the Democratic caucus transferred the power to nominate members for committee appointments from the Committee on Committees to the Steering
and Policy Committee. This reform was both an effort to
strengthen the party apparatus and an attempt to weaken the
powerful Ways and Means Committee. Traditionally, Ways and
Means members occupied the Committee on Committees and
handled committee appointments when it came time to organize the party for each Congress. The Speaker was also granted
various powers: to nominate members to the Rules Committee;
to set time limits on committees for considering legislation; and
to refer bills to more than one committee, so-called multiple
referral.[6]

These reforms apparently indicated a resurgence of the
speakership, giving the Speaker more tools to organize the majority party and coordinate the legislative process. The Speaker's formal powers in the post-reform period would be more
extensive than at any time since the revolt on Speaker Cannon
in 1910. He would have a formal hand in committee assignments—a power potentially useful for sanctioning disloyal
party members. The Speaker's increased leverage over the
Rules Committee seemed to hark back to days when powerful
Speakers dictated the congressional policy process with direct
control of scheduling and rules for floor debate.

Yet these procedural changes must be viewed in the broader
context of the reform period. The Speaker's new powers were
counteracted by the many changes that democratized the
House. Thus, even though the Speaker was chairman of
the Steering and Policy Committee, he could not make committee assignments without the input of an independent and
expressive group of members representing diverse preferences.
In their study of Democratic committee assignments in the
post-reform era until 1980, Steven S. Smith and Bruce A. Ray
found that, "despite the opportunities for direct intervention by
the Speaker, the size of the Steering and Policy Committee
makes it difficult to control."[7] Since the results of Smith and
Ray's study were published, the Speaker's influence on the

Steering and Policy Committee appears to have become more formidable. But in the immediate aftermath of the reforms, the Speaker's formal powers of appointment were restrained by conditions that encouraged widespread member participation. The Speaker's capacity to exercise control over the Rules Committee did not compare with the powerful Speakers at the turn of the century. Unlike the czar speakers the post-reform Speaker would not chair the Rules Committee, and his nominees to Rules would be subject to approval by the Democratic caucus. Furthermore, the Rules Committee itself was a target of reform, as the House limited its discretion over crafting rules for floor debate.

Therefore, the effects of the Speaker's new organizational powers were uncertain. In one sense, reforms provided the Speaker with only "front end power"; the changes "by no means guarantee either organizational or policy integration unless party leaders are extraordinarily prescient in their appointments or referrals."[8] The Speaker's ability to lead, with these modest powers, was compounded by the inherent tension between reforms that served the aims of integration and reforms that facilitated expression. At the most, the Speaker's enhanced position increased his discretion and provided some authority to counteract the participatory reforms passed by the House. At the least, these powers were merely symbolic, giving the Speaker little real capacity to integrate a fragmented policy process. How far these new powers improved the Speaker's ability to lead the majority party would depend ultimately on political and policy-related conditions and on the Speaker's individual qualities.

Budgeting before the Budget Act

The Budget Act was both an attempt to improve the integrative capacity of lawmaking within Congress and to strengthen Congress's position in relation to the president. At least since the passage of the Budget and Accounting Act of 1921, Congress had shared responsibility for the budget with the president, though the president assumed the leading role. The president submitted a budget to Congress, where it was divided up among the various authorization, appropriations, and tax committees. Aaron Wildavsky has described a stable budget process guided by established rules and informal norms.[9] The process was executed by government agencies and congressional committee experts who played clearly defined roles and who were guided by a concept called "fair shares." The agencies systematically submitted inflated program estimates to the Bureau of the Budget (BOB), where they were screened and packaged into the president's budget. Each government program was allotted an expected annual percentage increase or decrease relative to changes in expenditures for other government programs. The results of the process were predictable— incremental changes in spending fostered by steady economic growth.[10]

Within Congress, authorizing committees typically acted as claimants and recommended generous amounts for programs under their legislative jurisdictions. The Appropriations Committee, on the other hand, was the guardian of the federal Treasury and was responsible for cutting the inflated program requests of executive agencies.[11] The committee conducted deliberations in closed hearings and worked toward consensus by following the norm of minimal partisanship. Because the committee was well adapted to the expectations of the House, members regularly approved most of the Appropriations Committee's outcomes with little dissent, and appropriations bills usually passed without much debate or amendment on the House floor. The Ways and Means Committee conducted its business in a similar fashion with respect to tax legislation. The committee's deliberations were also conducted in closed sessions and its outputs normally received support from the House.[12]

This stable budgetary system broke down during the 1960s and early 1970s in what Allen Schick calls the "seven-year budget war."[13] It is difficult to characterize this critical period in a few words. Suffice it to say, the number of participants in the budgetary process increased, budgetary information became more widely dispersed, and economic growth halted. As the percentage of uncontrollable spending and the size of the deficit increased, the appropriations and tax committees in both chambers clashed over who was to blame. Finally, President Nixon's impoundment of congressionally appropriated funds challenged the Congress's power over the purse. These developments led to budgetary reform that culminated in the Budget Act.

The Budget Act of 1974

When Congress entertained the question of budget reform, the issues were diverse and complex.[14] Although the time had arrived for Congress to reform its budgetary procedures, the provisions of a budget reform bill would have to balance the interests of many players. There were at least six different reasons why members wanted budget reform: increases in spending and deficits; the lack of control in the appropriations process; the inability to set national priorities; the incapacity to make fiscal policy; the need for an independent source of information and analysis; and the presidential abuse of power.[15] Before the House reached a consensus on budget reform, the Budget Act was modified to suit nearly all of these needs. Allen Schick explained:

The new process would have to bring substantial improvement without openly depriving established power holders of the advantages they derived from the status quo. Congress had to seek coordination, but avoid centralization. It had to continue giving many interests a part of the budget power, but also it had to harmonize these interests into a reasonably consistent budget policy. . . . The debate would be waged over rules and procedures, but at stake would be the programs and interests for which funds were to be allocated in the budget process.[16]

A leading advocate of budget reform, Speaker Albert typically played the role of middleman, balancing the various competing interests at stake. He worked behind the scenes to reconcile conflicts between senior committee chairmen (who jealously guarded their policy jurisdictions) and young liberal Democrats (who suspiciously watched as the new power arrangements took shape).[17]

Both liberal and conservative members wanted Congress to have more control over the budget, but they differed over the existing problems with budget policy-making and the goals to be achieved by reform. The liberals argued that Congress lacked the power to set national priorities: they planned to use the budget process to propose spending increases for domestic programs. The conservatives complained about the growth of spending and the large deficits: they preferred spending reductions and tax cuts to stimulate the economy. A third group of "process-oriented" legislators sought to control backdoor spending, develop information sources, and improve coordination of the separate authorization and appropriations processes.[18]

The issue of budget reform also exposed differences between the jurisdictional privileges and various goals of the authorization, appropriations, and tax committees. These differences emerged in deliberations conducted by the thirty-two-member, bipartisan, bicameral Joint Study Committee on Budget Control (JSC), an ad hoc advisory group created to draft a proposal for budget reform. Twenty-eight of the JSC's members were from the House Appropriations, the House Ways and Means, the Senate Appropriations, and the Senate Finance committees. Only four members represented authorization committees. Hence, as W. Thomas Wander notes, "the deliberations of the JSC were dominated by the interests of the fiscal committees in Congress."[19]

The tax committees viewed the problems with the existing budget procedures differently than the spending committees did. Representatives of the tax committees blamed the spending committees for the desperate fiscal situation. They argued that a lack of spending control placed pressure on the budget deficit and restricted Congress from offering tax reductions to stimulate economic growth. They wanted a budget process that placed a ceiling on total government spending before the appropriations subcommittees considered separate spending bills. Representatives of the appropriations committees countered by arguing that they were unfairly held accountable for the growing deficits. They claimed that the Appropriations Committee had lost control over spending and tax decisions, in its battles with Ways and Means and authorization committees over the previous decade. Hence they wanted tougher provisions for backdoor legislation, more control over annual appropriations bills, a process that coordinated spending and revenues, and more orderly procedures that required authorization bills to be passed prior to appropriations bills.[20]

The four JSC members representing the authorization committees lacked a definitive reform plan. As the JSC proceeded with its deliberations, these members discovered that their only realistic objective was to limit any potential damage that reform could have on the power of the authorization committees.

The JSC eventually reached a compromise between the different objectives of the spending and tax committees. It recommended creating a budget committee for each chamber, with two-thirds of the membership representing tax and spending committees and one-third representing the various authorization committees of each chamber. The tax committees achieved spending control through a budget resolution (to be passed prior to the appropriations process) that included ceilings on total budget outlays, new budget authority, levels of total revenue and debt, a total amount of deficit or surplus, and ceilings for the separate legislative programs in the budget. Appropriations bills drafted by each subcommittee were required to meet the ceilings in the budget resolution, or be subject to a point of order, which could be waived only by a two-thirds vote of the membership.

The appropriations committees succeeded in passing a provision that channeled most of the existing backdoor legislation and all new backdoor programs through the regular appropriations process. This stipulation of the JSC proposal stripped spending privileges from the authorization committees. But the House Ways and Means Committee and the Senate Finance Committee retained jurisdiction over their backdoor programs, including social security. Overall, in what Schick refers to as a treaty between the warring factions of the JSC, "the preferences of the tax committees prevailed."[21]

But the JSC's ambitious budget reform proposal faced several challenges when it was submitted to the House and Senate. Commenting on the prospects of the JSC report, Wander points out, "the strategic position of the relevant institutional players changed substantially, as did the content of the reform package as a result of a new round of deliberations in each house." Ultimately, enacting budget reform required balancing the competing wishes of the traditionally powerful fiscal committees with the demands of the emerging liberal Democratic Study Group (DSG).[22]

Rules Committee Review of Budget Reform

The JSC's proposal was taken up first by the House Rules Committee. As the committee began deliberations, chairman Ray J. Madden (D-Ind.) noted the urgency of enacting budget reform: "The decisions about government spending and the priorities for that spending have never been so important. The time has come for Congress to assert clear authority and responsibility for control over these decisions. In order to do so we must initiate new procedures that are equal to the task."[23]

Madden's stress on the resurgence of Congress in budget policy-making and the importance of sound budget procedures highlighted the critical nature of the budget reform bill. Indeed, those two purposes went hand in hand—if Congress wished to challenge the executive in fiscal policy-making, it would need sound procedures.

But the goal of designing an effective budget process was entangled in a political and ideological thicket. Although the basic outline of the JSC report survived, several components of the tough-minded package had to be compromised to pass the final bill. The DSG soon notified the Rules Committee that the JSC proposals were "not acceptable to liberal Democrats in the House." The JSC report turned back the clock to the dark days of committee government, according to the liberals who complained that the JSC bill would create a super budget committee composed primarily of conservative members from the Appropriations and Ways and Means committees. The new budget committee would become "the most powerful committee in Congress—a super elite . . . the committee makeup would be unrepresentative of the House as a whole . . . the committee would be dominated by conservatives."[24]

Congressman Donald Fraser (D-Minn.) presented the liberal view to the Rules Committee. He argued that a budget committee and a budget timetable would "increase [Congress's] inability to face the real problems facing the United States." The real problems with the existing congressional budget process, according to Fraser, resided in an imbalance of spending priorities favoring national defense, and an unfair tax system that benefited the wealthy. Fraser added, "these problems can be solved with solid, carefully thought-out initiatives backed up with firm support from the Members." To this end, Fraser favored maintaining the existing authorization and appropriations processes. He supported a more active role by the majority party caucus, the Democratic Steering and Policy Committee, and the party leadership in deciding between "hard political choices" and coordinating total revenues with total expenditures.[25]

Although Fraser's view did not prevail, it led to a compromise plan aided by members of the House Appropriations Committee. Jamie Whitten (D-Miss.), co-chairman of the JSC and ranking majority member on the Appropriations Committee, used Fraser's premise—that the JSC report created a super budget committee—in order to restore the Appropriations Committee's jurisdiction over spending priorities. He argued that "Congress is not going to surrender its rights and privileges to any committee." Whitten added, "when you set up a super-duper committee, you run counter to every element in Congress with which I am familiar and you just haven't got a chance [of passing a budget reform bill]." Thus Whitten proposed weakening the JSC report by limiting the new budget committees' activities to a "macroeconomic advisory role." In other words, the budget committees should draft a budget resolution that contained only spending and revenue totals; they should not establish ceilings for separate spending categories. Specific policy decisions, according to Whitten, should be left up to the authorizing committees and appropriations subcommittees.[26]

The Rules Committee rejected Whitten's proposal and suggested a bill that continued to allow the Budget Committee to make spending recommendations for both the macro-economic figures and the separate program functions of the budget. But this bill combined the DSG's concern for diffusing committee power with Whitten's flexibility toward the JSC report. The final Rules Committee bill reduced the percentage of Budget Committee members representing Ways and Means and Appropriations committees from two-thirds to less than 45 percent. This adjustment enhanced representation from the authorization committees. The final bill also proposed a rotating membership on the Budget Committee by limiting each member's service on the committee to two terms (or four years) over a ten-year period. (In 1978, Congress changed the term length for each member from two to three terms per ten-year period.) The objectives of the rotation system were to broaden participation in budget policy-making and to restrain the power of the Budget Committee.

The Rules Committee's budget reform proposal also revised the JSC's procedures for formulating the congressional budget. A first budget resolution would contain aggregate spending and revenue targets (rather than ceilings) and recommendations for nineteen separate budget functions. The adoption of the targets in the first budget resolution, rather than the ceilings proposed by the JSC report, weakened the force of the Budget Committee's first concurrent resolution. The budget functions represented broad estimates of national priorities and still gave the appropriations subcommittees flexibility to make separate spending decisions for particular programs. The functions serve as guidelines rather than binding constraints for appropriations decisions on individual programs. Spending ceilings for overall budget figures (total budget authority, outlays, revenues, and deficit or surplus levels) and separate policy functions were to be set by a second resolution enacted after the appropriations process went through its annual cycle. This final Rules Committee bill passed quickly on the floor with only two minor amendments.[27] After House and Senate conferees settled differences over the question of presidential impoundment, both chambers overwhelmingly approved the Budget Act.

Guidelines of the Budget Act

We should take a moment to summarize briefly the major provisions of the Budget Act and explain how the formal budget process was designed to work.

BUDGET COMMITTEES. The act created two budget committees, one in each house. The budget committees were given the responsibility of drafting the congressional budget. The House Budget Committee had twenty-three members—five members each from the Ways and Means and Appropriations committees, eleven from authorization committees, and one member each from the majority and minority party leadership.

CONGRESSIONAL BUDGET OFFICE (CBO). The CBO was created to analyze and furnish budget information. It was assigned the task of reviewing the president's budget and recommending its own economic projections. These projections are based on economic assumptions that include annual estimates for rates of inflation, interest, unemployment, and economic growth. The CBO was designed to serve the informational needs of all members of Congress, but most of the CBO's work was directed toward the tasks of the budget committees. A CBO director, to serve a four-year term, would be appointed by the Speaker of the House and the president pro tempore of the Senate based on the recommendations of the budget committees.

BUDGET TIMETABLE. Under the budget timetable (see table 1), the new fiscal year begins October 1 and ends September 30. By November 10 of each current fiscal year, the executive branch was required to submit a "current services budget," an estimate of the cost of maintaining existing government programs at current levels after indexing for inflation. On January 20, the president submits a budget to Congress, including any changes in the current services budget.[28] The authorization committees and appropriations subcommittees were required to issue estimated spending reports for programs under their jurisdictions to the budget committees by March 15. The CBO's report was due April 1. Before drafting a first budget resolution, the House and Senate budget committees reviewed the president's budget, the CBO's analysis, the Joint Economic Committee's recommendations, and requests by individual committees. By April 15, the two budget committees were scheduled to report a draft of their resolutions to the House and Senate. After each chamber passed a first budget resolution, budget committee conferees would meet to put together a final report. A conference version of the first concurrent resolution should be approved by May 15.

The first budget resolution consisted of non-binding targets for the upcoming fiscal year, which were divided into two parts: macro-economic figures and budget functions. The combined macro-economic figures (overall targets for total budget authority, total outlays, total revenues, total federal debt, and an annual budget deficit or surplus) are essentially a statement of fiscal policy. The budget functions (that is, national defense, agriculture, health, and so on) reflect budget priorities. Once the conference report for the first budget resolution was passed, the budget committees translated the budget functions into program estimates and distributed them to authorization committees and the Appropriations Committee.[29] The estimates served as guidelines for considering separate legislative proposals.

The budget timetable was essentially layered over the existing authorization and appropriations processes. All authorization committees should report legislation to the House by May 15. The only exception to this rule was social security and entitlement legislation, which would not be reported to the floor until after the first budget resolution was passed. The May 15 deadline for reporting authorization bills could be waived, at the recommendation of the Rules Committee, by a majority vote in the House. Committee hearings for appropriations bills actually begin in January, but appropriations bills could not be reported from the Appropriations Committee to the House floor until after the first budget resolution was passed. Once the spending bills were reported, the regular appropriations process continued. This process included House floor action, Senate action, conference debate, and final passage of conference bills. The bills were scheduled for final passage by the middle of September, a deadline that could be waived if the authorization process was delayed.

After completing work on the authorization and appropriations bills, Congress was scheduled to pass a second budget resolution by September 15 (two weeks prior to the beginning of the fiscal year). The second resolution could either reaffirm or revise the targets of the first resolution. Reconciliation procedures could be used if the total spending or revenue levels enacted in the authorization, appropriations, and tax processes, or in any one of these, did not match the totals passed in the second resolution. Under the reconciliation process, the budget committees could instruct one or more committees to change spending or revenue levels for certain programs. The original objective of reconciliation was to ensure that the total amount of spending and revenue approved by Congress on separate legislation conforms with the ceilings passed in the second

resolution.[30] If the reconciliation instructions applied to only
one committee, then that committee would draft a reconciliation bill recommending the necessary changes. If two or more
committees were involved in reconciliation, each committee
would report changes to the Budget Committee where they
could be packaged in the form of a reconciliation bill and
submitted to the House for a vote. Reconciliation should
be completed by September 25, one week before the fiscal
year begins.

Budget Reform and the Speaker's Role

In the debate over budget reform, several proposals sought to
strengthen the Speaker's role in the new process. The main
concerns were the Speaker's control over committee assignments and his input in the budget resolution. But discussion of
these issues was sporadic and did not result in a more definitive
role for the Speaker. Any proposals that defined an explicit role
for the Speaker were tempered by the political necessity of
passing a budget reform bill.

The most widely discussed issue concerning the Speaker's
role in the budget process focused on committee appointments.
On this issue, the JSC proposals gave the Speaker more power
than the Budget Act did. The JSC report stipulated that the
Speaker would appoint seven at-large members to the Budget
Committee. During the Rules Committee hearings, at least
two members—Spark Matsunaga (D-Hawaii) and Thomas
Rees (D-Calif.)—argued that the Speaker should retain the
privilege of appointing the at-large members of the House Budget Committee.[31] But the Rules Committee's budget reform
bill dropped the JSC provision giving the Speaker direct control over Budget Committee appointments. Thus the Speaker's
ability to affect Budget Committee appointments, like all other
committee assignments, depended on the extent of his influence on the Steering and Policy Committee.

Perhaps the most critical factor in making Budget Committee assignments is the limited term length for each member assigned to the committee. The frequent turnover of the Budget Committee might offer an opportunity to shape the composition of the committee. If the Speaker gained influence over appointments through his position as chairman of the Steering and Policy Committee, then he could select members to the Budget Committee who would promote his budget priorities. On the other hand, if committee assignment power is diffused by widespread participation among members of the Steering and Policy Committee, then the Speaker would have far less influence over the composition of the committee. In the latter case, regular membership turnover on the Budget Committee might prohibit a long-term institutional relationship between the Speaker and the committee. Hence, the fixed length of term on the Budget Committee could either help or hinder the leadership's prospects for advancing a coherent budget plan, depending on the Speaker's general influence over committee assignments.

Any proposals that involved the Speaker directly with the Budget Committee confronted the political realities of passing a reform bill. For example, David Martin (R-Neb.), ranking minority member on the Rules Committee, suggested placing the Speaker and the minority leader on the Budget Committee and making the Speaker chairman. He said, "It seems to me that the leadership on both sides of the aisle should be directly involved in this [making Budget Committee recommendations] because this involves leadership determinations and decisions." But George Mahon (D-Texas), chairman of the Appropriations Committee, opposed Martin. While Mahon believed that the Speaker would be kept informed of the Budget Committee's business, he thought that placing the Speaker on the Budget Committee would make it a leadership committee. According to Mahon, such an arrangement would signal a centralization of power in the Speaker's hands and would ruin prospects for passing a reform bill. Martin conceded to Mahon, "Whatever package we report out to the House for consideration, we have to keep in mind *practical political considerations* [my emphasis] as to how far we can go in making the changes in the House structure and the committee structure, and so forth, in order to get it approved."[32]

Political scientist Robert Peabody recommended the most ambitious proposal for institutionalizing the Speaker's role in the budget process. Assessing the Budget Act within the broader context of congressional reform, Peabody argued that party leaders should have a definitive role in the budget process in order to facilitate party leadership. He noted, "[The leaders'] lack of involvement would drastically retard [other] current efforts designed to strengthen the hands of the party leaders and through them, wider party caucuses." Peabody testified that party leaders should be involved at the committee stage of the budget process so that they could establish the party's priorities. He warned that, "unless the party leadership becomes involved in the early stages of this all-encompassing legislation, they are likely to be on the defensive for the balance of consideration, inhibited in the most meaningful participation until it is almost too late [to establish priorities]—floor action." He proposed that the Speaker should not only appoint all members of the Budget Committee but serve as a member of that committee along with the minority leader. Furthermore, the Speaker should be given additional professional staff to monitor the Budget Committee's activities. The Budget Committee should be responsive to the party leadership. In short, Peabody said, "What I am really recommending is an institutionalization of much of what would have to preoccupy a Speaker . . . during the months that the congressional budget was under consideration."[33]

But budget reformers were reluctant even to discuss the possibility of strong central leadership by the Speaker, let alone to institutionalize it. Congressman Richard Bolling (D-Mo.) commented, "I think the great dilemma that we confront here is to do something that will be *practical* and *effective* [my emphasis] and yet it is almost impossible to achieve the ideal."

The debate following Peabody's proposal shifted to questions of multi-year budgeting, the four-year term length for committee membership, and the budget timetable.[34]

Claude Pepper (D-Fla.) speculated about the potential of the budget process as an instrument for exercising party leadership.

In the past no leader of the House has had the authority to do anything like this [establish budget priorities] because he only had a persuasive power. He might have had a persuasive authority by calling in all of the chairmen and the like, but without some vehicle like this the leadership heretofore hasn't had this authority. But now with the majority of this Budget Committee of the dominant party in each of the bodies of Congress, right away they are going to be making recommendations. The recommendations are going to have a considerable effect, a definitive effect.

The parties are going to begin to take a position and it will lead, in my opinion at least, either in that stage when the recommendation of the Budget Committee is made, to a majority recommendation, or when the House acts on the concurrent resolution.

Of course, that will reflect the majority party and the minority party vote or how the vote may divide on these recommendations, but it will almost inevitably, it seems to me, lead the leadership of the respective parties to taking a position and advocating that position, maybe through their members on the Budget Committee and certainly to their members in the House when they come to consider the concurrent resolution.[35]

This long quotation offers a preliminary idea of the potential influence a Speaker might exercise in the new budget process. The budget resolution provides a planning mechanism through which the Speaker could work with the Budget Committee to advance the majority party's priorities. He may then rely on the committee members or employ either the party caucus or perhaps the whip system to gain support for the leadership's recommendations on the floor. Both co-chairmen of the JSC, Whitten and Al Ullman (D-Ore.), agreed with Pepper as to how the party leadership would respond to the new budget process. They also agreed that party leadership would strengthen congressional budgeting, as it would enable the House to sponsor a coherent budget policy.

Perhaps the most important aspect of the deliberations over the Budget Act is that they did not define the Speaker's role in the budget process. Pepper's insights reveal that the Budget Act provided the majority party leadership with only the potential tools to recommend a majority party program. The extent to which the Speaker could harness this potential would hinge on the way the budget process was actually put into practice.

Summary

The Budget Act was passed in a context that valued expression more than integration and that created an ambiguous process. As Schick points out, "Every party to the 1974 treaty has been compelled to jockey for advantages, to assert prerogatives and ward off intrusion by others." Consequently, "Not the least of the reasons why Congress was able to accommodate diverse interests in the Budget Act was the ambiguous and permissive process that was established." Roger Davidson concurs, "With such divergent motivations and differing jurisdictions to protect, it is little wonder that a giant question mark existed with regard to what the new process was supposed to do." Assessing the process after about seven years, Davidson found that "much like the budget itself, the process is a 'moving target'; each year since 1980, the process has changed."[36]

What was so ambiguous about the Budget Act? First, the role of the budget committees in the new process was unclear. Would they assert control over budget priorities, thereby challenging the prerogatives of other committees? Or would they be content to sketch the broad economic estimates of the budget resolution and allow the authorization committees and appropriations subcommittees to determine the allocation levels for specific programs? Or did they even have a choice between the two alternatives? As Schick points out, "the Budget Act ordains neither outcome." Second, there was uncertainty over how the authorization and appropriations committees would respond to the budget timetable. No institutional means were created to manage the conflict that would inevitably develop as the budget process was layered over the existing authorization and appropriations processes. Rather than provide a mechanism to manage conflict, Schick adds, "the new process marks the institutionalization of budget conflict within Congress." Speculating on how the budget process would operate amid this uncertainty, Schick observed, "it all depends on how the parties interact with one another in the congressional arena."[37] In other words, the inherent gaps of the Budget Act would have to be filled as the process was put into practice.

It is within this uncertain context that the Speaker's roles in the budget process were forged. The ambiguities inherent within the Budget Act suggested that the House would need a leader to explain the new process and clarify its purpose. One should also expect the House to incur problems during the implementation of the budget process as House members clashed over budget priorities and jurisdictional boundaries. Congressman Pepper's expectation that the party leadership would become involved in making substantive recommendations to the first budget resolution eventually came about during the 1980s when the Speaker became the opposition party leader. Thus we search in vain for a definition of the Speaker's role in the debate over budget reform and in the provisions of the Budget Act. Those roles unfolded after the Budget Act was passed, as the House adapted and the Speaker responded to problems and opportunities in the budget process.

3

From Nurturer to Process Manager:

The Speaker's Roles, 1975–80

In the capacities of both nurturer and process manager, from 1975 to 1980, the Speaker assisted the House in dealing with the unanticipated or neglected consequences of budget reform. The term *nurturer* is given by former congressman Richard Bolling, one of the founders of the Budget Act. "When the budget process first began it was going to start out like an infant. And, like any infant, it had to be nurtured." He went on, "I knew the way it was designed there wasn't any place the power was going to come from to get [the budget process] started except from the Speaker."[1] The nurturer role is characterized by three supportive functions: explaining the complex procedures of the Budget Act to participants in the new budget process, organizing the committees for action, and moderating fears about the uncertain potential of the Budget Act.

But the novelty of the Budget Act was only one of the factors shaping the Speaker's roles in the budget process. Political and policy conditions also affected these roles. After the Speaker helped get the budget process on its feet, problems began to emerge in the operation of the process. Intra-party disagreements over Democratic budget priorities called into question the House's ability to pass budget resolutions, a critical first step in the process. The Speaker concentrated primarily on trying to build and maintain coalitions so that the House could meet the basic requirements of the new process. Eventually, alarm over the detrimental effects of a growing deficit fueled a movement to reduce federal spending, which in turn created more conflicts in the budget process. The House needed a leader to manage these conflicts in order to maintain the process. The Speaker was called upon to perform several important managerial tasks: mediating policy and procedural disputes between committees; trying to prevent breakdowns in the budget schedule; and reminding committee chairmen that their spending decisions should meet the guidelines of House-passed budget resolutions.

In this chapter I assess the conditions under which the Speaker's role in the budget process evolved from nurturer to process manager. I begin with a broad overview of the policy, political, and institutional conditions that shaped budget politics in the late 1970s. I proceed to describe the development and performance of the Speaker's roles in terms of the interactive effects of conditions and the individual leader qualities of Speakers Albert and O'Neill.

The Context: A Broad Overview, 1975–80

During the latter half of the 1970s, the Speaker's roles in the budget process were affected by a variety of conditions (see table 3). The nurturer role was influenced largely by the novelty of the budget process itself and the assistance it demanded. The most critical conditions leading up to the Speaker's role as process manager were the ideological divisions within the majority party; the growing federal deficit; and the use of reconciliation procedures to control spending.[2] The latter two factors changed the nature of the budget process itself and uncovered the problem of how to manage conflict, which was never fully resolved by the Budget Act. Let us consider generally how these conditions affected the Speaker's role in the budget process.

TABLE 3
Speaker's Roles in Relation to Changes in Policy, Political, and Institutional Conditions, 1975–1980

	Nurturer 1975–76	Nurturer/Manager 1977–79	Manager 1980
POLICY CONDITIONS			
Priorities	Mixed	Mixed	Deficit
Deficit	Non issue	Emerging	Issue
Economy	Poor	Unstable	Poor
POLITICAL CONDITIONS			
President's Party	Republican	Democrat	Democrat
Net gains in	1974 (49D)	1976 (1D)	—
House seats	74 New Dems[a]	1978 (15R)	—
Majority party unity	Low	Low	Low
Minority party unity	High	High	High
Ideology of HBC Democrats compared with all House Democrats	More conservative	More liberal	More liberal
INSTITUTIONAL CONDITIONS			
House norms	Resurgent members vs. committees	Participatory mood	Committee conflict
Relationship between Congress and president	Divided party	Conflict	Cooperation
Purpose of the budget process	Establish procedures/ Meet timetable	Coordinate committees	Reconciliation

Note: This table is intended to provide a broad overview of how variations in conditions affected the Speaker's roles. The chapter will illustrate more precisely how these conditions influenced the development of the Speaker's roles over time.
[a]The 1974 congressional elections brought seventy-four freshmen Democrats to the House, who facilitated the participatory reforms described in chapter 2.

INSTITUTIONAL CONDITIONS. Congressional reforms altered power arrangements within the House and the institutional relationship between Congress and the president. Within the House, the new participatory norms clashed with the collective goal of making Congress a more responsible legislative body. Conflicts between committee chairmen and a resurgent membership persisted throughout the period. Tensions peaked in 1980 when the House voted to attach reconciliation instructions to the first budget resolution. Under the Budget Act, reconciliation was to be used at the end of the budget schedule in case the sum of the separate appropriations, authorizations, and tax decisions approved by Congress failed to match the aggregate spending and revenue ceilings of the second budget resolution. Using reconciliation with the first resolution (as Congress did in 1980)—to instruct authorizing committees to make spending reductions in existing legislation—placed the House majority in direct conflict with the committees. According to the established ways of legislating, committees should recommend legislation to the House, not the other way around.[3] The Speaker wound up awkwardly in the middle, trying to mediate the tensions between committee chairmen and the majority, while holding back his own budgetary preferences.

The relationship between Congress and the president was obscured by the mood of congressional resurgence on Capitol Hill. Prior to the Budget Act, at least since Franklin D. Roosevelt, the president was deemed the programmatic leader of his party. A president may have encountered difficulties enacting his programs because of divisions within the congressional party, but in theory he was responsible for setting the party's legislative agenda. With the passage of the Budget Act, however, Congress developed the potential to formulate its own budget. It was relatively easy for House Democrats to challenge President Ford's budget priorities; there were both partisan and institutional imperatives to do so.

With the election of Jimmy Carter in 1976, Democratic majorities in both the House and Senate faced the problem of deciding whether to follow or challenge the president's budget. Speaker O'Neill described the dilemma between President Carter and the Democratic Congress. On the one hand, O'Neill said of Carter, "We want to work to make him a great president." On the other hand, O'Neill pointed out, "with the War Powers Act and the new budget process Congress is proving that it is capable of operating on an equal footing with the Executive. Common sense and the Constitution demand Pennsylvania Avenue remain a two-way street."[4] O'Neill's assessment of the situation indicated the uncertainty about where the leadership on the "Democratic" budget should come from—Congress or the White House.

POLICY AND POLITICAL CONDITIONS. Policy and political conditions complicated the conflicting institutional objectives of the post-reform Congress. President Carter and Budget Committee Democrats differed significantly over policy objectives. Carter campaigned on a balanced budget platform and, although the specific priorities of his budgets varied from year to year, he maintained a fiscally conservative posture throughout his presidency. But liberal Democrats in Congress were unprepared to make the spending cuts necessary to achieve a balanced budget. Democrats on the House Budget Committee were considerably more liberal than the House Democratic membership as a whole (see table 4). Consequently, Carter's balanced budget pledge was ignored by the House Budget Committee for the first two years of his administration. In 1977 and 1978 (Carter's first two years in the White House), the Budget Committee voted to increase spending for domestic program functions beyond Carter's requests.

TABLE 4
Mean Liberal Ideology
All Members and House Budget Committee (HBC) Members by Party

Year	Democrats			Republicans		
	House	*HBC*	*New HBC*[a]	*House*	*HBC*	*New HBC*
1975	57.5[b]	55.6	—	18	11.5	—
1977	53.5	70.6	74.8	17	7.8	5.4
1979	53.2	66.0	60.6	14	12.3	11.3

Source: Conservative coalition voting scores, *Congressional Quarterly Almanac* (Washington: Congressional Quarterly Inc.), (various years).
[a]"New HBC" is the category for newly appointed Budget Committee members.
[b]Figures indicate mean "liberalness" for each group of members as measured by conservative coalition opposition scores; the higher the score, the more liberal the group.

The new congressional budget process was also severely tested by turbulent economic times. Unprecedented budget deficits were perceived to be linked to high interest rates, inflation, and unemployment (see table 5). Fiscal policy choices were neither clear nor promising. A policy aimed toward reducing inflation ran the risk of exacerbating the recession. On the other hand, an economic stimulus plan threatened to fuel inflation.

In the midst of economic turmoil, nearly everyone in Congress claimed to be a fiscal policy expert. Leading House Democrats expressed divergent views on how to balance the budget and improve the economy. Eventually, members began to test the institutional capacity of the budget process beyond the point of simply meeting deadlines. Some members perceived the budget process as a forum for advocating national priorities, while others used it to express their particular interests. In both cases the result was the same—a greater demand for floor amendments to the Budget Committee's first budget resolutions.

The heavy amending activity, combined with a lack of cohesion and with ideological differences among House Democrats, increased the uncertainty of passing budgets on the House floor.[5] Compared with House Republicans, Democrats

TABLE 5

Major Economic Indicators and Federal Budget Deficit, 1976–80

Indicator[a]	1976	1977	1978	1979	1980
Inflation[b]	5.8	6.5	7.7	11.3	13.5
Unemployment	7.7	7.0	6.0	5.8	7.1
Prime rate[c]	6.8	6.8	9.1	12.7	15.3
GNP growth	5.4	4.8	5.0	3.2	−.2
Deficit[d]	53.6	59.2	40.2	73.8	78.9

Source: U.S. Bureau of the Census, *Statistical Abstract of the United States: 1981,* 102d ed. (Washington: United States Government Printing Office, 1981).
[a]All figures except the deficit are percentages.
[b]Inflation rate based on Consumer Price Index.
[c]Prime rate is the rate charged by banks.
[d]Deficit is in billions of dollars.

lacked unity on roll call votes for the Budget Committee's first budget resolutions (see table 6). Weak party unity was rooted in ideological divisions within the Democratic party.[6] From one year to the next, House Democrats were not even close to a consensus on the budget issue. The "nay" votes on first budget resolutions were shared by liberals, moderates, and conservatives (see table 7). Thus, party leaders needed more time to accommodate more interests in order to pass budget resolutions and maintain the validity of the budget process.

A movement to balance the budget during the last two years of the Carter administration exacerbated existing partisan divisions over national priorities. Many budget makers argued that deficits were fueling inflation. As the Consumer Price Index, the leading indicator of inflation, grew from 6.8 percent to 9 percent, Carter's goal of a balanced budget became more appealing. By 1980, the debate shifted from the question of whether to balance the budget to how and when to balance the budget.[7] When the harsh realities of fiscal conservatism set in, members grimaced at the prospect of cutting funds from their favorite programs and they tried to protect their policy preferences. Conservatives favored increases in defense to abate a Soviet military buildup, whereas liberals sought to salvage tra-

TABLE 6

Percentage of Members Voting against Their Party's Majority on House-passed First Budget Resolutions, 1975–80

Calendar Year	Democrats	Southern Democrats	Republicans
1975	25.7	43.2	2.3
1976	17.5	37.5	10.5
1977	22.0	22.8	5.5
1978	23.6	43.9	2.2
1979	19.2	20.0	6.3
1980	23.4	10.0	14.4

Source: Roll call votes in the *Congressional Record*, 1975–80.

TABLE 7
*Number of House Democrats Voting against Passage of First
Budget Resolutions by Ideology, 1975–80*

Calendar Year	Liberals	Moderates	Conservatives[a]
1975	21	13	34
1976	10	9	25
1977	21	16	21
1978	10	14	37
1979	22	6	22
1980	39	14	9

Source: Roll call votes in *Congressional Record* and conservative coalition scores in *Congressional Quarterly Almanac*, 1975–80.
[a]The three ideological categories are calculated by using conservative coalition opposition scores (the higher the score, the more liberal the member). Categories are defined by the following classification scheme:
  Liberals = scores ranging from 67–100
  Moderates = scores ranging from 34–66
  Conservatives = scores ranging from 0–33

ditional human needs programs. Eventually, when the budget committees instituted reconciliation procedures to reduce the House's appetite for spending, chairmen of the authorization committees protested that their jurisdictional boundaries were violated.

This capsule summary of the broader context of the 1970s lays the foundation for assessing the Speaker's roles in the budget process. Whether acting as nurturer or process manager, both Speakers had to respond to problems of exercising budgetary procedures within the context of economic crisis, partisan division, and institutional fragmentation.

Carl Albert: The Speaker as Nurturer

Speaker Albert played the first critical role as nurturer when the House initiated the budget process on a trial basis in 1975. It was difficult to nurture the process through its formative stages, given the institutional and political conditions. The participatory reforms were complemented by the 1974 congressional elections, which produced seventy-five freshmen Democrats eager to participate in House politics. Speaker Albert's assistance was needed to smooth the House's transition from a long period of entrenched committee government to a wide-open but hopefully more efficient legislative body.

Transition periods often harbor conflicting expectations about the course and relative speed of change. In such periods, leaders struggle to accommodate the various expectations at once. As Speaker Albert entered his final two years in office (1975–76), younger members wanted the reforms implemented rapidly, while senior members resisted swift change. Albert was sensitive to both views, but he was not wholly supported by all factions of the Democratic party.[8] The freshman class of 1974 created most of the Speaker's problems. A gain of forty seats for the House majority party is normally welcomed by the Speaker, but the 1974 elections brought a different breed of congressman to the House. As House Republican Barber Conable (R-N.Y.) warned, "A lot of expectations that people have now including the fierce 75 will go aglimmering. They're going to find out among other things that 75 doesn't constitute a majority and that they all don't agree with each other."[9]

Before long, freshmen complained about Albert's failures to initiate creative policy proposals and control committee chairmen.[10] In June 1975, twenty-five freshmen Democrats issued Albert a list of ways to improve the party's leadership: identify a set of top priority issues; adopt a party position and seek support for it; consult more with members; increase efforts to build winning coalitions; have the Speaker appoint party spokesmen for key issues; improve identification and communication of the daily roll call schedule; and work five days instead of three or four days per week.[11] Albert met with the freshmen in January 1976 to allay their anger and inform them that his top priorities were to meet the requirements of the budget timetable and to pass all the thirteen appropriations bills before the start of the fiscal year.[12]

The Speaker's commitment to the budget process had actually become evident a year earlier, in 1975, when Congress had put the process through its first trial run. Albert's concern for the process reflected his personal interest and the House's expectation to achieve the task it had set itself—to pass an annual budget resolution and meet the deadlines of the timetable established in the Budget Act. In this case, the goals of the leader coincided with the expectations of most members. Fortunately for the new budget process, Albert identified his role as nurturer and ably performed the functions associated with getting the process started.

One of the biggest problems was the lack of understanding about the procedures and purpose of the Budget Act. Albert's first move was to recruit Brock Adams (D-Wash.), an energetic and intelligent member experienced with economic issues, to be chairman of the House Budget Committee. In early March, after the House was organized to begin the Ninety-fourth Congress, Albert and Adams met with all the standing committee chairmen and appropriations subcommittee chairmen. Bolling described the meeting:

Albert did an incredible job of organizing the leadership of the committees for the transition into the new budget process. In 1975, after we organized the committees, he had a meeting of all the committee chairmen with regard to the Budget Act and it was a phenomenal experience. These guys had all voted for it, it had been going on for about six months, and they didn't know the first thing about the Budget Act. One of them knew a little. So, quite obviously, if it wasn't for the Speaker there wasn't going to be any Budget Act. It wasn't going to last.[13]

Albert's objectives for the meeting were to educate the chairmen about the budget process, acquire an initial idea of their spending requests for the fiscal 1976 budget resolution, and motivate them to meet the deadlines of the budget timetable.

In this first meeting, Albert solicited two funding estimates from the chairmen: realistic estimates of what each committee needed to finance their programs, and wish lists. The Budget

Committee added up all the requests for each list. The total sum of the requests for each list constituted the total amount of federal spending estimated for two different fiscal 1976 budget resolutions—a realistic budget and a wish-list budget. Albert proceeded to call a second meeting of the chairmen. This time, Adams explained, "his objective . . . was to show that if we granted all of the requests from the wish lists, the deficit would be outrageously high, something like $75 billion."[14]

Speaker Albert also realized the need to explain the limitations of the new process and its chief purpose—to offer a rival congressional budget to the president's budget. Nurturing the budget process required Speaker Albert to moderate any fears the committee chairmen had as the House began this new process. Adams commented, "The Speaker was incredibly important in communicating the idea that the [Budget] Committee was not designed to compete with the other committees in the House. He wanted to make clear and carry out the view that the first resolution was a planning tool, a response, an alternative to the president's budget."[15]

Even though the Budget Act gave House Democrats the opportunity to challenge the Republican president's budget, Albert was not interested in initiating or even advocating particular budget priorities. The Speaker was concerned only with the survival of the process—an objective he clearly emphasized in a speech he delivered on May 1, 1975, during the first floor debate on a budget resolution:

Mr. Chairman, I do not take this time to comment on the amendments either pending or prospective, but upon what I think is one of the most necessary actions that this House can take during this session, and that is to pass a concurrent budget resolution and do it on time. . . . I am not attempting to make a brief for any particular provision or position. Nevertheless, I must assert, as the elected leader of the House, on behalf of this House and the future of the Nation, that it is essential that we pass a budget resolution, and that we finish our procedures within the time contemplated in the act itself. For only by supporting a budget resolution can we continue the development of the vitally important overall budgetary process in this Congress.[16]

Passing the fiscal 1976 first resolution required more than an inspiring speech by the Speaker. A whip count taken prior to the vote revealed that the leadership lacked support for the Budget Committee's resolution. In order to attract the votes of liberal Democrats, majority leader Tip O'Neill (D-Mass.) proposed an amendment that lifted cost-of-living-adjustment (COLA) ceilings on social security benefits and federal employee salaries. Then Adams and the leadership team lobbied members on the floor to produce a slim victory (200–196).

Once the budget resolution was passed, Speaker Albert played a supporting role for the budget process. He commissioned Adams to oversee the separate spending decisions made by the appropriations subcommittees. Adams recounted his job: "I was told [by Albert] to go on the floor and speak out against bills that exceeded the targets. Albert backed me in that. . . . He could use the Rules Committee to keep waivers down to a minimum and told the committee chairmen they couldn't go over the initial estimates."[17]

Thus, from the very beginning the Speaker played an important role in nurturing the budget process. The House needed a leader to explain the formal procedures, to clarify the purpose of the Budget Act, and to coordinate the existing committee system with the new budget timetable. The nurturer role rested on the expectation that Congress should fulfill the formal requirements of the Budget Act and that the Speaker was suited to perform that role.

Even though the conditions determined the Speaker's role, it was important for Albert to respond favorably and to use his faculties to nurture the budget process. Albert realized that the credibility of the House rested on its success or failure to make the budget process work. In Albert's view, "If we didn't make [the budget process] work we were going to be a laughing stock."[18] As the House accepted the responsibility of enacting its own budget, he was committed to getting the process started. Albert preferred Rayburn's style of meeting in small groups or individually with committee chairmen. His extensive and cordial relationships with most members enabled him to implement that style effectively.[19] Both Bolling and Adams, two of the people most involved in the budget process at that time, credit Albert for nurturing the process in its earliest stages. Bolling points out, "Albert was the guy who was bailing it out, he got it started and was enormously important." Adams concluded, "the Speaker, at that time, was a primary moving force in the budget process, a great factor in making the budget process successful."[20]

In short, regardless of the complaints over his lack of leadership, Speaker Albert should be credited with recognizing the need for the Speaker's involvement in the new process and for using his personal skills to perform the nurturer role. In its infancy, the budget was not a powerful planning tool, nor did the members expect it to be. Albert accepted the process for what it was, a mechanism to achieve a modicum of coordination among the separate authorization, appropriations, and tax decisions in the House. A different Speaker with a different understanding of what conditions demanded and a weaker commitment to the Budget Act might well have been less successful in nurturing the budget process.

Tip O'Neill: From Nurturer to Process Manager

Speaker O'Neill inherited a post-reform House with an indefinite purpose, a House torn between individual demands to participate and collective expectations of congressional resurgence. The context of the late 1970s was defined by intra-party divisions over budget priorities; an ambiguous, sometimes hostile relationship between Congress and President Carter; economic decline; and eventually a bulging deficit. Under these conditions policy controversies grew louder and more frequent. Committees violated the budget timetable as members became more concerned with the content of budget decisions than with procedural guidelines. As demands on the budget process intensified, members called on the Speaker to reconcile procedural and policy disputes. Members expected the Speaker at least to keep the trains running, even if they did not run on time.

Speaker O'Neill's actions are illustrated best in his efforts to serve two functions: to help pass first budget resolutions, and to coordinate the separate spending and tax bills of the standing committees with the overall figures and priorities approved in the first budget resolution. O'Neill's style and ability to perform the roles of nurturer and process manager depended both on the particular circumstances and on his leadership qualities. A brief description of O'Neill's qualities is needed to assess his actions in the budget process.

By most accounts, Tip O'Neill was a highly partisan Speaker, committed to protecting a Democratic tradition upheld by the liberal economic and social policies of the New Deal and Great Society. Members from both parties expected O'Neill to be more aggressive and partisan than Albert. For Republican minority leader John J. Rhodes (R-Ariz.), O'Neill's appointment signaled trouble for Republicans. Rhodes described O'Neill as "the most partisan man I have ever known. . . . In contrast to Speaker Albert, who maintains a fair-minded approach towards all Members regardless of party, Tip can be impossible to deal with if you are in the minority."[21] For Democrats, O'Neill potentially offered a clearer direction for the party. One Democrat noted, "O'Neill is a dyed in the wool gut liberal. He'll be leading the party in the House and will be out front on issues the way Albert wasn't." O'Neill certainly had high aspirations for his new job: "I intend to be a strong Speaker. I hope to make some imaginative changes around here."[22]

Despite his partisan reputation and ambitious leadership goals, O'Neill was sensitive to the conditions that shaped the House and needs of the House membership. He confidently expressed his ability to adapt to the post-reform House: "You can teach an old dog new tricks and this old dog wants to learn." Appropriately, at a time when the Watergate scandal damaged the image of all government institutions, O'Neill responded by making his first legislative priority a new code of ethics for the House.[23]

O'Neill's view of leadership coincided with the prevailing participatory mood of the post-reform era. He once said, "The House is not the most efficient institution, but it is the freest. . . . My policy will be an open-door policy. I am easy to talk to." He described the importance of listening to the members, "Anyone who comes into your office with an idea, and it may be the silliest idea in the world, listen to them and never ridicule them." O'Neill later reflected on his open-door policy, "I certainly tried to make the House a more open and effective place, and I believe I succeeded."[24]

O'Neill had political skills in dealing with members, but he lacked budgetary expertise. He did serve on the Budget Committee, as majority leader, during its first years of operation, and during that time he proposed a few amendments to budget resolutions. But O'Neill was involved in congressional budgeting in its formative years, and his brief experience on the Budget Committee did not prepare him for the intense budget battles of the late 1970s and the 1980s. One staff person described the limitations of O'Neill's budgetary experience: "Tip was not unmindful of the process, but he was not a detail-oriented person, and he was on the committee when the pie was perceived to be growing."[25]

Other observers described O'Neill's acquaintance with budget policy in less generous terms. One Budget Committee staff person said, "From the gut, Tip just didn't relate to [the budget]." He went on to describe O'Neill's posture toward the budget-deficit problem in 1980, during meetings between congressional leaders and Carter administration officials:

Tip personally throughout this whole process never could understand what the fuss was about the budget. To a great extent that reflects the fact that when he was cutting his spurs politically, the budget was not a big issue. It was something real boring they did in the Massachusetts House that you knew you had to have, but it really didn't make much difference. . . . I don't think he ever really understood in a gut sense what was important or why all the members of Congress were concerned about this issue.[26]

How did O'Neill's personal qualities affect his leadership role in the budget process? O'Neill's openness fitted well with the participatory mood of the House. He preferred to share leadership functions with other members of the leadership team and involve other members in task forces.[27] A stalwart partisan with traditional Democratic values, O'Neill sought to protect federal expenditures for social welfare, education, and employment programs designed to help lower- and middle-income people. During leadership meetings, O'Neill would remind Budget Committee chairman Robert Giaimo (D-Conn.) to remember the principles of the Democratic party when the Budget Committee drafted its first budget resolution. But O'Neill's limited budgetary experience prohibited his taking a direct role in instructing the Budget Committee on specific policy issues. His relationship with the Budget Committee rested mostly on his trust in Giaimo to represent his broader policy objectives on the Budget Committee. As the deficit began to pose constraints on domestic spending, however, even Giaimo did not concur with O'Neill's preferences, and this created tension between the chairman and the Speaker.

At times, O'Neill's ideological views conflicted with his role as process manager. As the House was pressed to reduce spending in the latter years of the Carter administration, traditional Democratic programs came under attack. In this context, members expected the Speaker to facilitate a reconciliation process that would reduce spending for some federal programs that O'Neill supported. O'Neill initially expressed misgivings about the use of reconciliation and voiced reservations about the fiscal 1981 first budget resolution. His lack of support may have hindered the process, it is impossible to say for sure. The situation certainly depicted a role conflict that leaders of a representative body often confront in trying to reconcile their personal policy preferences with institutional roles.

Passing First Budget Resolutions on the Floor

During the 1970s, the Speaker's roles as nurturer and process manager included the traditional functions of party leadership—to build and maintain winning coalitions for bills sponsored by the majority party.[28] In one sense, the Speaker was merely applying these tasks to budget decisions by trying to build partisan support for the Budget Committee's resolutions. Yet, the Speaker's efforts to build majorities went beyond partisan objectives; they were motivated also by the goal of maintaining the budget process. Given the ideological divisions within the House Democratic party and the growing number of floor amendments, passing timely budget resolutions was perhaps the most acute problem with congressional budgeting during the 1970s.[29] If the House failed to pass timely budget resolutions, the process itself would be undermined. There would be no congressional budget, and no guidelines for the committees to use in formulating authorization, appropriations, or revenue bills. Thus the Speaker's coalition-building task was aimed not only at uniting the party behind the Budget Committee's prescribed budget priorities, but also at securing enough votes to pass budget resolutions so that the House could proceed with other business in an orderly fashion.

Since an average of only about ten Republicans voted in favor of first budget resolutions during each year of this period (see table 6), O'Neill had to rely primarily on an ideologically divided Democratic party in order to build support for first budget resolutions (see table 7). He was quite familiar with the dimensions of the problem. O'Neill described the House Democratic Party as "five parties in one. . . . We've got about 25 really strong liberals, 110 progressive liberals, maybe 60 moderates, about 45 people just to the right of the moderates and 35 conservatives."[30]

The fashioning of a majority coalition was hindered also by reforms that opened up the amendment process in the House. In 1970 the House passed an amendment to the Legislative Reorganization Act (offered by O'Neill acting as a member of the

Rules Committee), which allowed twenty members to call for a recorded teller vote on any amendment. Coupled with the participatory mood of the House, the rule change produced drastic increases in recorded teller votes and floor amendments.[31] This trend of increased amending activity was reflected in House floor votes for first budget resolutions (see table 8). Up until 1980, when the Rules Committee issued its first closed rule for floor consideration of first budget resolutions, the floor was open to amendments; and members took advantage of that access. Amending activity peaked in 1979, when thirty-five amendments were offered to the Budget Committee's first budget resolution. In that year, after nine days of floor debate on the budget, majority leader Jim Wright observed, "a budget is a devilishly difficult thing not only to put together but to keep together."[32]

Throughout the late 1970s, the Speaker used numerous strategies to recruit enough votes to pass budget resolutions: leadership appeals to support the process, leadership amendments on the House floor, inclusion, and Speaker's task forces.[33] On two occasions, not even these strategies were enough to pass the Budget Committee's first budget resolution when it initially came to the floor. Yet, without the Speaker's efforts the chances of failure would have been even greater.

TABLE 8
Floor Amendments to House Budget Committee Resolutions, 1975–79

Year	First Budget Resolution Fiscal Year	Number of Amendments Offered	Number of Amendments Passed
1975	1976	3	1
1976	1977	9	2
1977	1978	12	6
1978	1979	7	2
1979	1980	35	9

Source: Lance T. LeLoup, *The Fiscal Congress* (Westport, Connecticut: Greenwood Press, 1980), p. 74.

64 *The* SPEAKER *and the Budget*

PASSING THE FISCAL 1978 FIRST BUDGET RESOLUTION.
The problem of building coalitions to support the Budget
Committee's resolutions was evident in the first year of
O'Neill's speakership. In spring 1977, Congress departed
from the normal budget process and passed a third resolution for fiscal year 1977, which amended the ceilings of the
fiscal 1977 second resolution that had been passed the previous fall. The budget revisions included a two-year $31.2
billion economic stimulus plan of combined tax cuts and
spending increases worked out by congressional leaders and
White House officials. The Budget Committee later modified Carter's plan by raising his estimates for government
jobs programs from $1.8 to $3.5 billion. This decision reflected the liberal bias on the committee—as a matter of
choice, liberal Democrats preferred government spending
to tax cuts as a means of stimulating the economy.

The third resolution was approved easily by the House.
But the Budget Committee's first budget resolution for fiscal
year 1978 failed miserably on the House floor by a vote of 84–
320. O'Neill's problems stemmed from two sources. First,
President Carter's indecisive fiscal policy and hostile approach
to Congress disrupted the previous agreement between congressional Democratic leaders and the White House to offer
the stimulus plan. Second, there were clear ideological differences between the budget priorities of the liberal House
Budget Committee and the more conservative Democratic
membership.

In the early months of 1977, the Carter administration took
two actions that caused disarray over the budget. First, about
one month after the House had already passed a conference report on the revised third resolution and the House Budget
Committee had drafted its version of the budget resolution for
fiscal 1978, Carter withdrew his support for most of the stimulus plan. Urging Congress that the economy was picking up
and that "we do not need to proceed in Congress with the $50
tax rebate, nor the optional business tax credits," the president

dropped $11.4 billion of the original $13.8 billion stimulus plan for fiscal year 1977. In the process of trying to mobilize public support for his balanced budget plan, Carter proceeded to offend House Democrats by warning, "I will resist to the utmost of my own ability excessive spending by Congress in fiscal year 1978. . . . I am going to oppose strongly . . . any substitution of this money for spending projects that might be nonvital and which might initiate permanent programs or expenditures that can't be controlled in the future."[34]

These actions angered Budget Committee chairman Robert Giaimo and Ways and Means chairman Al Ullman, who had both worked hard to build support for Carter's tax rebate. Giaimo described the effect of Carter's actions on the House Democratic party: "A lot of Democrats were asking, what's going on here, what do we stand for as the Democratic Party . . . I think the administration has to cooperate much better with us in Congress."[35]

Carter's decision to drop the tax cuts was poorly timed, because the House was just about to consider the Budget Committee's fiscal 1978 budget resolution. When the tax cuts were removed, Giaimo had to adjust the figures for the fiscal 1978 budget on the spot. His new budget plan increased outlays and the deficit by $1.5 billion. The higher deficit figure in the hastily revised fiscal 1978 first budget resolution alienated conservative Democrats. Many of them had already expressed reservations about the Budget Committee's original fiscal 1978 budget resolution because it reduced Carter's proposed defense authorization request by $4.1 billion.

While conservatives were irritated by the higher deficit figure, liberals were frustrated with another move made by the Carter administration. Days before the floor vote on the budget resolution, the defense secretary Harold Brown lobbied the House Armed Services Committee for a higher defense authorization. The House subsequently approved Omar Burleson's (D-Texas) amendment to restore Carter's original defense expenditure request to the Budget Committee's version of the fiscal 1978 first budget resolution. Liberals thought that the Burleson amendment created an imbalance between defense and domestic spending. According to Giaimo, the Burleson amendment resulted in "breaking a delicate balance between defense and domestic spending proposed by the Budget Committee." He went on to say,

Quite rightly, a great many moderate and liberal members felt that the restraint they had shown with respect to spending for urgent domestic needs was not going to produce a similar restraint on the part of the defense establishment. . . . For any one sector—such as the defense establishment—to be given special treatment destroys our entire effort to provide for a reasonable balance among all competing interests.[36]

But Giaimo's view of what constituted a reasonable balance between defense and domestic spending interests was not entirely accurate. Part of the problem with building support for the Budget Committee's resolution could be traced to the ideological differences between the committee and the Democratic caucus (see table 4). Evidence suggests that the Budget Committee's resolution reflected the preferences of liberal Democrats, rather than a careful balance of domestic and defense spending. For instance, Carter's defense request was the only program function in his entire budget that the committee reduced. Yet Carter gained support for his defense request outside the Budget Committee. Following Brown's testimony, the House Armed Services Committee voted 35–2 to report a defense authorization matching Carter's request. The House proceeded to pass the committee's authorization bill three days prior to the floor vote on the budget resolution. Hence, as one report would have it, the Budget Committee was "out of step with the House, with the Democratic administration and the American people with its defense recommendations."[37]

After this initial failure, the Budget Committee went back to the drawing board and drafted a compromise resolution that bridged the gap between liberals and conservatives. The committee increased defense by $1.15 billion in budget authority and $300 million in outlays from the original estimate and reduced the deficit target from $68.6 to $66.4 billion. These two provisions allowed the leadership to gain support from enough conservative Democrats to pass the revised fiscal 1978 first budget resolution.

The Speaker was not directly involved in reconciling the differences, but majority leader Jim Wright urged members to vote in favor of the committee resolution and "redeem the commitment of the House to make the process work." Wright sent a letter to House Democrats appealing to their interests and emphasizing the need to support the budget process. "If the budget resolution should not be adopted, we'll be prevented under law from proceeding with the appropriations process. Bills of all sorts will be stymied, and Congress itself would be a victim of self paralysis."[38] On its second attempt, the Budget Committee's fiscal 1978 budget resolution passed the House by a vote of 213–179.

PASSING THE FISCAL 1979 FIRST BUDGET RESOLUTION. In 1978, the following year, Speaker O'Neill used the whip system, a task force, and personal persuasion to protect the House Budget Committee's resolution amid pressures on the House floor to cut the budget. During several days of floor consideration, the Speaker and the leadership team fought off numerous attempts to reduce the Budget Committee's spending recommendations for fiscal 1979. First, a Republican substitute offered by Marjorie Holt (R-Md.), which reduced the committee's spending estimate by $21.4 billion in budget authority and $13.1 billion in outlays and cut the deficit by $9.9 billion, lost by a narrow 197–203 vote. Then the Speaker lobbied enough support to reverse a previously passed amendment by John Ashbrook (R-Ohio), which reduced budget authority and outlays for the Department of Health, Education, and Welfare by $3.15 billion. Finally, the House defeated (195–203) an amendment by Democrat Joseph Fisher (D-Va.) to reduce spending across the board by $8 billion in budget authority and $7 billion in outlays. On both the Ashbrook and Fisher amendments, the Speaker used whip counts to determine which members could be persuaded to support the leadership position. At-large whip Tom Bevill (D-Ala.) emphasized the Speaker's importance in defeating the two amendments that would have jeopardized the Budget Committee's resolution: "In a close case, the prestige of the Speaker is very great."[39] The Speaker also appointed a task force, chaired by Butler Derrick (D-S.C.), to build support for the committee's resolution, which then won by a narrow margin of 201–197.

PASSING THE FISCAL 1980 FIRST BUDGET RESOLUTION. By 1979 pressure was building to reduce spending, but with the help of Speaker O'Neill, liberal Democrats remained a formidable obstacle to President Carter's goal of a balanced budget. It was the only year during the Carter presidency that O'Neill became actively involved in budgetary politics prior to floor consideration of the first budget resolution. Carter announced in his budget message, "a policy of restraint is not a casual one. It is imperative if we are to overcome the threat of accelerating inflation."[40] His budget, including spending cuts in every policy area except defense, was denounced by lobby groups for workers, minorities, and the elderly, and it was criticized as unfair by liberal Democrats, including Speaker O'Neill. O'Neill directly challenged Carter's budget:

I'm not going to allow people to go to bed hungry for an austerity program . . . no way. If unemployment goes up to 6.5 percent and I hear nothing from the White House, I'll be calling the [Democratic Steering and] Policy Committee to come forward with our own economic stimulus program and have a public works program of our own and we'll put it on his desk.[41]

Although the movement to reduce spending had begun, O'Neill still had a relatively strong liberal following in the House. The Budget Committee continued its pattern of endorsing a more liberal budget package than Carter. The committee reduced the president's defense request from $138.2 billion to $134.2 billion and restored funds for education, health, and urban development. O'Neill influenced this course somewhat, through a meeting over lunch with Budget Committee Democrats when he "made an impassioned plea for saving social programs."[42]

The Speaker was directly involved in several efforts to ensure passage of the Budget Committee's fiscal 1980 first budget resolution. First, Speaker O'Neill and other members of the leadership team sent a letter to all House Democrats encouraging them to defeat the Republican substitute. Then, in an effort to build support among conservatives and liberals, the leadership sponsored a floor amendment that added $2.2 billion in budget authority and $1.5 billion in outlays to purchase two destroyers, increased targeted fiscal assistance for high unemployment areas of the country, and allowed for unexpected costs of disaster loans and food stamps. Finally, Speaker O'Neill appointed a task force, this time chaired by Norman Mineta (D-Calif.), to build support for the Budget Committee's plan.[43] The task force was designed to communicate to liberal Democrats the idea that, although defense spending was high, domestic spending was realistic and the Republican alternatives were worse. Mineta explained, "the bottom line is, do you want a budget written by the Democratic majority . . . or the Republican minority?"[44] The effort paid off: 211 Democrats voted in favor of the Budget Committee resolution, which passed in the House by a vote of 220–181.

This victory was short-lived, however, which indicated yet again the uncertainty of maintaining a Democratic coalition. After a compromise with Senate conferees produced a more conservative budget—one that added funds for defense and reduced spending limits for function 500 (the category including estimates for education, training, employment, and social services)—David Obey (D-Wis.) led the liberal DSG to upset the House coalition in support of the fiscal 1980 first budget resolution. The conference report went down by a vote of 144–260, with 152 Democrats voting "nay." After $350 million was

restored to function 500, the House approved a revised conference resolution by a vote of 202–196.

PASSING THE FISCAL 1981 FIRST BUDGET RESOLUTION.
By 1980 it was clear that Speaker O'Neill's ideological
views ran counter to the fiscally conservative movement in
Congress. Chairman Giaimo described the national mood:
"The head of steam behind spending limits is stronger than
ever. We're in an intolerable inflationary period. And voters
think that government spending is one of the causes.
They're saying 'get it down.' "[45] Democratic support swung
away from traditional liberal programs and toward concern
for a balanced budget.

In his January 1980 budget message, President Carter temporarily relinquished his goal of a balanced budget for fiscal
year 1981. But, after the OMB reported the January 1980 economic figures showing an inflation rate of 18.2 percent, Carter
and his economic advisers reassessed his original budget plan.
The economic crisis brought together White House officials
and congressional budget leaders. The group met continuously
during the first two weeks of March to negotiate a deficit reduction package. Based on the outcome of these meetings,
Carter's revised budget plan, announced on March 14, included $14 billion in spending cuts from his original January
budget. After altering projections for inflation and unemployment, these cuts produced enough savings not only to balance
the budget but also to achieve a projected $10 billion surplus
for fiscal 1981.[46]

Giaimo led the charge to balance the budget in the Budget
Committee's markup sessions. Using the format agreed upon
at White House–congressional meetings, the Budget Committee's fiscal 1981 budget resolution included reconciliation instructions calling for $6.4 billion in spending cuts and $4.2
billion in revenues. For the first time, the Budget Committee
plan received bipartisan approval by a vote of 18–6, with the
six "nay" votes coming from liberal Democrats.

With House Democrats appealing to fiscal conservatism, Speaker O'Neill initially faded into the background. O'Neill disagreed with the movement to balance the budget, and he did not partake in the meetings with White House officials. He believed balancing the budget would "dismantle the programs I've been working for as an old liberal." He also remained aloof from the Budget Committee's deliberations over the budget resolution. Unlike the previous year when he encouraged support to salvage traditional New Deal and Great Society programs, in 1980 O'Neill did not even attempt to sway Budget Committee Democrats. The Speaker had neither the authority nor the following to reverse the conservative momentum that had developed. For Speaker O'Neill, the only consolation in the Budget Committee's decision (to use reconciliation to reduce the deficit) rested in his belief that the House "lacked the discipline to actually make those cuts."[47]

But although O'Neill's personal preferences placed him at odds with the mandate approved by the president and Budget Committee Democrats of his own party, eventually he played a critical role in approving the 1981 first budget resolution. Indeed, the Speaker's assistance proved to be essential to make the budget process work.

One of the critical strategic decisions of 1980 was for the Rules Committee to issue a modified closed rule to limit the number of floor amendments to the Budget Committee's first resolution. In past years, floor amendments had steadily increased—a clear reflection of the participatory spirit that propelled the reform period. But in 1979, after a backlog of amendments caused the House to take nine days to pass one budget resolution, the situation was clearly out of hand. Even Speaker O'Neill, who was instrumental in initiating reforms that opened up the amendment process, criticized the distinct political purpose of the amendments: "Everyone's getting in on the act. It's great for home consumption to get in on this." By 1980, Giaimo realized that a closed rule was necessary in order to pass a budget resolution that included reconciliation

instructions. He argued, "We can't have a free, wide open rule.
We would be here literally for weeks balancing one interest
against the other."[48]

Giaimo's proposal for a closed rule revived a still-unsettled
conflict over the purpose of the Budget Act, which had originally been fought between the junior members (with participatory aims) and senior committee chairmen. The debate
revealed tension between the legislative jurisdiction of House
committees and the privilege of members to participate in formulating the budget resolution. Rules Committee Republican
Robert E. Bauman (R-Md.) protested the use of a closed rule,
saying that it "flies in the face" of the Budget Act, which he
argued intended to provide a forum for debating priorities.[49]
But others claimed that members were abusing the privilege to
participate in the budget process by proposing amendments for
specific programs. In their view, the amendments undermined
the purpose of formulating a comprehensive budget plan and
actually threatened the legislative autonomy of the authorization committees and appropriations subcommittees. They believed that line items in the budget should first be reviewed at
the committee stage and then be introduced when separate appropriations and authorizations bills are offered on the floor.

The Rules Committee—the Speaker's arm for coordinating
House business—was responsible for reconciling the tension
between committees and the House membership over the purpose of the Budget Act. The central question was how to
provide enough opportunity for members to offer legitimate
amendments to the committee's budget—an acknowledged
right of members—but also to prevent them from abusing the
right to express their narrow interests.[50] The number and type
of amendments offered under the closed rule were arrived at in
a collegial fashion with O'Neill, Wright, Bolling, Giaimo, and
majority whip Thomas P. Foley (D-Wash.) acting as the principal arbiters in the case.[51] From twenty-four requests, the
rule granted eight amendments. The Republicans were allowed
four amendments, including one substitute that reduced total spending and domestic funds, and another that increased

the defense budget. Democrats proposed the remaining four amendments, including an amendment to consider Carter's original budget; an amendment by David Obey to increase spending for social programs by $1.2 billion; an amendment by Giaimo to make technical corrections in fiscal 1980 estimates for military and trade adjustment aid; and a motion to strike reconciliation instructions from the budget resolution.

Despite all the clamor over the closed rule, it passed easily on the House floor. The only amendment to pass was Giaimo's technical adjustment to the budget resolution. Although O'Neill privately supported Obey's amendment to increase spending for social programs, he did not actively lobby for votes on the floor. According to one report, O'Neill was persuaded by House budget leaders not to announce his support for the amendment, as they thought it would upset the chances of passing the whole first budget resolution.[52] The budget resolution passed on the floor by a vote of 225–193. Twenty-two Republicans voted for the resolution, the highest number of Republicans ever to vote for a Budget Committee resolution. The thirty-nine liberal Democrats who voted against the resolution (see table 6) resented the conservative bent of the committee's budget resolution backed by the majority party leadership. House Budget Committee member Bill Gray (D-Pa.) articulated this view: "It was very clear that the Democratic leadership felt that they did not need the liberal vote because they were going to seek the votes on the Republican side."[53]

From the standpoint of passing a budget resolution, it was imperative for the leadership to build a coalition of conservative Democrats and Republicans. As much as Speaker O'Neill disagreed with the fiscally conservative movement in the House, there simply was not enough support for the liberal Democratic position. The Speaker's responsibility was to facilitate passage of first budget resolutions, and this was an institutional commitment that superseded his personal preferences. An attempt to satisfy the needs of liberal Democrats could have obstructed the budget process in a situation that clearly called for a conservative budget policy. As process manager, O'Neill had a role to prevent breakdowns in the budget process, even if he had to set aside his own policy preferences to perform that role. By withholding support for the Obey amendment, O'Neill tacitly sided with the majority of House Democrats.

For the second consecutive year, the House-passed resolution fell apart in conference with the Senate. The Senate Budget Committee Democratic conferees, led by their recently appointed chairman Ernest Hollings (D-S.C.), stood firmly behind the Senate's much higher defense figure. House conferees were without the services of Chairman Giaimo who was ill during conference proceedings. Five House Budget Committee Democrats—William Brodhead (D-Mich.), Richard Gephardt (D-Mo.), Norman Mineta, Leon Panetta (D-Calif.), and Timothy Wirth (D-Colo.)—refused to sign the conference report that included the Senate's defense request. O'Neill realized that, without the backing of these key House Democratic conferees, the budget resolution would be difficult to pass on the House floor: "It's a tough hard fight. . . . You really lost some good solid people who really have some clout in Congress."[54]

Democratic leaders were divided over the conference report: Wright, Foley, John Brademas (D-Ind.), and Bolling supported the conference plan, while Carter and O'Neill were opposed. The president and the Speaker complained that the conference report recommended too much for defense spending and too little for domestic programs. On the day the conference report was scheduled for a vote on the floor, O'Neill told reporters, "The budget goes against my philosophy." The House rejected the conference report by a vote of 141–245. At least in Giaimo's view, O'Neill's actions disrupted the process of passing the budget: "If certain people in high positions had stayed out of the process, we'd be a lot closer."[55]

The prospect of revising the conference report was worsened by other events on the floor. Delbert Latta (R-Ohio) made a motion to accept the defense figure in the conference report;

Giaimo made a motion to table Latta's motion, but this was defeated by a vote of 123–165. Many liberal Democrats left the House floor before the vote was taken, and 57 conservative Democrats joined 108 Republicans to defeat the motion. The House then defeated Giaimo's motion to adjourn and accepted Latta's motion to instruct House conferees to support the Senate defense figure. Giaimo concluded that he now had two mandates—one from liberal Democrats who rejected the conference resolution because the defense figure was too high and another from conservative Democrats and Republicans who coalesced to pass the motion to support the Senate's defense estimate.

Giaimo, Hollings, and Carter worked out a compromise budget resolution that reduced defense by $800 million and added $1.3 billion for domestic programs. At that point, Speaker O'Neill finally got behind the Budget Committee and devoted his energy to passing the conference report. Barbara Sinclair observed, "At this point the ambivalence that had characterized his involvement in the process gave way to strong determination to pass the compromise." First, O'Neill mobilized the support of Steering and Policy Committee Democrats by stressing to them that this vote was a party issue. Then, he employed the whip system and appointed a task force to build support for the conference plan. He met with deputy and at-large whips to acquire feedback from their efforts to build Democratic support. At the next whip meeting before the vote was taken, the Speaker communicated the message that partisan support was expected on the conference report. Finally, O'Neill signed a letter sent to all Democrats emphasizing that "failure to adopt the first resolution would demonstrate clearly that the Democratic Congress cannot deal with the budget. It would discredit the party and the Congress."[56] After the task force worked to mobilize support on the floor, the House passed Giaimo's motion to accept the conference report by a vote of 237–161. Only twelve Democrats voted "nay," while the Republicans voted unanimously against the report.

The vote illustrated the importance of the Speaker's role in generating support for the budget process. The original House-passed first budget resolution for fiscal 1981 reflected a modest bipartisan coalition. But the vote on the first conference report indicated the fragility of that coalition. Once internal party differences receded to a reasonable level, O'Neill translated the urgency of passing the first budget resolution into an issue of majority party responsibility. After the budget resolution was approved, the House could proceed with the appropriations and reconciliation processes.

Enforcing Budget Decisions

Enforcing the budget process requires meeting the deadlines of the Budget Act and coordinating the separate authorization, appropriations, and tax decisions with the guidelines of the first resolution and the ceilings of the second budget resolution. Both objectives require coordination between the Budget Committee and the other committees in the House. The task of enforcing the budget process is easy, so long as the committees are willing to follow the formal procedures of the Budget Act. If the committees voluntarily comply with the guidelines of the Budget Act, the Speaker performs only the supportive functions defined by his role as nurturer. But when the committees ignore the guidelines or when their actions conflict with the preferences of the majority of House members, the Speaker plays a key role in managing the process.

For the first four years after the passage of the Budget Act, the process basically worked according to design. So long as the committees were not burdened by pressures to reduce spending in programs under their jurisdictions, they complied with the formal timetable established by the Budget Act. Although the committees typically submitted hefty spending requests in their March 15 reports to the Budget Committee, the reports were submitted promptly.[57] This allowed the Budget Committee adequate time to assess the reports before drafting the first budget resolution. Up until 1979, Congress generally met the deadlines for passing the first (May 15) and second (September 15) budget resolutions (see table 9).[58]

The second resolution was normally adjusted to accommodate whatever final allocations on separate spending bills the House approved during the budget cycle. In this context, the Speaker's role as nurturer reflected the modest expectations of the House membership, which were to follow the timetable established by the Budget Act.

The budget process ran according to the guidelines set by the Budget Act only so long as the priorities of the whole membership coincided with those of the separate committees. As Allen Schick points out, "a Congress bent on circumventing its own budget controls is not likely to be stopped by appeals to uphold the process or by various points of order implanted in the Budget Act."[59] The formal deadlines for the first and second resolutions were missed in 1979 and 1980, the first two years that the House majority pressed the committees to reduce spending (see table 9).

When the budget issue heated up in the latter half of the Carter presidency and the House eventually voted to use

TABLE 9
Dates the House Passed Conference Versions of First and Second Budget Resolutions

Year	Fiscal Year	First Budget Resolution (May 15)[a]	Second Budget Resolution (September 15)[b]
1975	1976	May 14	Dec. 12
1976	1977	May 13	Sept. 16
1977	1978	May 17	Sept. 15
1978	1979	May 17	Sept. 21
1979	1980	May 24	Nov. 28
1980	1981	June 12	Nov. 20

Source: Compiled by author from *Congressional Quarterly Weekly Report* (various editions).
[a]Under the Budget Act, May 15 is the date for passing the first budget resolution.
[b]Under the Budget Act, September 15 is the date for passing the second budget resolution.

reconciliation procedures to reduce spending, committees clashed over jurisdictional boundaries and legislative responsibilities. These conflicts led House members to reassess the ambiguous purpose of the Budget Act. The tension underlying the reform period—between traditional committee government and the vocal House membership—was played out on the increasingly intense field of budget politics. No procedure existed for settling the tension between the policy goals of the House majority and those of the committees. The members' broadly defined goal of reducing the deficit clashed with narrower concerns raised by the committees when their particular programs were put on the chopping block. In this context, the Speaker was called upon to manage a major problem left unresolved by the Budget Act: how to make the separate decisions of committees comply with the budget totals endorsed by the House in the first budget resolution.

From 1976 to 1979, the House and Senate budget committees tried to achieve spending control through "assumed legislative savings."[60] As the budget committees drafted the first budget resolution, they assumed that the authorization committees would reduce or maintain spending levels in selected entitlement programs. But since the committees treated the first budget resolution merely as a set of targets, they could ignore the assumptions of the budget resolution, and they normally did. And the leadership accommodated the committees, rather than enforce the assumed legislative savings of the first budget resolution. Consequently, the total spending target established by the first budget resolution was exceeded, and the imbalance between the assumptions of the first budget resolution and the committees' actions had to be adjusted in the second budget resolution.

In 1979, however, the leadership appointed a task force on legislative savings. During the drafting sessions on the fiscal 1980 first budget resolution Leon Panetta, the task force leader, maintained "if we go to the floor with a resolution that doesn't make a clear signal that we are committed to balancing the budget, we're going to get shot down."[61] Once the first budget resolution was approved by the House, the task force was in charge of pressing authorization committees to make cuts in existing legislation in order to meet the spending targets established by the budget resolution. Toward this end, the Budget Committee recommended that certain committees make reductions in specific details of legislation, so-called line items.

The task force's mission was bound to cause conflicts between the Budget Committee and the appropriations and authorization committees. The authorization committees not only demanded their independence in writing specific legislation, but they continued to request spending increases for their programs. The Appropriations Committee was also disturbed by the specific nature of the policy recommendations debated during floor consideration of the first budget resolution. With so much attention focused on specific programs, Appropriations Committee chairman Jamie Whitten challenged the members to reconsider the original purpose of the Budget Act:

My friends, practically all the debate on this resolution and the attitude of the Members has indicated that we have been voting for or against individual programs. I am fearful that many Members have completely forgotten the macroeconomic purpose of the Budget Act. There was absolutely no intention in the creation of the Budget Act that it would disintegrate into the kind of item debate we have seen here in the last few days.[62]

Whitten believed the Budget Act intended the budget committees to assess the authorization committees' March 15 requests, draft a broad budget plan with macro-economic estimates reflecting those requests, and then draft a second plan later in the year to confirm the separate work of the committees. The Appropriations Committee, not the Budget Committee, should decide spending levels for specific programs. The Budget Committee should only enforce procedural violations of the Budget Act; it had no authority to direct the authorization committees to reduce spending for specific programs.

In spite of Whitten's authoritative view as a key member of the JSC, however, the underlying intentions of the Budget Act were unclear. Some members believed the budget process should be used as a means of setting priorities, while others believed the objective was to control government spending. From either of these perspectives, members were tempted to amend the budget resolution to protect or advance their own policy interests. And in order for the Budget Committee to make macroeconomic estimates, it had to analyze and make recommendations on specific components of legislation. The debate over budget reform never clarified the proper means for handling jurisdictional disputes between the Budget Committee and the other committees. The problem emerged in the daily operation of the budget process as the Budget Committee attempted to enforce fiscal discipline, and it would have to be addressed in that context.

If the targets of the first resolution are to be used as guidelines for the congressional budget, blatant violations of those targets cannot be tolerated for long without undermining the process altogether. Under the Budget Act, the budget committees are responsible for tracking authorization and appropriations bills through the legislative process, to see if they follow the guidelines of the first budget resolution. In 1979, the Budget Committee was able to restrain excess spending recommendations of authorization bills with the help of outside allies. In one case, the Rules Committee declined to schedule for floor consideration a House Small Business Committee authorization bill for disaster loans, because the bill exceeded the amount estimated in the first budget resolution. In a second case, the Speaker's direct assistance was needed. Speaker O'Neill removed a child nutrition bill from the suspension calendar and ordered it back to the Education and Labor Committee after the Budget Committee reported that the bill failed to meet the estimated legislative savings under the budget resolution.[63]

O'Neill used the opportunity to establish a general rule for scheduling: "There had been scheduled today a suspension, but in view of the fact that it is the understanding of the Chair that it violates the Budget Act, the Chair will say to all committee chairmen that he will not recognize Members for bills under suspension that violate the Budget Act without the concurrence of the Budget Committee."[64] Because of the Budget Committee's weak institutional position in the House, it needed the support of existing entities to gain more than voluntary compliance from the other committees. Clearly, the Speaker was a primary source of support for the Budget Committee. He had the power to schedule bills and to use the Rules Committee to shape the rules for considering appropriations and authorization bills.

In 1979, however, Congress did not adopt rigorous procedural methods to reduce government spending. The budget committees met in conference in October to consider the second budget resolution, and as usual they found that the total sum of the separate committee decisions exceeded the aggregate spending and deficit targets approved by the first resolution. The conferees reached a deadlock: whether to use reconciliation to make the committees reduce spending or simply to adjust the ceilings of the second resolution to coincide with the committee decisions, as they had in the past. The Senate's second resolution recommended reconciliation to instruct certain committees to cut spending. But the House voted against reconciliation, and Giaimo supported the authorization committees, arguing that they had already created enough legislative savings and should not be asked to cut further. He concluded, "reconciliation is an important tool, but not this year."[65] House and Senate conferees essentially decided they would agree to disagree: the Senate included reconciliation language in its report and the House did not. The Senate later replaced reconciliation instructions with "a sense of Congress" clause to the second resolution. The clause recommended, rather than instructed, committees to lower spending to the level of the ceilings set by the second budget resolution.

By the end of the year, after the House defeated several attempts by authorization committees to make legislative savings, Giaimo regretted not having used reconciliation. It seemed that members endorsed the goal of reduced spending to lower the deficit but were unwilling to vote in favor of reductions in specific programs. The beleaguered chairman lamented, "I have long been troubled by the gap between congressional rhetoric on the need to exercise fiscal restraint and congressional performance in voting on specific spending bills." The lack of "congressional will" to reduce the deficit and the inability of the budget process to integrate separate spending bills with the aggregate totals in the budget resolution convinced Giaimo that "unless we devise stricter controls, we will not get a firm grip on federal spending."[66]

The balanced budget momentum carried over into 1980. By that time the budget deficit swelled to $73 billion, the Constitution subcommittee of the Judiciary Committee drafted a constitutional amendment to balance the budget, and the blame for long-term debt was placed squarely on the growth in entitlements.[67]

In 1980, entitlements posed perhaps the biggest obstacle for Congress in reducing the deficit. Entitlements are commitments by the government to transfer payments directly to individuals or agencies that meet eligibility requirements specified by law. Since the budget classifies entitlements as "relatively uncontrollable" under existing law, they are not subject to annual review in the appropriations process. Whereas regular appropriations bills can be altered each year they come up for review, most entitlements can be reduced only if Congress changes the laws themselves.[68] Changing laws to cut entitlements can be difficult for congressmen, particularly for members of authorization committees who are normally the most staunch proponents of programs within their jurisdiction. Cutting entitlements can be a painful political exercise also because it entails repealing benefits that people in need or groups representing people in need have come to expect. As Panetta observed, "you've got constituencies that are built into these programs. The reality is that you aren't going to cut them."[69]

Giaimo recognized, however, that spending for entitlements had to be reduced in order to reduce the deficit. Reconciliation provided a means whereby a House majority could instruct authorization committees to change entitlement laws, instead of depending on the committees' good faith. Although the authorizing committees claimed their right to achieve legislative savings on their own—that is, without any instructions from the Budget Committee—Giaimo shot back, "I'm no longer willing to give them the benefit of the doubt."[70]

In April 1980, the committees revealed their disapproval of reconciliation. Sixteen committee and subcommittee chairmen signed a letter to Speaker O'Neill protesting the use of reconciliation with the first resolution. The letter read in part:

Invoking reconciliation in the first step of the congressional budget process undermines the committee system, reposing in the Budget Committee authority to legislate substantively with respect to the nature and scope of federal activities. Such a procedure, which infringes on the legitimate roles of authorizations and appropriations processes, is not required to balance the budget. Balancing the budget should be accomplished by the spending committees in light of their evaluations of the priorities of the activities in their jurisdiction.[71]

The committees had their chance during floor debate to strike reconciliation instructions from the House Budget Committee resolution. Morris Udall (D-Ariz.), House Interior Committee chairman, said, "you don't change the rules in the middle of the game and you don't dismantle the committee system."[72] But Udall's amendment to scratch reconciliation procedures failed by a vote of 127–289. Most of the votes in favor of the amendment came from senior Democrats and committees affected by reconciliation. Senior members were considered to be more sensitive to committee autonomy, whereas members of the affected committees feared retrenchment for their programs. Against these objections, the House decided it would use reconciliation to make spending cuts in order to reduce the deficit.

Although the House approved of reconciliation as part of the first budget resolution, the instructions would not be enforced automatically. Obey, a Budget Committee Democrat who voted against the fiscal 1981 first budget resolution, pointed out, "To get reconciliation you have to have the support of the committees. You had better get them on board, or you might have a balanced budget now [when the first budget resolution is passed], but you won't have one in September."[73]

Obey was referring to the nature of the reconciliation process, which depended on the committees to follow instructions. Under the Budget Act, reconciliation was designed to reconcile the separate decisions of the committees with aggregate ceilings passed in the second budget resolution. In 1980, however, the first resolution included reconciliation instructions that recommended reducing $6.4 billion from existing legislation. Once the budget resolution was approved by the House, these instructions directed eight House and ten Senate authorizing committees to alter legislation for programs under their jurisdictions so that the savings could be achieved.[74] The committees were responsible for reporting the savings back to the budget committees by a specified date. The budget committees would then package all the savings into an omnibus reconciliation bill, which would be voted on by both chambers and then, like any bill, be signed by the president.

Giaimo realized that the Speaker's help was necessary if the House was going to be successful in enforcing reconciliation. Giaimo noted, "Nothing is going to happen in legislative reform unless the leadership forces these committees to do it [go along with the reconciliation instructions]."[75] The Speaker's assistance in resolving committee disputes became apparent soon after the first resolution passed.

The case of the Post Office and Civil Service Committee illustrates the importance of the Speaker's authority in persuading the authorizations committees to comply with reconciliation instructions. House and Senate leaders agreed earlier in the year that the budget committees should instruct the Post Office and Civil Service Committee to cut $500 million from Saturday mail delivery subsidies.[76] This provision was specified in the reconciliation instructions passed along with the first budget resolution. But Post Office and Civil Service resisted the instructions and was supported by Jamie Whitten, chair of the House Appropriations Committee. In principle, Whitten strongly opposed the idea of the Budget Committee's issuing specific instructions to an authorizations committee. As a symbolic gesture, intended to defy the House Budget Committee and the party leadership, the Appropriations Committee voted against cutting $500 million from appropriations for Saturday mail delivery for fiscal 1981.

Although the Appropriations Committee's vote had no direct effect on the legislation drafted by the Post Office and Civil Service Committee, Giaimo feared that Post Office and Civil Service would now assume it was no longer obliged to follow the instructions of the first budget resolution. Giaimo complained, "Appropriations can't live in its own little world and not work with us or the leadership." Speaker O'Neill initially supported Whitten's actions, but Giaimo convinced O'Neill that violations of this kind were intolerable if reconciliation was going to succeed. The Speaker said he would use his influence to ensure that the Post Office and Civil Service Committee met its obligations, and he set forth a general rule: "The legislative committees remain under an obligation to report the legislative savings voted by the House."[77]

The Speaker's efforts to get the committees to comply with reconciliation procedures was strengthened by the vote against the Udall amendment and the fiscally conservative mood of the country. Thus, when O'Neill organized a meeting with Giaimo and the committee chairmen affected by reconciliation, shortly after the first resolution was passed, the chairmen generally agreed to comply with the reconciliation procedures. Although many committee members affected by reconciliation instructions complained, the committees reported the necessary savings back to the Budget Committee. Barbara Sinclair observed, "Pressure from the leadership and the Democratic membership at large . . . was too strong for the committees to resist."[78]

The next step in the reconciliation process—packaging the committee reports into a reconciliation bill—also required the Speaker's assistance. The Rules Committee decided whether to package all individual program cuts into a single omnibus reconciliation bill (to be voted up or down by the House membership) or to allow separate floor amendments to restore funds that the reconciliation instructions ordered to be reduced. This was a critical procedural question because it would be far more difficult for members to vote for each separate spending reduction than to vote for all of them at once. Voting in favor of an omnibus reconciliation bill was a vote to reduce the deficit; voting in favor of cutting funds for specific programs forced members to discriminate among priorities.

The Budget Committee requested a closed rule on the reconciliation bill. But twenty-four witnesses came before the Rules Committee, and most of them requested amendments to restore cuts made in the reconciliation bill.[79] With bipartisan support, the Rules Committee voted 8–7 to allow an amendment to restore the COLA for federal retirees. Three Democrats—Joe Moakley (D-Mass.), Shirley Chisholm (D-N.Y.), and Leo Zeferetti (D-N.Y.)—voted in favor of the COLA amendment. This decision placed the entire process in jeopardy because, if the COLA amendment was offered, then other members could make legitimate claims to offer their amendments.

Again, the Speaker was called upon to manage the dispute. In this case, O'Neill exercised his powers in two ways. First, he rescheduled floor consideration on the reconciliation bill, in order to cool the tension created by the COLA amendment. The bill was originally scheduled for July 30, prior to the August recess. The bill was rescheduled until the House returned from recess, so that the leadership could have more time to build support for a rule that would limit the number of amendments. Second, O'Neill reminded Rules Committee Democrats that he had the power to nominate members to the Rules Committee, and that he expected their cooperation. Although he was unable to reverse the committee's decision to offer the COLA amendment, he was able to convince them not to allow any further amendments.[80]

The leadership had already secured enough support for passing the reconciliation bill when it reached the House floor on September 4, so long as the bill was offered under the restricted rule. In order to secure passage of the rule on the House floor, a majority of the House had to vote in favor of the previous question. Without a vote on the previous question, the rule itself would be subject to debate and amendment. The vote on the previous question was the focus of Bolling's speech on the floor as the House moved toward closing debate on the rule. Although he disagreed with the reconciliation cuts, he respected the "overwhelming majority of this institution [that] spoke and said: This is the reconciliation we want." He emphasized that the House Democratic party was responsible for maintaining the process and he urged strong partisan support for a procedural vote. Most important perhaps, he explained that the alternative to the leadership's rule—a rule issued by Latta—would be even worse. He announced that voting down the previous question "is not going to help the liberals over here with whom I sympathize. Many of the programs that are cut in this reconciliation are my favorite programs, too. [Voting down the previous question] is not going to help anybody that wants to do something different."[81]

Bolling's motion to order the previous question, which would end debate and call the House to vote on the rule, passed 230–157, with only fourteen Democrats voting "nay." The leadership had lobbied vigorously for support, on the grounds that the motion to order the previous question was a procedural vote and that losing would mean giving the Republicans a chance to control the floor.[82] The rule was also adopted, by a vote of 206–182, with thirty-nine Democrats voting against. Both the COLA amendment and the reconciliation bill passed with bipartisan support.

By 1980, it was clear that the Speaker had become an important player in managing the problems incurred in the budget process. Although O'Neill, like Bolling, was not enthusiastic about the policy effects of reconciliation, he was obliged to support the House's position. The budget had come to dominate the business of the House, and the Speaker, with the help of the Rules Committee, was called upon to clarify the distinction between procedure and substance. By setting the precedent that committees should comply with the will of the majority, and then by using the powers of his office to carry out that will, the Speaker was able to build support for the budget resolution and reconciliation bill.

Summary

In the first six years following the passage of the Budget Act, the Speaker concentrated mostly on addressing internal institutional and partisan problems stemming from the prevailing conditions underlying budget-making. As the House adapted to the many reforms passed earlier in the decade, the Speaker's role as nurturer reflected the modest expectations of the members, which were to meet the basic procedural guidelines of the Budget Act. Soon, intra-party divisions and increasing floor amendments summoned the Speaker to devise strategies for passing budget resolutions. While coalition building was a traditional task for the Speaker, new techniques (such as the use of task forces) were employed to get the job done. The Speaker's efforts were motivated not only by partisan interests but also by concerns for maintaining the budget process. Thus, while in some cases the Speaker appealed to the process to unify the party, in others he appealed to party unity to build support for the process.

As the period progressed, external pressures—mainly economic troubles and fiscal constraints—induced House members to use the new process as an instrument for reducing federal spending. This development created tensions between the parts and the whole and raised questions about the purpose of the Budget Act. The Speaker emerged as process manager, reconciling intra-party procedural and policy differences, both between committees and between committees and the membership. In this capacity, the Speaker began to use the Rules Committee more aggressively to manage the process.

Yet, while the Speaker's roles as nurturer and process manager were defined by the context of budget politics, the style and the success of a Speaker's performance in those roles are determined partly by individual factors. Speaker Albert's commitment to making the process work aided his ability to perform the nurturer role defined by the conditions of the day. Without question, the House budget process benefited from his ability to educate committee chairmen and coordinate the committees for action in the budget process.

Conditions may also shape leader roles that conflict with a leader's personal preferences. Speaker O'Neill confronted this situation in 1980 when his role as process manager clashed with his personal budget priorities. Even though he preferred to maintain spending levels for certain traditional Democratic programs that the committees were instructed to cut, he was responsible for facilitating the reconciliation process. Such dilemmas are not uncommon for leaders of representative bodies whose roles are often created to resolve institutional or party-related problems.

On the whole, both Speakers Albert and O'Neill conformed mostly to a collegial leadership style and adhered to the middleman hypothesis. On only one occasion, in 1979, did O'Neill attempt to challenge his president's budget and meet personally with Budget Committee Democrats to promote traditional Democratic programs. His appeal was general, however; it was directed more toward salvaging existing spending levels than initiating new policies. Besides, sentiment to reduce the deficit was only just beginning to spread among House Democrats. The major policy change was the move to cut spending in 1980, a decision that O'Neill did not support let alone initiate. The Speaker remained apart from high-level negotiations between White House officials and congressional budget makers. As it turned out, O'Neill's role conflict was relatively easy to resolve. After his own president and the House majority approved reconciliation, the Speaker had little choice but to go along. Although O'Neill did not initially endorse reconciliation, he conceded to the will of the majority of House Democrats and carried out the tasks associated with managing the budget process.

4

The Speaker Under Stress:

Budget Politics in 1981

Reflecting on his experience as Speaker of the House during 1981, Tip O'Neill stated, "In all my fifty years of public life, this was absolutely the lowest point in my career."[1] O'Neill's frustration stemmed from his futile efforts to stop the House from approving unprecedented spending cuts in social welfare, education, and health programs endorsed by President Ronald Reagan. Using his personal skills, public popularity, and an effective White House operation, Reagan took advantage of a favorable set of policy, political, and institutional conditions to gain congressional approval of his conservative economic mandate.[2] The same conditions underlying Reagan's success adversely affected Speaker O'Neill's influence over budget outcomes. O'Neill confessed, "I screeched and I hollered and I fought his program every way I could, but there are times that you just can't buck a trend."[3]

The 1980 elections left Speaker O'Neill opposition party leader of an ideologically divided majority party. In fact, on budget issues, O'Neill lacked a majority in 1981. Reagan formed his own majority in the House by recruiting conservative Democrats to join with a unified minority Republican party. The Speaker continued to play the role of process manager, trying to facilitate budget decisions and resolve conflicts between committee chairmen and between chairmen and the House majority. But the conflicts grew more intense when the White House used reconciliation to seize legislative authority from congressional committees. Under these conditions, O'Neill had to struggle to balance competing roles as opposition party leader and process manager. He also had to reconcile his personal commitment to traditional liberal programs with his responsibility to carry out the choice of a House majority to cut many of those programs.

I begin this chapter by describing the conditions that facilitated Reagan's presidential leadership. I proceed to assess how O'Neill adapted to Reagan's four major budgetary victories in 1981: the fiscal 1982 first budget resolution (Gramm-Latta I); an omnibus reconciliation bill including major reductions in domestic spending (Gramm-Latta II); a three-year tax plan providing tax breaks for individuals and depreciation allowances for businesses; and further spending reductions attached to an omnibus appropriations bill. O'Neill's strategies for managing the budget process and leading the opposition party against the Reagan juggernaut stemmed partly from his lack of expertise in budget policy and partly from his conception of leadership. Yet the bulk of the Speaker's troubles can be traced to an overwhelming transformation in the political context, in which the president became the dominant force.

Conditions for Presidential Leadership

Reagan's leadership of Congress in 1981 was prefaced by favorable policy, political, and institutional conditions. The conservative policy mood of the late 1970s—characterized by domestic spending restraints, defense increases, and dissatisfaction with the sluggish economy—crystallized with the 1980 elections. Public opinion polls revealed that voters clearly favored Reagan over Carter on economic and defense issues.[4] Reagan defeated Carter by nearly 10 percent of the popular vote and carried forty-four states totaling 489 electoral college votes. The Republicans unexpectedly gained eleven seats in the Senate, giving the party its first majority in either chamber since 1954. Republicans gained thirty-four House seats, as twenty-seven Republicans defeated Democratic incumbents, while only three Republicans lost bids for re-election. Christopher Buchanan, an elections analyst, described the group of fifty-two new Republicans to enter the Ninety-seventh Congress as "articulate spokesmen of the Reagan line on government spending and defense."[5]

The gain in Republican House seats weakened the Speaker's capacity to perform a vital leadership function, that of building a majority coalition to support the Budget Committee's first budget resolution. The 1980 elections reduced the House Democratic majority from 276–157 to 242–189, a margin of only fifty-one seats. Consequently, the Budget Committee's version of the first budget resolution could be defeated if as few as twenty-six Democrats voted against it. From 1975 to 1980 an average of fifty-five Democrats, and no less than forty-four Democrats in any given year, voted against the House Budget Committee's first budget resolutions. Although Democrats were usually divided over budget priorities during the 1970s, each year the Speaker eventually found enough votes to pass a Democratic budget resolution. But given the relatively small margin of Democrats to Republicans during the Ninety-seventh Congress, combined with the momentum generated by Reagan's electoral victory, the Speaker could anticipate problems with coalition building.

The most formidable challenge for Speaker O'Neill came from the conservative wing of the Democratic party. Southern conservatives, so-called Boll Weevils, were the most likely Democrats to coalesce with House Republicans. In 1978 and 1979, for example, the conservative coalition of Southern Democrats and Republicans nearly approved Marjorie Holt's (R-Md.) substitute amendments to the Budget Committee's fiscal 1979 and 1980 budget resolutions.[6] After the 1980 elections, a vociferous group of forty Southern Democrats led by Charles Stenholm (D-Texas) formed the Conservative Democratic Forum (CDF). The CDF urged Speaker O'Neill to "use his appointive powers to get a better balance [of conservatives to liberals on key committees]."[7] O'Neill accommodated Stenholm by seeing to it that three conservative Democrats—Beryl Anthony (D-Ark.), Phil Gramm (D-Texas), and Bill Hefner (D-N.C.)—were appointed to the Budget Committee in 1981. O'Neill also remained neutral in the race for Budget Committee chairman that pitted conservative Jim Jones (D-Okla.) against liberal counterpart David Obey. House Democrats elected Jones on the third ballot, exhibiting the party's lukewarm preference to have a conservative chairman at the helm.

In addition to the conservative policy environment and Republican electoral gains, Reagan also had the advantage of reconciliation, a device the Democrats used along with the first budget resolution in 1980. Reconciliation enables Congress to package spending reductions into a single omnibus bill, thereby mitigating the problems associated with passing each of them separately. OMB director David Stockman saw reconciliation as the "procedural innovation" for swift action to "rubber stamp" the Reagan mandate.[8]

Leaders Interpret the Conditions

Although Reagan was elected by a landslide and Republicans made impressive gains in congressional elections in 1980, many elections analysts interpreted Reagan's victory as a rejection of Carter's poor performance rather than as a mandate for Reagan's supply-side economic policy.[9] Speaker O'Neill certainly held this view. He said, "After Reagan won, the press of America, the media of America, were saying it was a mandate for the fiscal change of the last fifty years. That wasn't what it was about at all. It was about the unpopularity of Jimmy Carter."[10]

O'Neill's interpretation of the 1980 election undoubtedly affected his strategy as opposition party leader. The Speaker believed that, although a newly elected president deserves an opportunity to define the nation's priorities, Congress should also be consulted on budget policy. In O'Neill's view, solving the economic problems of the country required the cooperative efforts of a popular president and a formidable Congress. After a meeting with Reagan shortly following the election, O'Neill announced, "I told [Reagan] I would not criticize him for six months and that we would work to turn the country around. We want to get him off on the right foot."[11]

O'Neill may have misinterpreted the situation. Others, including political scientists Warren E. Miller and E. Merrill Shanks, argue that the 1980 elections reflected an "underlying structure of conservative preferences" rather than a vote to disapprove of Carter. Most important, regardless of how O'Neill interpreted the election results, Reagan planned to operate on the premise, perceived or real, that the elections signaled a mandate from the people.[12] Although Reagan realized the necessity of building congressional support for his economic agenda, he made it clear early in 1981 that he was not about to compromise with Democratic leaders. Reagan announced in his budget message, "When considering the economic recovery package, I urge the Members of Congress to remember that last November the American people's message was loud and clear. The mandate for change was not my mandate; it was our mandate." He predicted that his budget, consisting of reductions in federal spending and tax cuts, combined with a "stable" monetary policy, would produce a "return to prosperity."[13]

Congress: Politics as Usual?

Despite the president's call for a restructuring of fiscal policy, budget policy-making in the House during the first few months of 1981 appeared to be politics as usual. The Budget Committee was prepared to offer its own budget proposal as specified by the Budget Act. Budget Committee Democrats, led by Chairman Jones, were aware of the fiscally conservative trend Reagan identified in his budget message. Yet, despite Reagan's professed mandate, the Budget Committee disagreed with some details of the Reagan budget and set out to devise a feasible conservative alternative. In relentless pursuit of the president's mandate, a skillful White House staff eventually undermined the committee's efforts. After months of political maneuvering by budget makers, the House decided, for the first time ever, to approve a president-sponsored substitute to the Budget Committee's first budget resolution.

Hoping to draw support from the Boll Weevils, Chairman Jones criticized the measures recommended in Reagan's budget as too extreme and drafted a modified conservative alternative first budget resolution. He immediately expressed disfavor with the Kemp-Roth tax plan, endorsed by Reagan, which reduced personal income taxes by 30 percent over three years. Although Jones supported lower capital gains taxes and depreciation allowances for businesses, to make American companies more competitive in the international market, he disagreed with a long-term tax plan in a period of rising deficits.[14] He also denounced Reagan's proposal to increase defense by $23.3 billion. He argued, "the Defense Department has to be called on the carpet to deal with this problem of waste and duplication in the same way as other departments."[15]

House authorization committees also resisted Reagan's proposals to reduce spending for domestic programs. As usual, the March 15 committee reports to the House Budget Committee estimated spending levels above the president's requests. The most pronounced attack on Reagan's budget came from the House Education and Labor Committee, which held jurisdiction over many of the programs high on the list of David Stockman's "black book," a catalogue of itemized reductions in government spending. Among these programs were child nutrition, elementary school aid, grants and loans to college students, and employment and job training. The committee's March 15 reports requested a total of $42.4 billion for all its programs, exceeding Reagan's budget by $18 billion.

The first budget resolution offered by the Budget Committee differed from Reagan's budget in several ways. First, the Budget Committee rejected the OMB's three-year extended economic forecast underlying Reagan's budget. Democrats of all stripes were skeptical of Stockman's rosy scenario for the country's economic future, embodied in a set of economic assumptions used to estimate total spending, revenue, and deficit levels for the budget. Liberal Democrat Tom Downey (D-N.Y.) called them "hallucinogenic," and conservative Democrat J. J. Pickle (D-Texas) referred to them as "jelly-bean talk." Chairman Jones announced, "We're not going to put out a budget based on mirrors and magic which six months or a year from now will be held up to ridicule."[16] Jones decided to use the CBO's more "realistic" economic assumptions for drafting the Budget Committee's first budget resolution. The CBO's assumptions projected higher inflation, unemployment, and interest rates, and lower GNP growth than those of the OMB (see table 10).

The Budget Committee also estimated a lower deficit figure for fiscal 1982 (−$25.6 billion compared to Reagan's −$45 billion) and changed the budget priorities endorsed by Reagan. The committee opted for only a one-year tax cut in contrast to Reagan's three-year cut, and the budget resolution restored some of Reagan's proposed cuts in social programs. The Budget Committee estimated significantly more spending for the income security function and the education, training, employment, and social services function than Reagan's original budget (see table 11). At the same time, the Budget Committee increased estimated outlays for defense over Reagan's budget by nearly $900 million.

TABLE 10
Economic Assumptions for Fiscal 1982 (in percentages)

Source	Inflation	Unemployment	GNP	Interest Rate
Budget Committee	10.4	7.3	2.3	12.0
Reagan Budget	8.3	7.2	4.2	8.9

Source: *Congressional Budget Office* data reported in Gail Greg, "GOP Senators Successful in Heading Off Attempts to Restore Veterans' Funds," *Congressional Quarterly Weekly Report*, March 28, 1981, p. 550.

TABLE 11
Fiscal 1982 Budget Outlays by Function (in billions of dollars)

Budget Function	Reagan Budget	Gramm-Latta Budget	HBC Budget
National defense	$188.8	$194.10	$189.75
International affairs	11.2	11.00	11.20
General science, space, and technology	6.9	7.00	7.05
Energy	8.7	9.50	6.85
Natural resources and environment	11.9	12.70	12.35
Agriculture	4.4	5.15	5.10
Commerce and housing	3.1	4.25	4.30
Transportation	19.9	20.65	21.10
Community and regional development	8.1	9.35	9.50
Education, training, employment, and social services	25.8	26.60	29.40
Health	73.4	73.80	74.45
Income security	241.4	243.85	247.65
Veterans benefits	23.6	23.60	24.05
Administration of justice	4.4	4.35	4.55
General government	5.0	4.95	4.90
General purpose fiscal assistance	6.4	6.45	6.15
Interest	82.5	91.90	90.10
Allowances	1.8	1.70	.70
Undistributed offsetting receipts	−32.0	−34.20	134.60
Total	695.3	16.70	714.55

Source: Gail Gregg, "New Round of Budget Bargaining Begins," *Congressional Quarterly Weekly Report*, April 25, 1981, p. 706.

Speaker O'Neill played a minimal role in formulating the priorities of the fiscal 1982 first budget resolution. He was poorly positioned to encourage Jones to work for a liberal budget reflecting the Speaker's priorities. Political scientist Steven Smith observed, "O'Neill . . . believed that the public was demanding a new direction in federal spending although he personally dreaded the actions he felt that demand dictated." Under the circumstances, O'Neill accepted the committee's resolution as a viable alternative to Reagan's budget, one that would allow Americans to "get a college education, to own a home and earn a decent living."[17] As in previous years, the Speaker was mostly involved with developing strategies for passing the resolution on the House floor. Toward this end, O'Neill joined with conservative Budget Committee Democrats in persuading Jones to recommend a defense outlay higher than Reagan's as a way to attract conservative Democratic votes.

During the committee's deliberations over the budget, the strategy of drafting a conservative alternative to Reagan's budget seemed to be working. The Budget Committee passed Jones's budget resolution by a vote of 17–13, with the support of every Democrat except Phil Gramm. The committee also rejected a bipartisan substitute worked out by Gramm and Stockman and sponsored by Delbert Latta. Hence, even though three of the seven new Democrats appointed to the House Budget Committee in 1981 were conservatives, all but Gramm cooperated with Jones. Meanwhile, Reagan was losing ground in the Senate. Three Senate Budget Committee Republicans—William L. Armstrong (R-Colo.), Charles E. Grassley (R-Iowa), and Steven D. Symms (R-Idaho)—rejected Reagan's budget because the deficit figure was too high.

White House Victory: Gramm-Latta I

Despite the apparent shortcomings of Reagan's budget, leading administration officials expressed dissatisfaction with the Budget Committee's first budget resolution. Secretary of the Treasury Donald Regan called the committee's effort "well intentioned but inadequate." Stockman accused the Democrats of "changing their words, but still singing the same old tune" of more taxes and spending.[18] Since Reagan's original budget was floundering in Congress, the White House decided to seek a fresh alternative to the Budget Committee's budget resolution.

Jones realized that a Republican alternative could jeopardize the fragile support he received from conservative Democrats. Originally, Jones was optimistic about passing the committee's budget in the House. But with the White House decidedly against compromise, Jones admitted, "I don't think there are 218 votes for anything right now." Wendell Belew, the Budget Committee chief counsel, observed, "Because it gave the administration 75 percent of what it wanted, Jones was very surprised the Republicans opposed the proposal so strongly. But they apparently thought they could get more momentum for later battles, especially for taxes, from a total victory."[19]

"Total victory" was what the Reagan administration wanted and "momentum" was the key ingredient to achieving that end. A description of the events that took place after the Budget Committee completed its work (April 9) and before the whole House considered the first budget resolution (May 1) illustrates how the president won the battle over the budget.

Initially, Reagan confronted problems by trying to form a conservative coalition of Republicans and Southern Democrats to support a substitute to the Budget Committee's resolution. The Boll Weevils were skeptical about Reagan's generous tax breaks and thought a −$45 billion deficit was too high. Many of them favored the Budget Committee's first budget resolution because the deficit was nearly $20 billion below Reagan's. Furthermore, Speaker O'Neill would promote a floor amendment by Bill Hefner to increase defense by an additional $6.6 billion. Offering the Hefner amendment was a deliberate strategy to entice Southern Democrats to vote for the Budget Committee's resolution.[20]

But President Reagan's multifaceted coalition-building strategy undercut the Speaker's attempt to attract Southern Democrats. Gramm, Latta, and Stockman revised Reagan's original budget, adopting even more optimistic economic assumptions. The so-called Gramm-Latta substitute reduced the original budget-deficit figure from $45 to $31 billion. Stockman later explained, "Gramm felt he couldn't win on the floor unless they had a lower deficit, closer to Jones's deficit, so they got it down to $31 billion by hook or by crook, mostly the latter."[21] The Gramm-Latta substitute also increased defense by more than $5 billion over Reagan's original request and more than $4 billion over the Budget Committee's estimate (see table 11).

Meanwhile, the White House Congressional Liaison Office worked feverishly to solicit votes from the Boll Weevils. The president became personally involved, telephoning members directly and inviting them to the White House. Reagan promised Southern Democrats that he would not campaign against them if they supported his budget. White House political director Lyn Nofziger coordinated a massive grass-roots lobbying campaign to promote the Gramm-Latta substitute in fifty-one carefully targeted House districts. Forty-five of those districts were represented by Southern Democrats and held constituents who voted heavily for Reagan in 1980. The White House believed that these Southern Democrats would be the swing votes on the budget resolution. Nofziger contacted conservative interest groups and business associations in these districts. Those groups then arranged speaking engagements to arouse support and used direct mail and telephone calls to reach individuals who donated to Reagan's presidential campaign. Individuals and interest groups were instructed to write letters and call their congressmen in support of the Gramm-Latta budget substitute.[22]

Finally, Reagan spoke before a joint session of Congress on April 28, just two days before the Budget Committee resolution and the Gramm-Latta substitute were scheduled for consideration on the House floor. The president criticized the Budget Committee's resolution because it "falls short of the essential actions we must take." He asked members to approve the bipartisan Gramm-Latta substitute because it closely approximated his mandate for economic recovery, which would "restore our economic strength and build opportunities like none we've ever had before."[23]

Meanwhile, as the House was about to vote on the first budget resolution, Jones and O'Neill quarreled over the effects of Reagan's lobbying campaign. O'Neill, who had just returned from a two-week trip to Australia, all but conceded victory to Reagan. He lamented, "Support the President—that's the concern out there and Congress can read that. I've been in politics an awful long time and I know when you fight and when you don't fight." While O'Neill appeared willing to concede victory to the White House, Jones attempted to salvage the waning morale of his House Democratic colleagues. Jones explained that O'Neill "had an erroneous perception of the situation," and the vote on the budget resolution "will be very close."[24]

The debate over the fiscal 1982 first budget resolution lasted six days on the House floor. Member after member gave five-minute speeches either in favor of or against the Gramm-Latta substitute. For O'Neill, the debate provided an opportunity to reverse his previous skepticism and try to rescue the Budget Committee's resolution. He really had no choice but to support Jones, even if the trend had swung away from the Budget Committee resolution.

In the final speech before the vote was taken on the Gramm-Latta budget, O'Neill attempted to unite the party by urging a modification, though not a rejection, of traditional Democratic principles and by warning members of the negative consequences of the Gramm-Latta substitute. He praised New Deal programs that pulled America out of the depression, and "made this country great." Although he admitted that his party failed to implement these programs effectively in recent years, he asked members not to eliminate them. He recognized that times had changed and Congress now had to tighten its hold on federal expenditures. In his view, however, the Gramm-Latta substitute was not the answer to the nation's fiscal problems. He criticized the architects of Gramm-Latta for using phony economic assumptions and refusing to cooperate with the Budget Committee. As for the effects of the Gramm-Latta cuts on the poor and the elderly, O'Neill argued, "You close the door on America with the Latta bill." O'Neill concluded with an endorsement of the budget resolution drafted by Jones. That budget accomplished the goal of fiscal conservatism and offered an "honest" alternative to Reagan's economic plan.[25]

But O'Neill's words did not convince enough members to support the Budget Committee's resolution. Sixty-three Democrats, forty-nine from southern and border states, joined all of the Republicans to pass the Gramm-Latta substitute by a vote of 253–176. The House then gave final approval to the budget resolution (270–154), with eighty-four Democrats voting "yea" and only one Republican dissenting. At a reception for House members following the vote on the budget resolution, Reagan announced, "I think we've made a little history. Thanks to you, we've made it clear that spending can be controlled and that our system works. The voice of the people can be heard here in the Capitol."[26]

THE FAILURE OF O'NEILL'S LEADERSHIP. While Reagan celebrated his victory, Democrats began to blame the leadership for failing to defeat the Gramm-Latta substitute. Although the Budget Committee's first budget resolutions were rejected in the past, 1981 was the first year the House approved a substitute in place of a committee-sponsored resolution. Some Democrats criticized majority leader Jim Wright for recommending Phil Gramm's appointment to the Budget Committee. Others blamed O'Neill for traveling to Australia for two weeks while Reagan built support for the Gramm-Latta budget. Others wondered why the Speaker did not appoint a task force to build support for the committee's resolution, as had been the case in previous years. Liberals criticized O'Neill for trying to build conservative support by promoting the Hefner amendment. Liberal Democrat George Miller (D-Calif.) argued, "this country can't afford to pay the price for these twenty or thirty [conservative Democratic] members."[27]

Were these valid criticisms of O'Neill's leadership? Or were the conditions facing the Speaker insurmountable? While conditions limited O'Neill's strategies, and perhaps even dictated his approach, a different Speaker might have acted differently in a similar situation. As opposition party leader, O'Neill was in a position to challenge Reagan's budget, but he preferred to allow the president a fair opportunity to make a case for his economic program.[28] Rather than publicly denounce Reagan's spending cuts, O'Neill took a low profile. He contacted interest groups, requested committees to study Reagan's budget proposals carefully, and urged the media to expose the specific programs Reagan planned to cut. Finally, as the middleman hypothesis would predict, O'Neill placated conservative Democrats, believing that they had earned a more prominent place in deciding the party's priorities. Certainly, he could have pushed for a more liberal alternative or expressed more public criticism of the president's economic plan, as Majority Leader Wright did. Thus, O'Neill's behavior in the early months of 1981 was not entirely bound by conditions but conformed at least partly with his conception of leadership.[29]

The issue of leadership failure is more difficult to assess. It appeared to depend more on conditions beyond the Speaker's control than on his personal decisions. There is enough evidence to dismiss, or at least excuse the Speaker for the criticisms voiced by party members. First, Wright backed Gramm, under the premise that he would support the Democratic party as he had promised. (Gramm had written to the Steering and Policy Committee before being appointed to the Budget Committee, saying, "I'll try to make my case, but if I lose, I'll be a team player.")[30] But after losing in the Budget Committee, Gramm violated his promise. When Budget Committee Democrats realized that Gramm was consorting with Stockman, they ostracized him from Democratic committee caucus meetings. Second, O'Neill's trip to Australia was planned two years in advance of the first budget battle of 1981, before Reagan was even nominated the Republican candidate, let alone elected president. Third, a task force was seemingly unnecessary in this case, because members were aware of the contents of the Budget Committee's resolution and the Speaker's staff generally knew how Democrats planned to vote.[31]

One could argue that the Speaker, the majority party leadership, and the Budget Committee chairman Jim Jones devised a sensible strategy to challenge the president. Regardless of

dissension from liberal Democrats and O'Neill's personal
views, the Speaker did not attempt to stonewall the conservative sentiment that was growing among many House Democrats. In an effort to accommodate this conservative trend in
the 1980 elections, O'Neill consented to appoint three new
conservative Democrats to the Budget Committee in 1981. The
average liberal rating for all Democrats on the Budget Committee in the Ninety-seventh Congress was lower than ever
before.[32] Of all the conservative Democrats on the Budget
Committee, only Gramm voted against Jones's budget; the others initially supported the Budget Committee resolution because Jones accommodated their preferences. Finally, the
Speaker attempted to placate conservative Democrats by stag-
ing the Hefner floor amendment to increase defense spending.

Conceding victory to Reagan before the floor vote was perhaps the one strategic flaw O'Neill was rightly criticized for.
The opposition party leader sets the tone for his party's position, and O'Neill's announcement that there was no sense in
fighting against the White House lobbying team may have been
premature. On the other hand, by that time whip counts indicated that the committee's resolution stood little chance of
passing any way.[33]

A plausible argument could be made that all of these problems were minor events, which became significant only within
a broader context that favored the policy views of a popular
president with an effective White House operation. Reagan's
highest public approval scores for 1981 were recorded just before and after the May 7 House vote on the first budget resolution (see figure 1).[34] The constituency pressure generated by
the White House congressional liaison team also contributed to
Reagan's victory.

Finally, in 1981, O'Neill faced the same problem—of trying to juggle the various factions of the Democratic party—
that had frustrated the majority party leadership in the 1970s.
Hefner pointed out, "even when the Democrats are together,
we're still fragmented." He believed the problem was structural: "We're a party made up of liberals, moderates and con-

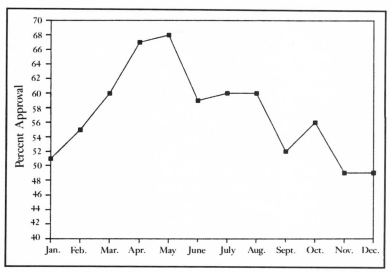

FIGURE 1. *Reagan's public approval ratings, 1981. Data from Gallup Report, December 1984, p. 10.*

servatives. We don't have the luxury of the Republicans, who know exactly what their constituency is."[35] O'Neill tried to implement strategies for building a winning coalition in a fractured party. But in 1981, there were thirty-four fewer Democrats. When the time came for a final tally on the first budget resolution, Reagan's persistent efforts paid off. With Reagan's energetic presidential leadership, under the prevailing policy and political conditions, the Democrats were simply too divided to withstand the White House lobbying effort. Or as one Budget Committee staff person recalled, "There was nothing we could have done to change that policy outcome. We just didn't have the votes."[36]

The Politics of Reconciliation

Reconciliation procedures for the fiscal 1982 budget resolution were similar to those used the year before. The Gramm-Latta budget resolution instructed various committees to reduce spending levels for programs within their jurisdictions and recommended the program changes that would meet those levels. But so long as the committees complied with the spending levels issued by the reconciliation instructions, they could exercise discretion over specific changes in legislation. The committees were instructed to report their recommendations for legislative savings to the House Budget Committee, where they were packaged into a reconciliation bill to be voted on by the House. The reconciliation bill would become law if approved by both chambers and signed by the president. These actions were scheduled to take place within sixty days after the conference report on the first budget resolution was passed by both chambers.

But the content of the reconciliation instructions contained within the Gramm-Latta substitute far exceeded the spending cuts approved by Congress the previous year. The reconciliation instructions issued by the fiscal 1981 first budget resolution called upon eight House committees to make spending reductions totaling $6.4 billion. In contrast, Gramm-Latta called for $36.6 billion in reductions from among sixteen committees for fiscal 1982. Gramm-Latta also projected spending cuts for three years rather than just the upcoming fiscal year. Spending was to be reduced by additional amounts of $48.2 billion in fiscal 1983 and $58 billion in fiscal 1984. Furthermore, unlike the previous year when reconciliation instructions requested committees to cut annual outlays for existing programs, the drastic cuts under Gramm-Latta required the committees to change the legal requirements of the programs themselves. This meant cutting eligibility standards for recipients of federal funds, for example, or worse, eliminating certain programs that the government had been authorized to fund under existing laws.

The depth and severity of the spending cuts in the Gramm-Latta budget resolution created conflicts between committees and the House membership. Most committee chairmen simply disagreed with the Gramm-Latta reconciliation instructions approved by the whole House. In 1981, for the first time, a significant number of committee chairmen voted against the first budget resolution passed by the House (see table 12). In the previous year, although the Budget Committee's fiscal 1981 budget resolution contained reconciliation instructions, only three committee chairmen voted against it—Ronald Dellums (District of Columbia), Carl Perkins (Education and Labor), and Peter Rodino (Judiciary). But in 1981, thirteen of the sixteen committee chairmen who were instructed to make spending reductions voted against the Gramm-Latta fiscal 1982 first budget resolution (like most of the Democrats). Thus the conflict in preferences between the House majority and the committee chairmen would be more intense than ever before.

TABLE 12
Votes by Committee Chairs on House-passed First Budget Resolutions (fiscal years 1976–86)

Year	Fiscal Year	Yeas	Nays	Unrecorded
1975	1976	17	2	1
1976	1977	17	1	2
1977	1978	19	0	1
1978	1979	17	0	3
1979	1980	18	1	1
1980	1981	17	3	0
1981	1982	5	15	0
1982	1983	2	17	1
1983	1984	19	0	1
1984	1985	20	0	0
1985	1986	20	0	0

Source: Congressional Quarterly Almanac, 1976–85.
Note: Votes from chairs of the following twenty House Committees: Administration, Agriculture, Armed Services, Banking, District of Columbia, Education and Labor, Energy and Commerce, Foreign Affairs, Government Operations, Interior, Judiciary, Merchant Marine, Post Office and Civil Service, Public Works and Transportation, Rules, Science and Technology, Small Business, Veterans Affairs, Ways and Means, and Appropriations.

THE SPEAKER'S ROLE IN RECONCILIATION. Reconciliation placed the Speaker at a critical juncture between the committees and the House membership. His role included mediating between the House majority that approved the Gramm-Latta budget cuts and the committee chairmen who objected to following its instructions. Similar to the situation in 1980, the tasks of the budget process manager also conflicted with O'Neill's policy preferences as opposition party leader. O'Neill wanted to maintain the traditional Democratic programs that were jeopardized by the Gramm-Latta budget cuts.

Yet, in 1981, the nature of the Speaker's role conflict was different than it had been in the previous year. In 1980, O'Neill's party (including the party's president) gave him a clear signal to set aside his personal preferences in order to support reconciliation. Thus O'Neill's role conflict was easy enough to resolve. Though he regretted the policy consequences, responding to the clear interests of the party's majority was compatible with O'Neill's middleman style of leadership. But in 1981, although the House approved the Gramm-Latta first budget resolution, the majority of House Democrats voted against it. Hence, the Speaker confronted the dilemma of trying to balance institutional responsibilities of facilitating the reconciliation process, on the one hand, with not only his own but many other Democrats' policy preferences, on the other. The role conflict was much more difficult to resolve and created the setting for indecisiveness and disagreement over the proper strategy for executing reconciliation instructions.

After considering numerous ways to implement the spending cuts issued by the Gramm-Latta budget resolution, the party leadership agreed to pursue a strategy that would limit the potential damage to traditional Democratic programs.[37] The damage-control approach included working within the budgetary constraints set by Gramm-Latta while protecting as many traditional Democratic programs as possible. This strategy seemed to be the best course for balancing the institutional responsibilities of the budget process with the policy interests of the party. On the one hand, damage control allowed the committees to carry out instructions approved by the

House majority. On the other hand, since committees could decide the specific programs to be cut, they could write legislation in a way that might salvage the programs favored by most Democrats.

Nevertheless, even this approach did not eliminate the problems encountered by the committees as they attempted to work out the details of the reconciliation instructions. Morris Udall, chairman of the House Interior and Insular Affairs Committee and a leading spokesman for committee chairmen against reconciliation in 1980, explained, "It's exceedingly difficult to cut programs, like environmental ones, that are emotionally charged. We have to tromp on hallowed ground—kick old friends in the teeth to achieve some of these cuts." Carl D. Perkins (D-Ky.), chairman of the Education and Labor Committee, also complained, "In all my years in Congress, I have never witnessed an action more ill-advised, more insensitive or more threatening to the rightful operation of the legislative process than these so-called reconciliation instructions." Perkins vehemently opposed reconciliation: "I've worked for years for the welfare of the people and now I'm seeing practically everything dismantled. . . . I'm just not going to vote to destroy these programs."[38]

The chairmen's reluctance to cut programs created scheduling problems that the Speaker needed to address. As one of O'Neill's staff persons put it, reconciliation gave the Speaker a "huge responsibility." More specifically, he said, "to get this thing [reconciliation] through takes a lot around here. [The Speaker was] constantly meeting with chairmen, setting deadlines, resolving jurisdictional conflicts to the goal of producing legislation."[39] A Budget Committee staff person described the purpose of the meetings with the chairmen: "He would tell them, 'Look I don't like making these cuts any more than you do, but the House voted for it and we are committed to making the changes.' . . . When committee chairmen revolted or were not submitting their directives, the Speaker would step in and enforce the process." The Speaker was responsible for facilitating the decisions of separate committees because "the Speaker needs to get things through so as not hold up all other legislation."[40]

Once the committees began to report their recommendations back to the Budget Committee, other problems cropped up. As committees devised ways to circumvent reductions in their favorite programs, they interfered with legislation that crossed jurisdictional lines with other committees. Instead of mediating between the parts and the whole, jurisdictional conflicts involved resolving tensions between the parts. The Speaker became a crucial actor in mediating differences between committees. Several of O'Neill's staff people point out that these jurisdictional disputes occurred constantly. One staff person remembered the telephone ringing off the hook as committee chairmen complained about other committees meddling with programs within their jurisdiction.[41] Another staff person explained:

On reconciliation there are an enormous number of questions about who has jurisdiction over what. Is committee A trampling on committee B's jurisdiction and if so what do we do about it, to the extent that the Speaker can tell a committee to drop something because it's something that it should not have done or have the Rules Committee make an order to excise it out.[42]

When the House uses reconciliation procedures, the Speaker is placed in a position to resolve committee conflicts because, as one of O'Neill's aides put it, "no one else could do it."[43]

Floor Debate and Gramm-Latta II

The tension over the extent of the spending cuts instructed by the Gramm-Latta budget resolution created disputes over how the reconciliation package should be handled on the House floor. The leadership would change its approach several times before bringing a rule to the floor. Ultimately, the Speaker's efforts failed again. Divisions within the Democratic party, conflicts between the membership and the committees, and the political posturing of the Reagan White House affected the leadership's strategy and success in devising a rule for reconciliation.

Originally, several committee chairmen argued that the House should vote separately on each proposed spending reduction, rather than on an omnibus bill. By offering separate amendments, the committees stood a better chance of restoring the cuts called for by the Gramm-Latta first budget resolution. The chairmen reckoned that members could easily vote for an omnibus bill that claimed to achieve the general aims of reduced spending and a lower deficit. But members would think twice about voting for specific program reductions that required them to discriminate between particular interests.

Speaker O'Neill initially supported a rule that would allow floor amendments to the reconciliation package. In particular, O'Neill planned to instruct the Rules Committee to schedule amendments for school lunch and student loan programs. In his opinion, "we should give the members of Congress an opportunity to vote on the programs that made America great." Following O'Neill's advice, the Education and Labor Committee decided to report back all the specific cuts instructed by the Gramm-Latta budget because, as Chairman Perkins observed, "We have received an absolute guarantee from the Speaker and the chairman of the Rules Committee that we will be allowed several votes on the House floor to reverse some of the worst cuts." But Chairman Jones disagreed with Speaker O'Neill, saying, "Democrats would be making a mistake if we adopted a process that allowed the unraveling of all aggregate cuts."[44]

The debate among Democrats over the rule for floor consideration of the reconciliation bill was settled temporarily as a result of pressure from the White House. Reagan officials, like the committee chairmen, believed the House lacked the will to reduce specific programs one by one. In order to ensure that the House voted on a single omnibus bill, rather than on a series of separate amendments, Stockman considered offering a substitute to the Budget Committee's reconciliation package. Stockman collaborated with Gramm on the reconciliation substitute (later referred to as Gramm-Latta II or the "Son of Gramm-Latta"). The omnibus substitute would essentially undercut the Speaker's strategy of allowing amendments to the Budget Committee's package. Members could simply vote against the leadership's rule and support the omnibus reconciliation substitute without having to vote on separate programs.[45]

The threat of a substitute reconciliation bill caused committee chairmen and the leadership to reconsider their strategy of allowing amendments. They reasoned that if the House rejected the rule, it would be one step away from passing the Gramm-Latta II reconciliation substitute. Their ultimate objective, of circumventing the spending reductions instructed by the first budget resolution, would surely fail if the House voted for the substitute instead of for the Budget Committee package. Under the emerging scenario, the committees would have relinquished their legislative authority to the director of the OMB, in collaboration with a select group of Republican legislators and Phil Gramm. Even though the committees disliked cutting into their favorite programs, if it was absolutely necessary, they preferred to do it themselves.

Thus, the leadership reversed its original position in favor of allowing amendments and decided to report the reconciliation bill under a closed rule. This decision prompted the committees to go back to the drawing board and revise their reports to the Budget Committee. Before the White House threatened to offer a substitute, the committees generally complied with the reconciliation instructions issued in Gramm-Latta I. Even though the committee chairmen voted against the Gramm-Latta I budget, the best strategy for limiting the damage of the spending cuts was to go along with the reconciliation instructions at the committee stage. Once the Budget Committee packaged the cuts and reported the bill to the House, the chairmen planned to offer floor amendments that would restore the cuts they originally recommended to the Budget Committee. With the closed rule in effect, however, they would have to be more discreet in their recommendations to the Budget Committee. Since there would be no chance to amend the reconciliation package on the floor, damage control would have to occur within committee. Hence, the committee chairmen revised their original recommendations for specific reductions in an effort to protect their favorite programs.

Republican leaders were dissatisfied with the revisions made by the committees. Minority leader Robert Michel (R-Ill.) argued that only about half the committees involved in reconciliation reduced entitlements by the levels anticipated by the Gramm-Latta budget resolution. President Reagan warned of "a clear danger of congressional backsliding and a return to spending as usual." If the Democratic leadership did not revise the committee work "so that it honestly and responsibly achieves the original spending goals," Reagan cautioned, "my administration will have no other choice than to support the proposal of a number of representatives in the House to offer a budget [reconciliation] substitute on the floor that matches the resolution they voted for in May."[46] The president was not going to be outdone by the authorization committees or the Speaker's Rules Committee.

President Reagan telephoned Speaker O'Neill to inform him that Stockman was working on a substitute draft of the reconciliation bill. Reagan told O'Neill, "I want a chance to send some substitute language up there on the budget [reconciliation bill]. The House has worked hard and done a good job, but it wasn't enough, and I . . . " O'Neill interrupted the president in mid-speech, saying, "Did you ever hear of the separation of powers? The Congress of the United States will be responsible for spending. You're not supposed to be writing legislation." Reagan shot back, "I know the Constitution." After accusing Reagan of disguising budget details and hiding his intentions in "vague generalities," the Speaker conceded to the president and instructed him to send the substitute to Jones and Bolling.[47]

Writing a reconciliation bill outside the congressional committees radically disrupted the traditional ways of legislating in the House. Even though the House approved the Gramm-Latta substitute as the first budget resolution for fiscal 1982, the Budget Committee was still responsible for coordinating the reconciliation instructions included in that budget. More important, the committees were still responsible for handling the spending cuts in programs under their legislative jurisdictions. A substitute to a Budget Committee first budget resolution that sets guidelines for spending decisions is one thing, but making specific legislative changes to meet those guidelines is quite another. In a sense, substitution for the Budget Committee's reconciliation bill amounted to abdicating the House's legislative function.

For the moment, the battle lines were clearly drawn. The Budget Committee planned to offer a reconciliation bill in a single package, and the Republicans would offer a substitute bill. With no better alternatives available, the leadership believed that the strategy of damage control rested on letting members choose between the mix of priorities outlined by the two omnibus bills.

But the problem of pitting the Budget Committee's package of spending cuts against the substitute bill was that the specific components of Gramm-Latta II were unknown throughout most of the Democratic leadership meetings on the closed rule. The only information available to the leadership came from a meeting of Stockman, Jones, and Panetta, which took place after the leadership agreed to a closed rule and about one week prior to the scheduled floor debate. Stockman informed Jones and Panetta that, among other cuts, Gramm-Latta II included larger reductions in social security and student loan programs than those instructed by Gramm-Latta I. The following afternoon, Minority Leader Michel vaguely described the terms of the Gramm-Latta II reconciliation substitute. It would make changes in the "unsatisfactory" reductions reported by the committees. He also said the substitute would include the cuts mentioned by Stockman.

With this scant information, the Democratic leadership considered yet again the strategy of offering a closed rule. Some Democrats thought that if the bill was considered as

a series of amendments, the Republicans would have to propose individual reductions in several politically sensitive programs, like social security. A Republican-sponsored initiative
to cut social security benefits would clearly be in the Democrats' favor.[48] Others thought the Republicans should not be
allowed to offer a substitute at all until House members had
had enough time to assess the specific components of Gramm-
Latta II. After much deliberation, the leadership changed its
strategy for a third time, deciding on a rule that required the
Republicans to offer the reconciliation substitute as a series
of amendments rather than as a single bill. These amendments potentially included the most difficult programs to cut:
social security, Aid to Families with Dependent Children
(AFDC), energy and commerce, school lunches and student
loans, food stamps, subsidized housing, cost-of-living adjustments (COLAs) in federal civilian and military pensions, and a
cap on pay raises.

On the morning of Thursday, June 25, the House floor became the forum for deciding the rule for considering the reconciliation bill. The Republicans accused Democratic leaders
of unfairly forcing them to report their package as a series of
amendments. They delayed the vote on the rule so that Reagan
could call more Southern Democrats to offer special legislative
favors and Stockman could make deals with moderate Republicans, so-called Gypsy Moths, restoring spending for certain
programs in exchange for their votes against the rule.[49]

Democrats, on the other hand, criticized the Republicans
for failing to provide the specific details of the reconciliation
bill. They stressed the importance of legislative responsibility.
The debate raised complex questions about the meaning of the
budget process and the balance of power between the president
and Congress. Rules Committee Chairman Bolling touched on
some of these issues in his speech just prior to calling a motion
to consider the previous question, which he favored:

The issue today is: Do we begin to accept the responsibility of members of the House of Representatives without regard to party, without
regard to a popular President? Do we have the guts to stand up for

what we believe in? Do we have the guts to stand up for the people
we represent? . . . or are we going to hide behind this parliamentary
game, this attempt to gag the House?[50]

The House answered Bolling by voting 210–217 to defeat
the previous question. By voting down the motion on the previous question, the House decided to continue debate on the
rule for the reconciliation proceedings rather than move to vote
on the leadership's rule. Consequently, the Republicans gained
control of the House floor and were able to pass their rule, including a single vote on Gramm-Latta II, the contents of which
had still not been revealed in full form. Speaker O'Neill was
amazed by the vote on the previous question: "I've never seen
anything like this before in my life, to be perfectly truthful."[51]

Obviously, O'Neill had not expected to lose the vote and
surrender the House floor to the Republicans. The majority
party normally supports the Speaker on procedural matters.
Furthermore, the leadership's strategy of allowing the Republicans to offer Gramm-Latta II as a series of amendments
seemed to balance the important concerns of all House members. The House maintained the responsibility to legislate; the
majority party's policy preferences could be protected; and the
minority party's ability to participate in the reconciliation process was preserved. It was unprecedented for the House majority party to relinquish the floor to the minority party,
especially on a bill of such importance that few members were
privy to.

The vote against the previous question can be explained by
a combination of factors: the leadership's shenanigans on the
rule; the institutional and political conditions underlying the
House's action on the reconciliation bill; and Reagan's ability to
persuade Southern Democrats to support Gramm-Latta II.
According to Stockman, the leadership's final decision to allow
amendments to the reconciliation bill backfired. Opening the
rule, he explains, was "a staggeringly dumb political blunder"
that "reversed the deteriorating situation" for the White House.
Stockman believed that the White House lacked the support

of enough Southern Democrats and Republicans to pass the Gramm-Latta substitute. Many Republicans (including Minority Leader Michel) and Southern Democrats disliked the idea of the OMB director doing the work of Congress. But they reassessed their views after the leadership changed strategy, forcing members to vote separately on politically sensitive programs like social security and Medicaid. Republicans thought the rule was unfair. Stockman described the response of the House Republican leadership to the open rule: "They didn't like it. It got their partisan dander up, and for the first time in weeks they felt the enemy was the Democrats, not me."[52] In hindsight, the Democrats' chances of defeating Gramm-Latta II may have been better had the leadership set up a head-to-head battle between Gramm-Latta II and the House reconciliation bill.

Yet Stockman's pat conclusion falls short of accounting for the institutional and political conditions O'Neill faced as the leadership developed strategy on the rule. An omnibus reconciliation bill allowed members to vote in favor of large spending reductions without having to go on record for cutting specific programs. Whether the House's bill was more or less appealing than the package of Gramm-Latta cuts was debatable, especially since the White House was constantly altering the bill's contents to attract the support of Southern Democrats. And again, the loss of Democratic House seats in the 1980 congressional elections limited the pool of members from which the Speaker could build support for managing House procedures. Although House Democrats had always been divided during O'Neill's speakership, before 1981 there were enough votes to compensate for members who dissented from the Speaker's position.

Most important, perhaps, the Speaker confronted an extremely popular president who had a well-organized and effective congressional liaison staff. Once again, the White House conducted an effective lobbying strategy. In contrast to the public campaign and aggressive grass-roots style of building support through constituency pressure for Gramm-Latta I (the first budget resolution), lobbying for Gramm-Latta II (the reconciliation bill) was more personal. Two days before the House voted on the rule, President Reagan held a breakfast for all sixty-three Democrats who had supported him on the first resolution. The night before the House voted on the rule, Reagan spent two and a half hours on the telephone, lobbying members. Where personal persuasion failed, the White House offered tangible rewards to members in exchange for their votes. Referring to the president's bargaining strategy, Chairman Jones observed, "the Democratic cloakroom had all the earmarks of a tobacco auction." These deals clearly influenced some members. When Louisiana Democrat John B. Breaux was asked why he supported the president he answered, "I went with the best deal." He explained that although his vote was not for sale, "it could be rented."[53]

The Gramm-Latta II substitute finally surfaced in full form at 11:30 on the morning of Friday, June 26. The House debated the bill later that afternoon. Democratic leaders warned the members not to accept the "hidden agenda," which some called a travesty and others called "the most shoddily put together piece of legislation this body has ever seen."[54] There was some truth to their wrangling. OMB Director Stockman later explained how the White House spent the two weeks preceding the vote, including the morning the vote was taken, making deals with Republicans and Southern Democrats who complained about the specific components of the substitute bill.[55] A reading of Stockman's account suggests that Gramm-Latta II was held up not only because the White House wanted to conceal its contents, but also because the contents of the bill were continually being reshaped to reflect the concessions to members in exchange for votes.

The criticisms against Gramm-Latta II were not persuasive enough. The reconciliation substitute passed by a vote of 217–211, with twenty-nine Democrats voting for the bill and only two Republicans voting against it. Reagan was able to hold together enough of his conservative coalition to score a second budgetary victory. The president sang the praises of victory:

"The simple truth is that Congress heard the voice of the people and they acted to carry out the will of the people."[56]

The Reagan Tax Cut

President Reagan's tax plan constituted a major part of his supply-side economic philosophy. According to supply-side doctrine, economic growth is contingent upon long-term tax reductions that provide incentives for individuals to save and for businesses to invest. Without his proposed three-year tax plan, the president's fiscal policy mandate would have been incomplete. The battle over Reagan's tax package mirrored the battles over the budget resolution. The Speaker volunteered his cooperation; the House Ways and Means Committee offered a modified alternative to the Reagan plan; the White House refused to collaborate with Democratic leaders; and, working his coalition-building magic for a third time, Reagan emerged victorious.

Reagan's original tax plan included an across-the-board 30 percent tax cut for individuals and accelerated tax write-offs for businesses over a three-year period. Overall, the plan yielded $44.2 billion in tax reductions for individuals and $9.7 billion for businesses in fiscal 1982. Echoing the claim once again that the 1980 election was a mandate for his economic policy, Reagan announced in April, "I am convinced the American people strongly support my program and don't want it watered down." Speaker O'Neill claimed that the House would comply with the president's wishes, saying, "we will ultimately send a [tax] bill to the president that he will be satisfied with."[57]

Dan Rostenkowski (D-Ill.), chairman of the Ways and Means Committee, introduced a preliminary version of the committee's tax bill in late March.[58] The bill contained tax cuts totaling $40 billion for fiscal 1982, with $28 billion going to individuals and $12 billion to businesses. Rostenkowski's plan was designed to take effect for one year, whereas Reagan's was a three-year plan. The chairman also announced that

the Ways and Means bill could be adjusted according to the
size of the budget deficit. If the deficit increased, Rostenkowski promised to seek ways of raising revenues, by closing
loopholes, reducing the tax cut, or finding additional savings
through spending cuts in programs under the jurisdiction of
Ways and Means, or by a combination of these methods.

Hence, Rostenkowski's initial response to Reagan's tax plan
was much like Chairman Jones's response to Reagan's budget.
Like Jones, Rostenkowski offered a conservative alternative to
the president's tax plan. And the president appeared inflexible,
much as he had in his response to the House Budget Committee's budget resolution. After Rostenkowski announced in
March that the "mood of the House" was not for a long-term
tax cut because of the unstable deficit situation, Stockman reported that Reagan would veto a one-year tax cut. In April,
Vice-President Bush reiterated Stockman's message, reporting
that Reagan is "in no mood to compromise." Bush said that if
Ways and Means offered only a short-term tax cut, the president "would give the veto very, very serious consideration."[59]

But the president had less support in Congress on the tax
plan than he had had on the budget. Although Southern Democrats supported the president's budget on ideological grounds,
many were not endeared to supply-side economic theory.
They were more concerned with lowering the deficit than with
increasing capital investment, and they feared the extended
three-year tax cut might result in revenue losses that would
drive up the deficit.[60] Given this initial skepticism among
Southern Democrats, there appeared to be grounds for nego-
tiation between the White House and Ways and Means.

The two parties met in May to compare revised versions
of their original tax bills. Following the same strategy as they
had on the first budget resolution (Gramm-Latta I) and the
reconciliation bill (Gramm-Latta II), Reagan's economic experts amended his tax plan to accommodate the Southern
Democrats. The primary objective was to reduce the estimated
budget deficit. White House officials retained the three-year
tax-reduction plan for individuals but changed the first-year

tax cut from 10 to 5 percent. They also curtailed the benefits that businesses received from depreciation allowances. The revised package reduced tax benefits by about $17 billion from the original bill and effectively reduced the projected deficit for fiscal 1982 to about $30 billion.

Meanwhile, Rostenkowski compromised to accommodate some of the demands made in the president's original proposal. Ways and Means Democrats agreed to extend Rostenkowski's one-year plan to two years. Rostenkowski also agreed to the idea of cutting individual taxes across-the-board. But the total tax cut would be only 15 percent over two years as opposed to the 25 percent over three years in the revised Reagan plan. Finally, at Speaker O'Neill's urging, the bill contained more tax breaks for middle- and lower-income families.[61]

Under pressure to accommodate various interests on both sides, negotiations between the White House and Ways and Means Democrats fell apart in early June. The president tried to restore some of the original tax breaks to businesses, and Rostenkowski abandoned the idea of across-the-board tax cuts for individuals. Ways and Means Democrats decided to draft their own bill and square up against the president on the House floor. At this point, Ways and Means Democrats appeared to have an edge on Reagan. Economic uncertainty was a roadblock for the Reagan administration, which was trying to hold together the conservative coalition that had formed on the previous two budget decisions. Some Republicans and Democrats continued to express concerns about how long-term tax cuts might affect rising deficit and inflation levels. Indeed, on June 7, Speaker O'Neill was quite confident that the Democrats could win on the tax bill: "If the vote were tomorrow, we could win it. Right now we have the votes. Can Reagan take them away from us? Let's wait and see."[62]

Whatever advantage the Democrats held in June, they had lost it by July 29 when the House voted 238–195 in favor of the president's tax plan. Once again, an extraordinary White House lobbying effort and Reagan's personal persuasion meant the difference between victory and defeat. Several days before the House voted on the tax proposals, Reagan invited fifteen Democrats to Camp David for a cookout and an opportunity to discuss their concerns about the tax package. Following the same strategy used on the reconciliation bill, the White House granted favors to members in exchange for votes. The White House made several deals with Southern Democrats that benefited farmers and oil producers.[63] On July 27, just two days prior to the House vote, the president appeared on television to ask the American people for their support. Business lobbies and private corporations organized telephone banks to call House members urging them to vote for Reagan's tax plan. What followed, according to Speaker O'Neill, was "a telephone blitz like this nation has never seen." He thought the constituency pressure on members was the deciding factor in the vote on the tax bill: "it's had a devastating effect." Or as White House chief of staff James Baker said, "The bottom line is, the president blew them away."[64]

Appropriations and the Presidential Veto

The president scored one more victory in 1981, this time in a battle over a continuing resolution—an omnibus appropriations bill providing funds to operate federal agencies and to finance government programs in fiscal 1982. But conditions had changed by fall 1981, and the politics surrounding Reagan's final triumph differed from the three previous cases. Whereas Reagan used persuasion and bargaining to build congressional support for the components of his economic plan, this time he exercised the veto to compel Congress to accept further reductions in the fiscal 1982 continuing resolution.

By September, reports of a sluggish economy caused President Reagan to seek a second round of spending cuts for fiscal 1982. Persistently high interest rates, recurring inflation, and a fifty-point decline in the stock market during August stifled the economic recovery anticipated by Reagan's fiscal policy and threatened to push deficits well above $100 billion by fiscal

1984. On September 24, the president delivered another televised address to Congress, this time calling for an additional
$10.4 billion in spending cuts ($8.4 billion in non-defense discretionary programs and $2 billion in defense) and a $3 billion
revenue increase for fiscal 1982.

By that time, however, both congressional parties had
begun to show signs of fatigue from the pressure to reduce
spending. Speaker O'Neill said, "the President will get his
day in court," but he expected Reagan to experience "tremendous problems" trying to build support for his latest proposals.
Republican Senate Banking Committee chairman Jake Garn
(R-Utah) also responded negatively to the president's latest
proposal: "How many times can you cut the same piece of
pie?"[65] Neither Senate Budget Committee chairman Pete
Domenici (R-N.M.) nor House Minority Leader Michel were
optimistic about achieving Reagan's second round of cuts. Domenici speculated that Congress might be able to pass about
half of the $10.4 billion in proposed spending cuts, $4 billion
of which would have to be in defense programs.[66] Meanwhile,
both chambers voted either to increase appropriations levels
or to prevent program reductions that were anticipated under
Reagan's original budget requests.[67]

Several members also began to call in their chips on the
favors promised by the White House in exchange for their
votes on previous budgetary decisions. Several moderate Republicans thought the president's new round of spending cuts
violated promises to protect Medicaid, mass transit, energy
conservation, and student loans. Their distrust of the president
threatened the strong party unity that had been demonstrated
by the House minority party throughout the year.[68]

By November, congressmen worried about continuing economic decline and the political problems associated with deficit
reduction. Unemployment reached 8 percent, its highest level
since 1975. The House Appropriations Committee reported a
continuing resolution that ignored the spending cuts Reagan requested in September. Republicans within the Reagan administration and Congress began to disagree about Reagan's latest

proposal to curtail deficit spending. Stockman reached a three-year deal with Senate budget leaders that included $80 billion in tax increases, and spending reductions of $30 billion for defense and $40 billion for entitlements. But House Republican leaders and Treasury secretary Donald Regan resisted any type of tax increase. And Secretary of Defense Casper Weinberger persuaded the president to accept only an $8 billion spending cut in defense over three years.[69]

To make matters worse, revelations concerning Stockman's doubts about supply-side economics and Reagan's intentions of devising a plan to benefit the wealthy suddenly surfaced in William Greider's infamous *Atlantic Monthly* article "The Education of David Stockman." Stockman admitted to using unrealistic economic assumptions to craft the fiscal 1982 budget and also to knowing that the Reagan plan to increase defense and cut taxes, without adequate provisions for reducing entitlements, would lead to a budgetary disaster. Stockman confessed, "none of us really understands what's going on with all these numbers."[70]

Greider's article gave Speaker O'Neill the ammunition he needed to blame the struggling economy on the Reagan administration:

The architect of the administration's economic program is admitting exactly what I and other critics have been saying for six months. . . . Mr. Stockman misled Congress and the American people as to the consequences of the Reagan economic program. His credibility and the credibility of the program he supports are in serious doubt.[71]

The public embarrassment was so great that Stockman offered to resign as director of the OMB.

With mixed signals coming from the White House about the future of the budget, the congressional budget process stopped dead in its tracks. By the second week of November, Congress had not passed a second budget resolution for fiscal 1982. Republicans and Democrats alike waited for the president to offer a compromise to break the deadlock over the budget. Domenici said, "We need some real official iteration from the White House on where this budget is going and what they expect us to do." Ranking Budget Committee Republican Latta announced, "Until the administration passes the word to me, I'm not in a position to take a position." House Reconciliation Task Force chairman Leon Panetta said, "The White House is going to have to play a role. Very frankly, I'm not prepared to move on the markup until I know where the White House stands [concerning reconciliation]."[72]

At this point Reagan decided to disengage from Congress. He could no longer depend on the support of House Republicans and Southern Democrats to pass his latest round of spending reductions, and he had completely lost the trust of the Democratic leadership. When White House chief of staff James Baker suggested using reconciliation to achieve the president's proposed cuts, Speaker O'Neill responded negatively, "by bitter experience you get burned." Rather than bargaining with members of Congress, Reagan pledged to veto any appropriations bill that "abuses the limited resources of the tax payers."[73]

Reagan's actions spoke louder than his words. The government shut down after he vetoed a continuing resolution on November 23 because Congress failed to meet a sufficient portion of his requested spending cuts. Several days later, on the eve of Thanksgiving, the president and Congress settled on a short-term continuing resolution that extended government spending for three weeks. This was enough time to let tensions cool and allow White House officials and congressional leaders to negotiate a final settlement on total spending for fiscal 1982. On December 10, the House finally passed a continuing resolution that included $4 billion in new spending cuts, less than a half of what Reagan had requested in September, but more than he would have got without exercising the veto.

Summary

Reagan's successful leadership of Congress in 1981 created obvious problems for the Speaker in his roles as opposition party leader and process manager. The House failed for the first time ever to approve a first budget resolution drafted by the chairman of the Budget Committee. The Gramm-Latta II reconciliation substitute marked a case in which the executive wrested the lawmaking function from the House. The Speaker's role as budget process manager expanded with the use of reconciliation in 1981, but he was clearly not in control of its outcome. The legislative work of the committees was wiped out by choices reflected mostly by the director of the OMB.

Speaker O'Neill made several strategic decisions that were based partly on his personal qualities and interpretation of the prevailing conditions. O'Neill did not try to obstruct Reagan's economic program during the early months of 1981, for he considered it democratic to "give it a chance to be voted on by the nation's elected representatives." But since O'Neill interpreted the 1980 presidential election as a vote against Carter rather than for Reagan's economic philosophy, the Speaker underestimated Reagan's ability to lead Congress. According to one view, O'Neill also failed to grasp the movement to cut spending, or the reconciliation procedures necessary to achieve that end. One prominent Budget Committee member recalls Speaker O'Neill's attitude during a press conference on the budget at the beginning of 1981:

I was sitting next to him [when] the press came in and the room was filled with photographers, cameras, and reporters. And he shook his head and said, "I don't understand why they are interested in this budget stuff." This was early in the process and he understood after. But things like a budget with spending cuts and having a fast-track process and using reconciliation, he was lukewarm to all that because it was counter to the previous ways of doing things.

O'Neill admitted later that he "wasn't prepared for what happened in 1981."[74]

O'Neill's lukewarm support for the Budget Committee's first budget resolution in the formative stages of the process may also have hindered Chairman Jones's ability to build a winning coalition. The past record on budget resolutions illustrated that the Budget Committee relies on the Speaker's support for passing budget resolutions. Although O'Neill promoted the budget resolution on the floor, he had already expressed doubt that the resolution would pass.

Yet, while O'Neill's miscalculation of the situation and limited background in budget policy explain partly how he responded in 1981, the Speaker's performance was clearly affected by the conditions he confronted. O'Neill was overwhelmed by political and institutional changes, procedural innovations, and effective presidential skills. A clear fiscal policy message, a convincing electoral victory, unexpected gains in the House and Senate, and weak Democratic unity combined with solid Republican unity enabled the president to claim a mandate and implement it quickly.[75] Reconciliation allowed the president to aggregate separate legislative decisions and ease the pain of the selective cutting of important programs.[76] Reagan's popularity, persuasive speaking ability, and a talented staff provided clear direction and executed skillful coalition-building tactics.[77] The president's control over the agenda forced a manageable and coherent set of economic issues on Congress.[78] The White House mobilized the support of activist groups that exerted constituency pressure on House members.[79] Thus, it is reasonable to conclude that the Speaker's poor preparation was less significant than the conditions that propelled Reagan's economic program. Under some conditions the Speaker simply cannot overcome the force of presidential leadership.

5

Speaker O'Neill: Opposition Party Leader and Process Manager, 1982–86

Divided party government and large budget deficits prevailed throughout the 1980s, making budget politics more centralized, partisan, and unstable. Under pressure to reduce the deficit, makeshift procedural devices and political strategies were invented nearly every year to displace the formal guidelines of the Budget Act. Ultimately, Congress revised the original budget timetable and created a deficit-reduction schedule with the Gramm-Rudman-Hollings (GRH) law of 1985. All the while acting as process manager, O'Neill was involved in various conflicts over budget priorities, appropriations decisions, and rules for implementing the budget process. At the same time, he became the leading spokesman of the opposition party, a role that expanded to include "policy-oriented" tasks both inside and outside the House. Inside the House, he participated more than ever before in the process of formulating the first budget resolution. Outside the House, he engaged in budget negotiations with Republican leaders and the president.

In this chapter I develop two central themes concerning the development and performance of the Speaker's role in the budget process during the remainder of O'Neill's speakership. First, though the Speaker's responsibility for managing the budget process was never more important, his primary concern was to protect and advance the party's interests. When the roles of process manager and opposition party leader came into conflict, the party leader role took precedence. At times, the Speaker struggled to maintain an orderly process, but he never placed formal procedures above the party's policy and political interests.

Second, O'Neill's style as opposition party leader was better suited toward fending off Republican attempts to undermine Democratic priorities, than to initiating new priorities or building support for his own preferences within the Democratic party. O'Neill's capacity to influence the Democratic party's budget priorities was limited by his lack of budgetary expertise and by his conception of leadership. He dealt with the Budget Committee only indirectly, relying on staff personnel to represent his priorities on the committee. Meanwhile, he encouraged all Democrats to participate in formulating the party's budget priorities by expressing their policy preferences, and he acted as a middleman leader, attempting to balance and accommodate the different priorities of House Democrats. While House Democrats recognized O'Neill's preference for traditional liberal programs, the extent to which they concurred with his priorities varied with short-term conditions: economic trends, President Reagan's popularity, the urgency to reduce the deficit, and the ideological bent of the House Democratic party.

I begin this chapter with a broad overview of the conditions that defined the remainder of O'Neill's speakership and a description of how O'Neill's individual qualities affected his role in the budget process. I proceed with an assessment of budget politics in 1982—a transition year that found the Speaker only beginning to recover from the problems incurred in 1981. Then I assess O'Neill's actions during the remainder of his speakership; I focus on his policy-oriented tasks both inside and outside the House and his role in managing the appropriations and reconciliation processes.

The Context: A Broad Overview, 1982–86

The rising deficits that began in the 1970s soared to unprecedented levels during the 1980s (see figure 2). Large deficits constrained new spending initiatives and perpetuated a movement from distributive to redistributive policy-making that was already underway in the late 1970s.[1] Intense conflicts over spending priorities led to a breakdown in traditional norms for reaching budgetary decisions.[2] The budget process became unstable, changing from one year to the next. Naomi Caiden observed, "As conflicts rise and uncertainties increase, timetables are disrupted, and budgeting becomes an ad hoc affair in which participants exploit every possibility of leverage to the detriment of consistent or orderly decision making."[3] The Speaker was called upon to deal with the policy conflicts and procedural problems that emerged under the strain of large deficits.

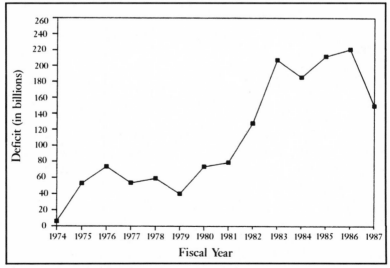

FIGURE 2. *Annual federal budget deficit, fiscal years 1974–87.* Data from *Historical Tables: Budget of the United States Government, FY 1990* (Washington, D.C.: GPO, 1989).

Amid the increased budgetary strife, the Democratic and Republican parties became more polarized and partisan. Beginning in 1983, high levels of partisanship were recorded for roll call votes, particularly on first budget resolutions (see figure 3).[4] After 1982 O'Neill was almost guaranteed partisan support for the Budget Committee's resolutions—a distinct contrast with the Carter years when O'Neill struggled to reconcile intra-party differences in order to pass first budget resolutions. The increases in party unity indicated a growing homogeneity of preferences among House Democrats and created expectations for the Speaker to engage more actively in policy leadership on behalf of the majority party.[5] Thus, the Speaker's primary emphasis shifted: it was less important to devise strategies for passing budget resolutions than to focus on

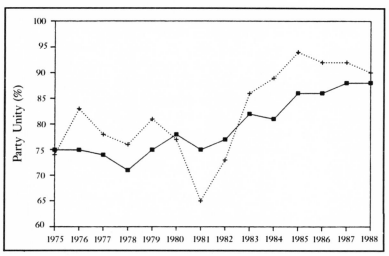

FIGURE 3. *House Democratic party unity and party unity on first budget resolutions, 1975–88. Note: Scores are normalized to account for absences on roll call votes: Unity = (Unity)/Unity + Opposition;* —■— = average Democratic party unity; "+" = party unity on first budget resolutions. Data from Harold W. Stanley and Richard G. Niemi, *Vital Statistics on American Politics,* 3rd ed. (Washington, D.C.: Congressional Quarterly Press, 1992), and *Congressional Quarterly Almanac* (Washington, D.C.: Congressional Quarterly Press, 1975–88).

formulating priorities and negotiating agreements with Senate leaders and the president. As partisan tensions over the deficit mounted, House Democrats expected the Speaker to represent their views and protect their interests from sabotage by leaders of the opposing party. Speaker O'Neill also attempted to protect Democratic House seats that were jeopardized by partisan attacks from the president and congressional Republicans.

Speaker O'Neill as Opposition Party Leader

O'Neill's response to the conditions enhancing the policy-making role of the speakership was affected by his policy expertise and conception of leadership. He lacked detailed knowledge of budget policy and promoted the values of an open and participatory House. He had neither the expertise nor the aspiration to initiate specific priorities on the Budget Committee. Instead, he relied on Steering and Policy Committee staff personnel for budgetary details. Rather than impose his own priorities on the Budget Committee, O'Neill preferred a collegial and middleman style of leadership, soliciting the budgetary preferences of committee chairmen and the party caucus. Yet he was a staunch partisan, committed to preserving traditional Democratic programs. He stubbornly resisted efforts by leaders from the opposing party to reduce spending for New Deal and Great Society programs.

Given these traits, O'Neill performed the opposition party leader role as a spokesman. The characteristics of the opposition party spokesman include (1) publicizing the leader's personal view of the party's principles, but allowing party members to participate in defining the party's budget priorities; (2) delegating responsibility over policy details to Budget Committee members or Steering and Policy Committee staff personnel; and (3) protecting the priorities of party members and their House seats in negotiations with opposing Senate leaders and the president.

Speaker O'Neill's style as opposition party leader is illustrated by the role he took in formulating budget resolutions. He performed two primary tasks in the process of formulating the House budget resolution: setting the general tone for debate over budget priorities and assuring that the Budget Committee's resolution endorses certain fundamental party priorities. The Speaker is interviewed by the press right after the president completes his budget address. Speaker O'Neill's response was based on preliminary reports of the president's budget, which had already been assessed by the Steering and Policy Committee and Budget Committee staff. Through his public statements, the Speaker would set the tone, in a very general way, for discussion of the budget in the succeeding months. As one of O'Neill's staff persons put it, this was the "first shot across the bow."

From that point, key staff personnel on the Budget, Appropriations, Ways and Means, and Steering and Policy committees identified the specific programs of the president's budget for which spending was notably altered from previous levels. The Speaker then met with his key staff personnel on the Steering and Policy Committee for a review of their analyses. For Speaker O'Neill, it was important to know how the president's budget influenced middle- and lower-class people. One participant in the process noted, "He would ask, who gets hurt most? Are they rich, or are they poor? Can they bear the pain?"

Soon after O'Neill was briefed by staff, the budget was reviewed in leadership meetings that were normally attended by the Speaker, the extended leadership (the majority leader, the majority whip, and the Democratic caucus chairman), and the chairmen of the Budget, Appropriations, Rules, and Ways and Means committees and their key staff personnel. The purpose of these meetings was to develop a strategy for putting together a Democratic budget to challenge the president. One of O'Neill's top staff people described how the typical leadership meeting illustrated O'Neill's collegial style: "The typical leadership meeting would be an all-afternoon event. . . . You would have a long discussion as to what to do. Speaker O'Neill did not typically start the meeting with a plan. He listened to everybody, he sort of let a plan develop."[6] To the extent that these meetings produced any consensus on budget priorities, Speaker O'Neill would endorse that consensus. The Budget Committee chairman would consider the information derived from the meetings when he drafted an initial mark for the first budget resolution.

Because of his limited budgetary expertise and his participatory leadership style, O'Neill was not directly involved in the day-to-day operation of the Budget Committee. O'Neill believed in the precepts of the New Deal—that government should take care of low-income, elderly, and disadvantaged people and provide educational and employment opportunities for middle- and low-income people. Yet, although he expected the Budget Committee to preserve a core set of traditional Democratic programs, he did not impose his personal priorities on Budget Committee Democrats. The Budget Committee was always deferential to the Speaker, but O'Neill did not believe a Speaker should intervene regularly in the business of any committee. As one Budget Committee staff person put it, "Tip was a gut politician. . . . As long as we were liberal on the committee, as long as we were taking care of the aged and elderly, he didn't have any problems. . . . He didn't have any specific [recommendations]."[7]

O'Neill did consult the Budget Committee chairman regularly to discuss the committee's progress and to repeat his views from time to time, but he did not give specific instructions for drafting first budget resolutions. As Jim Jones, Budget Committee chairman from 1981 to 1984, described his relationship with Speaker O'Neill: "We had a lot of private meetings through which I would keep him informed. . . . We [also] met privately to get the few things that were of importance on his list. But in terms of trying to direct me or the committee, he left that totally within my discretion."[8]

Basically, O'Neill viewed the Budget Committee as a special committee because it was engaged in drafting a budget resolution that reflected the Democratic party's priorities. But it was still a congressional committee and, for O'Neill, that meant the Speaker should respect its autonomy. O'Neill clarified the distinction between directing the committee and exercising discretion over the basic priorities the committee endorsed: "You didn't interfere with everything, that's not the process. But the things that you think the Party are really interested in must be in the bill [that is, the first budget resolution]."

Thus, Speaker O'Neill's most important influence on the substance of the House Democratic budget came after the Budget Committee finished drafting the first budget resolution. O'Neill exercised a final check, or informal veto, over the committee's final draft of the first budget resolution. Although O'Neill lacked a detailed understanding of the budget, he had capable staff personnel on the Steering and Policy Committee who, as he put it, "knew my philosophy and their philosophy was in tune with mine." O'Neill referred specifically to Ari Weiss and Jack Lew, whom he spoke of highly:

They knew everything I stood for and they were great people who could give me reviews. They could watch, report, and recommend as far as the budget was concerned. The Speaker needs that. The most important thing is to have a good watchdog like I had. I always maintained that I had a good watchdog to keep his eye on that thing. They wouldn't let it get out of hand, and could [find out] if there were things hidden in there that you didn't know about.

O'Neill used the information provided by staff personnel to decide whether to veto any of the committee's budget priorities. O'Neill explained, "That's where Ari [Weiss] and Jack [Lew] would come into it. They would tell me, '[the Budget Committee members] didn't put this in the budget and they didn't put that in the budget that you were interested in.' We'd call them in and say, 'Look, that's got to be in there.' "[9]

But regardless of O'Neill's final check on the Budget Committee's resolution, committee Democrats did not always adopt the Speaker's priorities. And, although the party demonstrated strong unity in support of the Budget Committee's resolutions after 1982, Democrats continued to debate over competing solutions for reducing the deficit. Throughout the period, the extent to which the Budget Committee and the House supported O'Neill's preferences for traditional liberal programs varied with short-term conditions.

Budget Politics, 1982

The economic and political climate of 1982 created a transitional role for the Speaker. Support for Reagan's supply-side policy dwindled among the voting public (see figure 4) and among the president's congressional coalition of Republicans and conservative Democrats, as they saw 7.2 percent unemployment, a $120 billion deficit, and no sign of inflation slowing down. In January, Delbert Latta, ranking minority member of the House Budget Committee, simply stated "the honeymoon is over" for President Reagan.[10] Congressional Democrats were divided as well. Although most Democrats generally agreed that Reagan deserved the blame for the deficit and economic downturn, they were undecided about the proper course to take on the budget issue.

Under these conditions, the Speaker's primary function continued to be coalition building, although his role in the budget process also began to expand. He exercised scheduling powers more successfully in the reconciliation process than he had the year before, and he played an important part in securing passage of a major tax bill. The Speaker also assumed a more active role in formulating the party's budget priorities, though his input came late in the process and was not backed by the House. Overall, the Speaker tried to balance his roles as process manager and opposition party leader. Yet, with the trauma of 1981 fresh on O'Neill's mind, he was less concerned with managing the process than with preventing further encroachments on traditional Democratic programs and protecting Democratic House seats.

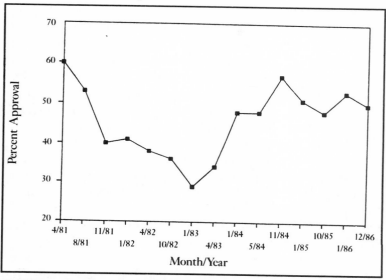

FIGURE 4. *Public approval of Reagan's handling of the economy, 1981–86.*
Data from *Gallup Report*, July 1988, p. 24.

O'Neill's capacity to challenge Reagan's budget priorities in 1982 was limited by the lack of cohesion among House Democrats. Democrats harbored four competing views of the party's budget priorities. First, the so-called human needs Democrats, the true liberals in the party, concurred with O'Neill's strategy to try and enact comprehensive social welfare, job training, and education programs. A second group of moderate, pragmatic Democrats, the so-called Atari Democrats, also advocated a Democratic budget alternative to Reaganomics, but they considered themselves more innovative and more economically prudent than the human needs bloc.[11] Rather than propose comprehensive domestic programs, their strategy was to target the most pressing domestic problems and find efficient ways to solve them. A third bloc of Democrats included responsible and cooperative conservatives, led by Budget Committee chairman Jim Jones. Jones represented those Democrats who were open to negotiating with the White

House and pursuing bipartisan alternatives to reduce the deficit. This group was flanked by a far-right-wing group of Democrats, the so-called Reagan Democrats, who unequivocally supported Reagan's economic plan in 1981 and staked their electoral fortunes on the president's popularity in their districts. They were the lost souls in the party—too embarrassed to support Reagan, yet too conservative and too unwelcome to join with other Democrats.

Amid the uncertainty over how to deal with a growing deficit and a struggling economy, debate between the parties proceeded on two different levels. On one level, the leading spokesmen of the parties—O'Neill and Reagan—articulated opposing views of the nation's priorities, one liberal, the other conservative. The two leaders fought an intense partisan battle, debating publicly the basic ideological views and differences in principle of their respective parties. Meanwhile, key budget policy makers met privately to negotiate budgetary details. Top White House officials and Democratic chairmen of the major congressional committees (Budget, Appropriations, Ways and Means, and sometimes Rules) worked toward a bipartisan compromise that would reduce the growing deficit.

The president and the Speaker would ultimately determine the prospects for compromise, however. As the budget battles wore on in the spring of 1982, the Speaker assumed a tough defensive strategy. It became clear that an important component of the Speaker's role was to decide the terms of agreement his party could accept in deficit-reduction negotiations with leaders of the opposing party.

In January 1982, the president and the Speaker appeared to set the tone for a partisan showdown between the new conservative philosophy and the old liberal New Deal philosophy. Reagan placed the blame for the deficit on "past policy errors" committed by previous Democratic administrations. He refused to increase taxes but asked members of Congress to persevere throughout another year of budget cutting. His fiscal 1983 budget included $56 billion in domestic spending cuts, a 13 percent inflation-adjusted increase in defense totaling

$44 billion, and no repeal of the 1981 tax cut.[12] O'Neill immediately criticized Reagan's plan, labeling it a "Beverly Hills" budget. Appearing on a televised film designed as a response to Reagan's State of the Union address, O'Neill proclaimed, "the administration is putting the [American] dream beyond the reach of most Americans. It is reserving that dream for the wealthy few."[13]

During the spring of 1982, President Reagan stubbornly resisted compromise, and Speaker O'Neill reciprocated. From his perspective as opposition party leader, O'Neill believed, "the president sees today's economic challenge as a test of strength between him and the Democrats. As long as he keeps his political saber drawn, I see no hope for compromise."[14]

Despite O'Neill's tough partisan posture, Congress was responsible for passing its own budget resolution, and in his capacity as process manager, the Speaker shared much of that responsibility. As an indication of O'Neill's effort to reconcile his roles as process manager and opposition party leader, the Speaker called for a summit meeting of leading House Democrats, House Republicans, and White House officials. Yet, it would soon become clear that O'Neill's primary objective was to protect Democratic policy and political interests, rather than facilitate the budget process.

Under pressure to produce a budget, the two parties finally came to the negotiating table in late March. These were the so-called Gang of Seventeen meetings—bipartisan deficit-reduction talks between administration officials and key Senate and House leaders. Among the most notable participants representing the Reagan administration were James A. Baker III (chief of staff), Kenneth M. Duberstein (presidential advisor), Senator Paul Laxalt (R-Nev.), Donald Regan (Treasury secretary), and David Stockman (OMB director). Senators Domenici and Dole were the principal representatives for congressional Republicans. Budget Committee chairman Jim Jones, Rules Committee chairman Richard Bolling, and Ways and Means chairman Dan Rostenkowski led the House Democrats. The meetings reflected the problem of establishing cooperation within a group of budget makers overshadowed by the harsh partisan rhetoric of Reagan and O'Neill. The negotiating group argued over budget priorities, but preliminary progress was made on some of the major issues—defense spending, entitlements, and taxes. Stockman recalled, "I got a pretty good hosing in those private sessions—as the Democrat leaders especially unloaded on my previous high-handed tactics. Still, they were willing to fashion a compromise plan if the President would back off partway on his 25 percent tax cut."[15]

As budget negotiators bargained in private under the pretense that everything was on the table, O'Neill and Reagan battled in public, maintaining their entrenched positions on taxes and social security. The two leaders essentially foreclosed compromises on the major issues before the Gang of Seventeen could reach any definitive agreements. Reagan announced, "You don't raise taxes in a recession." O'Neill responded, "I'm as firm on social security as the President is on taxes. I'm not going to balance the budget on the backs of the elderly." Thus any progress made behind closed doors was stalled by the public disagreement over priorities between the president and the Speaker. Chairman Jones described the situation: "Everything has been on the table for discussion, even the things that the principals [Reagan and O'Neill] have ruled off limits. But neither of the principals has changed his position on what is off limits." Likewise, Senate Budget Committee chairman Pete Domenici was optimistic about the chances of a budget agreement, "if we can get both Speaker Tip O'Neill and the president on board."[16]

After several weeks of bargaining, the Gang of Seventeen meetings collapsed. The two sides decided to make one more attempt to settle their differences. Reagan told reporters he would "go an extra mile" to reach a compromise with the Democrats. He invited O'Neill to the White House, and the Speaker accepted on the grounds that Reagan had "put the ball in my court."[17]

The meeting was on April 28 in the president's room of the Senate. Reagan was accompanied by Senator Paul Laxalt,

David Stockman, Ed Meese, James Baker, and Howard Baker. O'Neill's group included Richard Bolling, Jim Wright, and Ari Weiss, O'Neill's staff director of the Steering and Policy Committee. Reagan and O'Neill argued over ideological differences for two hours. Stockman described the exchange of blows:

Tip would say what made America great was the New Deal and all of the things that we have brought to the American people: Now everybody has a retirement pension; now everybody can go to college; people can get day care; they have health insurance. And then the president would say that we've been going to hell in a handbasket since 1932 when we started deficit spending and got government in all kinds of things it shouldn't be in.[18]

Both leaders stood firm by their priorities. Reagan guarded his tax cuts and defense budget, and O'Neill kept social security off the table. At one point during the meeting Reagan offered, "Tip, I feel like I'm going to pass a pineapple. But, okay, I'll agree to a temporary delay of the tax cut in return for these spending cuts." O'Neill then asked Reagan, "Mr. President, are you putting Social Security on the table or not?"[19] Reagan answered, "You're not going to trap me on that."

The meeting ended in deadlock. In Speaker O'Neill's view, "[the meeting] was a sham, the president had no intention of sitting down at that particular time. He had in the pocket of his vest a prepared statement for when the meeting was going to fall apart." O'Neill said that Reagan's "only concession was to allow a slight three-month pause in his program of giving billion dollar tax cuts to the rich." Laxalt summarized why President Reagan and Speaker O'Neill could not reach an agreement: "The philosophical differences were just too great to overcome."[20]

The president and the Speaker went their separate ways, but neither of them could offer a feasible alternative budget plan to their primary constituents. After the Senate Budget Committee unanimously rejected Reagan's budget, Domenici offered a budget resolution that included $95 billion in new revenues, and $40 billion reductions in social security over the ensuing three years. Reagan endorsed the plan, but House Republican leaders rejected it. O'Neill supported the House Budget Committee's plan that, compared with the Senate budget resolution, included higher revenues, larger defense cuts, fewer reductions in domestic programs, and no reductions in social security.

Floor Strategy, 1982

Speaker O'Neill faced a difficult task in trying to build a coalition of conservative and liberal Democrats to pass the Budget Committee's fiscal 1983 first budget resolution. As the deficit increased and the economy struggled, many Southern Democrats withdrew their support for Reagan's budget. Yet, the conservative Democrats who held the swing votes for the fiscal 1983 budget resolution were not prepared to support the party leadership either. One staff person described the situation: "We hadn't yet had another election, we didn't have any more votes. It was the year when Reagan no longer had control over the Boll Weevils, but they weren't home yet. . . . It could have gone either way. There was not a clear path you could march down and win."[21]

In response to the diversity of opinions on the budget, the Rules Committee drafted the so-called King of the Mountain rule, including sixty-eight amendments and seven substitutes to the Budget Committee's first budget resolution. The rule established the voting order for amendments and substitutes, with the last budget to receive a majority vote declared the House-passed budget resolution. The Budget Committee's resolution naturally was scheduled last, giving it an advantage under the King of the Mountain format. Thus, the rule allowed members to participate in formulating the budget resolution, vote in favor of more than one substitute, and still support the committee's proposed budget.[22]

After the first seven budgets failed, Speaker O'Neill closed the debate leading up to the final vote on the Budget Committee's resolution. The speech reflected O'Neill's attempt to balance his dual responsibilities to the House and the Democratic party. Even though the budget was not O'Neill's first choice, he urged the House to support it because "Our Nation is in a crisis." He said:

We have a final opportunity, we have a final vote . . . to demonstrate to the American people that this elected body can perform its duty; that we are able to act in their best interests. . . . I know the Senate has passed a budget. Now, we come to the moment of decision. The hour is late. Most Americans have retired for the evening. Tomorrow, when they wake up and find out that Congress did not do its job and did not pass a budget, I wonder what their feeling of frustration will be. . . . Truly, I think [supporting the first budget resolution] is the right thing to do for America. I do not speak as a Democrat. I do not speak as a partisan. I do not speak as a liberal. I just say to you that I think it is the best thing for America that we go and sit down at the conference table.[23]

Despite the Speaker's plea, the Budget Committee's plan was rejected by a vote of 159–265, with eighty-one Democrats voting "nay." The House had failed in its responsibility to pass a budget, sending the Budget Committee back to draft another alternative.

After concluding that "choices are altogether too tough to do it in a partisan way," Chairman Jones invited the White House to negotiate a bipartisan plan. Jones suggested that the two sides split the difference between the Budget Committee's resolution and the original Michel-Latta substitute. But Reagan rejected the offer. At that point, Speaker O'Neill decided to take charge of the situation in the House. O'Neill called upon the Steering and Policy Committee to draft a "true Democratic budget" including additional funds for housing, emergency jobs, unemployment compensation, Medicare, and education. This time the leadership decided on a closed rule that allowed only two alternatives: O'Neill's budget and a Republican substitute sponsored by Latta. O'Neill's budget was rejected 202–225 and the Latta substitute passed 220–207. After the vote, Chairman Jones remarked, "The Speaker found out that it's very tough to put together a budget that can pass the House."[24]

Although the recent history of passing budget resolutions certainly proved Jones correct, O'Neill's budget actually fared well in comparison with previous Democratic budget resolutions. Up until 1983, the House Democratic party had always found it tough to pass budget resolutions. Even when the Democratic party held large majorities in the House, the votes on first budget resolutions were always close (see table 13).

TABLE 13
Votes on House First Budget Resolutions: Fiscal Years 1976–81 Compared with O'Neill's "True Democratic" Fiscal 1983 Budget

Fiscal Year	House	Democrats	Republicans
1976	200–196	197–68	3–128
1977	221–155	208–44	13–111
1978	213–179	206–58	7–121
1979	201–197	198–61	3–136
1980	220–184	211–50	9–134
1981	225–193	203–62	22–131
O'Neill's budget 1983	202–225	199–39	3–186

Source: Congressional Record and *Congressional Quarterly Almanac* (1975–82).

There were actually fewer dissenting Democratic votes (thirty-nine) on O'Neill's budget than on any previous Budget Committee budget resolution. As I noted in the previous chapter, a crucial difference between the Carter years and the first two years of Reagan's presidency (in terms of passing budget resolutions) was that, prior to 1981, the Democrats had enough members to overcome ideological differences. The prevailing party disunity among Democrats caught up with the leadership in 1981 and 1982.

Reconciliation and Taxes, 1982

Despite O'Neill's problems with the fiscal 1983 first budget resolution, the Speaker scored two victories in combating Reagan's economic policy in 1982. First, he used his scheduling powers to oppose the reconciliation bill. The previous year the Democratic party had suffered a beating, and weeks of work by the authorizing committees had been negated, when the House approved the Gramm-Latta II reconciliation bill. In 1982, O'Neill vowed, "We're not going to allow ourselves to be put in that position again."[25]

Shortly after the fiscal 1983 budget resolution passed the House, including reconciliation instructions to cut spending by $6.57 billion, O'Neill announced that the committees involved in reconciliation should not be held accountable if they ignored spending cuts instructed by the budget resolution. The Post Office and Civil Service Committee took O'Neill seriously and refused to comply with reconciliation instructions that called for a 4 percent cap on the cost-of-living adjustment (COLA) to civil servants' pensions. Assuming the cap was adopted, the budget resolution anticipated that the committee bill would achieve $3.2 billion in savings over three years. By ignoring the cap, the committee decided to cut spending by only $113 million over three years. The committee's recommendations, along with those of several other committees, were packaged into the reconciliation bill.

O'Neill announced that the 4 percent cap on the COLAs could only be restored by a floor amendment. The House concurred with O'Neill, voting in favor of a rule that allowed a separate vote on COLAs for federal retirees. But the Republican leadership decided against offering an amendment that would cut spending for such a politically charged program as federal pensions. Instead, the Republicans submitted a motion to recommit the bill to the Post Office and Civil Service Committee and force the committee to comply with the budget resolutions' instructions. The House promptly rejected the motion and voted for the committee's much smaller $113 million spending cut in the pensions.

The Speaker was also instrumental in securing passage of the Tax Equity and Fiscal Responsibility Act of 1982 (TEFRA).[26] TEFRA, a deficit-reduction package including a

$98.3 billion tax increase, was a rare compromise between the Republicans and Democrats. The package was drafted primarily by Dole but required a bipartisan coalition to pass the House. O'Neill was critical in lobbying liberal Democrats. The House approved TEFRA by a vote of 226–207; House Republicans voted 103–87 and the Democrats voted 123–120.

In sum, Speaker O'Neill's roles as opposition party leader and process manager in 1982 combined existing trends with new tendencies. His new policy role was evident in negotiations with the president and in his effort to employ the Steering and Policy Committee to draft a budget resolution reflecting traditional Democratic principles. Yet the House failed to produce a Democratic budget for a second consecutive year. O'Neill's failure to attract support for his priorities indicated that the party lacked the necessary cohesion for the Speaker to provide policy leadership. O'Neill's actions indicated a continual struggle to manage the process and represent his party's interests. By and large, although House Democrats reached no clear consensus with regard to budget priorities, the Speaker's role as opposition party leader took precedence over his concern for managing the budget process.

The Speaker and Budget Policy-making, 1983–86

Throughout the remainder of O'Neill's speakership large deficits, divided government, and strong Democratic party unity created the opportunity for the Speaker to perform a more active policy role. Yet, the extent of House Democratic support for O'Neill's priorities varied with changes in short-term conditions. O'Neill's limited policy expertise and his participatory view of leadership prohibited him from using the budget resolution to shape the party's priorities. To his credit, O'Neill was capable of preventing further reductions in traditional New Deal and Great Society programs. Yet (with the exception of 1983), he lacked support within the party to advance those preferences, and he was not inclined to impose them on Budget Committee Democrats. His middleman style of leadership was evident as the House Democratic party formulated first budget resolutions. On the whole, while the Speaker's opportunities for policy leadership expanded, the constraints on leadership were also evident throughout the period.

Here, I would like to present a general overview of the major developments in budget-policy formulation in the House, from 1983 to 1986 (see table 14). Instead of going into great detail for each year, I have selected two critical cases, one from the Ninety-eighth Congress (1983–84) and one from the Ninety-ninth Congress (1985–86), to illustrate O'Neill's style and influence over budget priorities. His most influential role was in 1983 when House Democrats generally concurred with O'Neill's policy preferences. But the most important question is how the budget was put together. The process clearly exemplifies O'Neill's participatory, middleman style of leadership. O'Neill's least influential role was in 1986, his last year as Speaker and the first year the House considered the budget resolution after the GRH deficit ceilings were in place. In this case, the Budget Committee ignored O'Neill's plea to refrain from recommending a tax increase ahead of the White House. The analysis illustrates the limits of O'Neill's ability to shape the committee's preferences. I deal with the major events of the two other years—1984 and 1985—in the following section on settling conference disputes.

Traditional Democratic Principles, 1983

After a sluggish year in 1981, the economy declined through 1982 to the first quarter of 1983, reaching its lowest ebb in the period of months leading up to and succeeding the 1982 congressional elections. In October 1982, the unemployment rate reached double digits for the first time in forty years. Speaker O'Neill billed the November 1982 elections as a test of Reagan's economic plan, saying, "We believe that the results of the November 2 election will make it clear that the American people vastly prefer a 'back-to-work' program to the President's'stay the course' philosophy."[27]

TABLE 14
The Speaker and Major Developments in Budget Policy Formulation in the House, 1983–86

1983: New Deal/Great Society Resurgence

Speaker O'Neill takes advantage of a gain of twenty-six House seats in the 1982 midterm elections to organize the elements of an emerging consensus and advance traditional Democratic priorities in the fiscal 1984 first budget resolution. The Speaker uses whip meetings, a questionnaire distributed to House Democrats, and Steering and Policy Committee staff personnel to build support for a Democratic alternative to the president's budget.

1984: Deficit Response

The Budget Committee rejects a Steering and Policy Committee budget resolution sponsored by the Speaker in favor of George Miller's pay-as-you-go budget.

1985: Cautious Response

After Reagan won a landslide and the Democrats lost twelve House seats in the 1984 elections, the Budget Committee heeds O'Neill's advice to "lay low," and wait for the Senate to take the lead on proposals to reduce the deficit.

1986: GRH and the Call for Responsible Action

The year following the passage of GRH, the House Budget Committee proposes a tax increase to reduce the deficit and avoid a sequester, thereby ignoring Speaker O'Neill's warning that taxes will harm the party's electoral prospects.

The Democrats realized a net gain of twenty-six House seats in the 1982 congressional elections. Fifty-seven new Democrats were elected and only three of the nineteen new Southern Democrats were considered potential Boll Weevils. Analyst Alan Ehrenhalt said, "the new Democrats will go down as the group that resurrected traditional liberal issues from the graveyard." Voting scores for the ensuing Ninety-eighth Congress revealed that this was the most liberal group of new Democrats since the Class of 1974 (see figure 5). In the meantime, Republican party unity was shaken by the failure of Reagan's stay the course theme. And Reagan's economic performance ratings

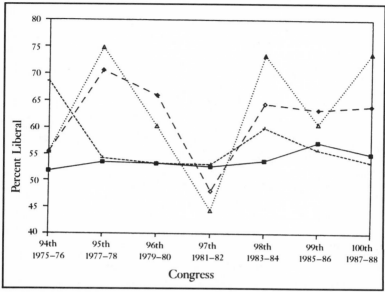

FIGURE 5. *Ideology of House Democrats, 94th–100th Congresses. Note: Liberal ideology is measured in terms of Conservative Coalition Opposition scores.* —■— = all House Democrats; – – – = all Freshman Democrats; –◇– = all Budget Committee Democrats; · ·△· · = all newly appointed Budget Committee Democrats. Data from *Congressional Quarterly Almanac*, 1975–88.

dropped to the lowest levels recorded during his two terms in the White House (see figure 4). New Budget Committee member George Miller observed, "Last fall's election really put the leadership in the driver's seat."[28]

When President Reagan delivered his budget message in January 1983, the deficit for fiscal 1983 was estimated at $200 billion and the country was in a recession (see table 15 for economic conditions). The domestic spending cuts passed by the reconciliation bills of 1981 and 1982 had begun to show their adverse effects. By February, nightly television news shows aired reports of emergency economic conditions— increased housing foreclosures, mentally ill people put out on the street, industrial plant closings, citizens waiting in unemployment lines, and people living in abandoned cars and under bridges.

150 The SPEAKER and the Budget

TABLE 15
Major Economic Indicators, 1981–86 (year end figures in percentages)

Indicator	1982	1983	1984	1985	1986
Inflation[a]	6.1	3.2	4.3	3.6	1.9
Unemployment	9.5	9.5	7.4	7.1	6.9
Prime rate[b]	14.9	10.8	12.0	9.9	8.3
GNP growth[c]	−2.5	3.6	6.8	3.0	2.9

Source: U. S. Bureau of the Census, *Statistical Abstract of the United States: 1988*, 108th ed. (Washington: United States Government Printing Office, 1987).
[a]Inflation rate is based on the Consumer Price Index.
[b]Prime rate is the interest rate charged by banks.
[c]Figures for GNP growth measure overlap of two years—the 1982 figure is for years 1981–82, for example.

The economic outlook had become so poor that even the White House reversed its laissez-faire economic policy. Baker and Stockman submitted several proposals to O'Neill, which included jobs programs and increased federal emergency aid to homeless and poverty-stricken people.

In this context, Speaker O'Neill's job was to organize the elements of a growing consensus that the government should act to redress the social problems affected by the ailing economy. O'Neill's first step was to use his power as Chair of the Steering and Policy Committee—the committee responsible for making nominations for Democratic committee assignments—to influence Democratic appointments to the Budget Committee. Though the Speaker does not have total control over Steering and Policy, he does have considerable discretion over Budget Committee appointments. Speaker O'Neill recalled, "On the Policy Committee, [the Speaker] almost always gets his own way, at least I always thought." O'Neill preferred Democrats who would protect traditional Democratic programs and still reflect the ideological composition of the party. O'Neill has said:

My job was always to make sure that there were members on the committee who weren't among that group that was fearful of Reagan and his popularity and ran away from the principles, policies, and past record of the Democratic party. The idea was always to get members of extreme competence who at all times would keep in mind what developed America, what made middle-class America.[29]

Of the nine new Democrats appointed to the Budget Committee for the Ninety-eighth Congress, seven were liberals and two were moderates (see table 16). O'Neill ensured that none of the "weak-kneed" party members who voted for Reagan's economic plan in 1981 were appointed to the Budget Committee in subsequent years. In 1983, O'Neill actively recruited Democrats Vic Fazio (D-Calif.), Mike Lowry (D-Wash.), George Miller, and Pat Williams (D-Mont.) to serve on the Budget Committee. These four members made up the human needs bloc of Democrats on the Budget Committee in 1983–84, oriented toward preserving traditional liberal Democratic programs.[30] In fact, there was a strong feeling among many Democrats that the Steering and Policy Committee stacked the Budget Committee against conservative Chairman Jones in 1983.[31]

Interestingly, one conservative Southern Democrat, John B. Breaux (D-La.), was denied a seat on the Budget Committee in 1983. Breaux voted for Republican substitutes to the Budget Committee's resolutions in 1981 and 1982. He also voted against the leadership on the previous question to suspend debate over the rule for the reconciliation bill in 1981. Breaux's failure to attain a position on the Budget Committee indicates Speaker O'Neill's concern for prohibiting the "weak-kneed" Democrats who were "willing to desert our basic principles and vote with the Republicans" in 1981.[32]

Yet, stacking the Budget Committee with liberals in 1983 was not simply an arbitrary act by the Speaker, designed to satisfy his personal policy preferences. O'Neill always maintained that he was responsive to the various ideological factions within the party. As the middleman style of leadership would predict, O'Neill's preferences for Democratic Budget Committee appointments reflected changes in the ideological composition of the party membership. O'Neill relied on election results and internal party demands to weigh the ideological mood of the House and the Democratic party. It just so happened that the ideological bias of the party in 1983 coincided nicely with O'Neill's own preferences.

This point is supported by the data in figure 5, which plots trends in the average liberal rating for three groups: (1) newly elected (the freshmen) Democrats, (2) newly appointed Democrats to the Budget Committee, and (3) all Democrats on the Budget Committee. Over time, changes in the ideological makeup of Budget Committee Democrats are quite balanced with the ideological trends in the membership of the House Democratic party as a whole. Compare the relationship between freshmen Democrats and newly appointed Democrats. For all three congresses in which O'Neill was Speaker during the 1980s, the average change in the ideology of freshmen House Democrats from one Congress to the next was positively correlated with that of the newly appointed Budget Committee Democrats. If freshmen Democrats were more liberal (conservative), new Democratic Budget Committee appointees were also more liberal (conservative).

After the Democrats regained twenty-six seats in the 1982 congressional elections, O'Neill was eager to appoint more liberals to the Budget Committee. The liberal trend within the party, measured by the ideology of freshmen Democrats, gave the Speaker sufficient leverage to recommend liberals for open seats on the Budget Committee. The sharp increase in the mean liberal score for freshmen Democrats in 1982 (see figure 5) was accompanied by the appointment of seven liberal Democrats to the Budget Committee (see table 16).

Once the Budget Committee was in place, O'Neill took several actions to involve more Democrats in the process of formulating the party's priorities and to move quickly to advance the party's agenda. O'Neill arranged party caucus meetings so that all House Democrats could "address the current economic and budget challenge." He instructed the Rules Committee to postpone hearings on reforming the budget process so that disputes over procedures would not obstruct the party unity that was developing on the budget issue. The Speaker's office dis-

TABLE 16
Ideological Groups of Newly Appointed House Budget Committee Democrats, 1981–86

First Year	Conservatives[a]	Moderates	Liberals
1981	(N = 3) Anthony (20)[b] Gramm (2) Hefner (19)	(N = 2) Benjamin (54) Donnelly (65)	(N = 2) Aspin (73) Downey (83)
1983	(N = 0)	(N = 2) Derrick (45) Frost (53)	(N = 7) Fazio (70) Ferraro (80) Gray (89) Lowry (86) Miller (83) Williams (77) Wolpe (88)
1985	(N = 2) Jenkins (21) Leath (4)	(N = 2) MacKay (52) Slattery (43)	(N = 5) Atkins (82) Barnes (86) Boxer (93) Russo (72) Schumer (90)

Source: Conservative coalition opposition scores, *Congressional Quarterly Almanac,* 1981–86.
[a]Ideological categories are calculated as follows:
  Liberal if member's score ranged from 67–100
  Moderate if score ranged from 34–66
  Conservative if score ranged from 0–33
[b]Scores are measures of "liberalness" calculated as an average of conservative coalition opposition scores for years preceding appointment and first year on the Budget Committee.

tributed to all Democrats a multiple-choice survey called "An Exercise in Hard Choices." The survey allowed Democrats to select from a number of alternative budgets, including spending levels for domestic and defense functions. Majority Leader Wright later said, "nearly every Democratic House member helped shape this budget."[33]

Information from the surveys was packaged and sent to the Budget Committee. From that point, high-level Budget Committee staff played an important role in allocating the specific amounts for each budget function. During a process called "spell down," in which the staff goes over estimates of the chairman's mark for each budget function, several key staff people raised the spending amounts for each of the domestic programs recommended by Jones. The staff persons realized that the new group of liberal members on the committee would approve higher levels of domestic spending than the chairman preferred.[34] The final resolution, labeled "The Democratic Plan for Economic Recovery," included a $33 billion increase in human needs programs over Reagan's request, only a 4 percent increase in defense (compared with Reagan's 14 percent increase), and $30 billion in revenues based on the assumption that the third year of the Kemp-Roth tax plan would be repealed.

The plan breezed through the Budget Committee by a straight party-line vote on March 17. It later passed on the House floor by a vote of 229–196 with only thirty-six Democrats voting "nay," the lowest number of Democratic dissenting votes ever recorded for a Budget Committee–drafted first budget resolution. Speaker O'Neill rejoiced in the victory: "The people believe that Reagan's policies are unfair and have gone too far. This evening the House voted to restore fairness and balance our national priorities."[35]

Budget Politics, 1986

Conditions that supported liberal policy preferences did not last long, however. Before the end of 1983 the economy had recovered and continued to grow, at least through Reagan's second term. The 1984 elections produced changes within the House Democratic party that symbolized a departure from the traditional liberal philosophy that Speaker O'Neill had been promoting throughout Reagan's first presidential term. Freshman Democrats were more ideologically moderate than their predecessors (see figure 5). In addition, after Reagan soundly defeated Walter Mondale and the Republicans gained twelve seats in the 1984 elections, a group of House Democrats led by Tony Coehlo (D-Calif.) and Richard Gephardt gathered to consider ways of moderating the party's liberal image.[36] Finally, many of the conservative Democrats who supported Reagan from 1981 to 1982, and who were abandoned by most House Democrats from 1983 to 1984, outwardly rejected Reagan's economic policies and began to cooperate with the party's mainstream.

As the expectations of House Democrats changed, O'Neill's New Deal and Great Society philosophy of governing was no longer in vogue. O'Neill acknowledged this reality in a speech to the Democratic caucus after the November 1984 elections: "We are a party of many philosophies. Our diversity is our greatest strength, but it is also the source of great tensions. . . . We need to listen to our Democratic colleagues." And, "we must find some new themes and some new directives for our party."[37]

O'Neill responded to these developments by supporting a group of Democrats to the House Budget Committee in the Ninety-ninth Congress (1985–86) who were more moderate than the liberals assigned in the Ninety-eighth Congress. The mean liberal score for new Budget Committee Democrats declined in 1985, along with a decline in the liberalness of freshmen Democrats elected in 1984 (see figure 5). Altogether, two conservatives, two moderates, and only five liberals were assigned to the Budget Committee in 1985 (see table 16). Speaker O'Neill explained why there were fewer liberals appointed after the 1984 election: "It was obvious then that the nation was moving to the middle. I didn't want the extremes [of either liberal or conservative] out there."[38] At the same time, although the new appointees to the committee in 1984 were less liberal than those of the previous Congress, O'Neill judged them to be extremely competent and generally committed to the party's basic principles.

This group was more independent of O'Neill and more concerned about the deficit problem than their predecessors. In 1986, pressured by the constraints of the GRH deficit ceiling,

House Democrats ignored O'Neill's position against tax increases. A look at how Budget Committee Democrats formulated the fiscal 1987 budget clearly illustrates O'Neill's limited influence over the Budget Committee's priorities during his final year as Speaker.

In January 1986, as one observer put it, Congress would go to work "under [a] budget cloud."[39] The budget cloud was the GRH deficit-reduction law passed in December 1985. GRH revised the budget timetable established by the Budget Act (see table 1) but, more importantly, created a six-year schedule for balancing the budget (see table 17). Automatic spending cuts would be enforced if the deficit exceeded the annual statutory ceilings established by GRH. Congress began the year with the task of meeting a fiscal 1986 deficit ceiling of $171.9 billion. If members failed to meet that ceiling, they faced the prospect of automatic spending reductions to be issued by the OMB as early as February 1.

The cloud of GRH grew darker when President Reagan submitted his budget. Reagan managed to shelter his priorities and still project a deficit of $143.6 billion, barely under the mandated ceiling of $144 billion for fiscal year 1987. His budget included, as usual, a defense increase of 8 percent above the rate of inflation, $32 billion in domestic spending reduc-

TABLE 17
Schedule of Deficit-Reduction Targets under the Original GRH Law
(deficit figures in billions)

Fiscal Year	Deficit Ceiling
1986	$171.9
1987	144.0
1988	108.0
1989	72.0
1990	36.0
1991	00.0

Source: Compiled by author from Wehr, "Congress Enacts Far-reaching Budget Measure," p. 2604.

tions, and no tax increase. The president also called for major tax reform in his 1986 State of the Union address. Reagan suggested the possibility of bipartisan negotiations to deal with deficit reduction, but he limited the area of compromise to the mix of cuts he requested for domestic programs. Reagan would not compromise on the defense increase, and he threatened those members who considered sending him a tax bill with his Dirty Harry imitation: "Go ahead, make my day."[40]

Speaker O'Neill responded by announcing that he would not schedule a tax increase bill unless the president initiated one. Despite the GRH deficit ceiling, O'Neill believed that a tax increase was politically unwise. Such a strategy, he thought, would invite criticism from the Republicans and threaten Democratic House seats in the upcoming midterm elections.

As a partisan gesture, Chairman Gray offered Reagan's budget on the House floor on March 13, and it was soundly defeated by a vote of 12–312. But the Budget Committee did not report its own budget resolution at that time. During the first week of April, O'Neill announced that the Democrats would continue to pursue a cautious strategy: "Our position is to wait for the Senate." Speaking on behalf of the leadership, Gray also announced that the House Budget Committee would not propose a tax increase without the president's initiative: "The President has got to provide leadership and he's got to holster that veto gun."[41]

But Budget Committee Democrats were not as patient as O'Neill thought. In May, an unlikely coalition of liberal, moderate, and conservative Budget Committee Democrats defied O'Neill's wishes and went forward with a $4.7 billion tax increase as part of the fiscal 1987 first budget resolution. The committee also approved a $285 billion defense budget, $35 billion lower than the president's request and $16 billion below the Senate-passed first budget resolution. Conservative Democrat Marvin Leath (D-Texas) was the key actor in the committee's decision to reduce defense and increase revenues. The liberal Democrats on the Budget Committee—George Miller,

Mike Lowry, Vic Fazio, and Charles E. Schumer (D-N.Y.)—
wanted a lower defense figure. Leath decided that reducing the
deficit was a higher priority than defense spending. He was
willing to split the difference in reductions for defense and domestic spending if liberal Democrats agreed to increase taxes.
In order to elude Reagan's tax-and-spend label, Budget Committee Democrats placed the revenues in a special tax account
to be approved only for the purpose of deficit reduction.

Thus, when Budget Committee Democrats realized they
had each other's support, they ignored O'Neill's cautious position on taxes. One member described the situation: "At the
first meeting with the leadership, they said, 'We can't do this
[raise taxes].' We said, 'What do you mean we can't do this?
We've got every Democrat on the Committee—from Leath to
Schumer—for it.' "[42] O'Neill apparently misread the situation, and the Speaker's informal veto on the Budget Committee's tax proposal was overridden. One observer asked Mike
Lowry if the leadership was going to tell the committee what
to do. Stephan Gettinger of *Congressional Quarterly* reported,
"Lowry winked and grinned, 'I think it's the other way
around.' "[43] The committee reported the budget resolution to
the floor, and to the surprise of Speaker O'Neill, the resolution
passed easily by a vote of 245–179.

In this case, Budget Committee Democrats assumed the
responsibility for making a difficult choice to reduce the deficit
in order to avoid a sequestration order. When asked if the deficit for the Budget Committee's fiscal 1987 first budget resolution would have been higher without the threat of the GRH law,
O'Neill said, "the deficit would be higher—no question about
it."[44] GRH provided a mechanism that triggered concern for
the budget deficit rather than caution against taking political
risks. The situation dictated bold solutions to meet the demands
of the mandated targets, and after initially disagreeing, O'Neill
acquiesced in the committee's decision to go for the higher tax
increase. It was a clear indication that Budget Committee
Democrats acted quite independently of Speaker O'Neill.

Resolving Conference Disputes

One of the critical problems with the budget process that required the Speaker's assistance during the 1980s was the conference committee. Intense partisanship and spending constraints posed by large deficits during the 1980s created conflicts between the Democratic House and the Republican Senate, which were too great for conferees to resolve without the assistance of party leaders. The longer conference disputes lasted, the more imperative it was for the Speaker to become involved in the decision-making process. From 1982 to 1986, Congress never approved a first budget resolution before the May 15 deadline established by the Budget Act (see table 18). But the longest delays in the process occurred in 1984 and 1985. In both cases, the Speaker played a vital role in defending the party's interests and breaking the deadlock between the House and the Senate.

Speaker O'Neill's negotiations with Senate leaders and the president over conference decisions indicated that he was primarily motivated by his party's interests. The budget process moved sluggishly and was delayed as the Speaker held out for a deal that favored the policy interests of House Democrats.

TABLE 18
Dates for Final Passage of First Budget Resolutions, 1982–86

Year	House (April 15)	Senate (April 15)	Congress (May 15)
1982	June 10	May 21	June 23
1983	March 23	May 19	June 23
1984	April 5	May 18	Oct. 1
1985	May 23	May 10	August
1986	May 17	May 10	June 26[a]

Source: Congressional Quarterly Weekly Report, various editions.
Note: The expected dates for passing budget resolutions are in parentheses.
[a]Expected deadline changed to April 15 by Gramm-Rudman-Hollings.

CONFERENCE SETTLEMENT ON FIRST BUDGET RESOLU-
TION, 1984. The deadlock over the fiscal 1985 first budget
resolution stemmed from procedural delays and policy disputes. In 1984, the budget committees in both houses decided to ignore formal budget procedures and to work on a
reconciliation bill before approving the fiscal 1985 first budget resolution. Each house used its first budget resolution
as a baseline for negotiating the deficit-reduction package.
But Congress would not pass a first budget resolution until
the two houses had agreed on the terms of a reconciliation
bill. The new procedure was employed as an emergency
tactic to address the deficit problem.

Differences between the House and the Senate were rooted
in a Reagan-endorsed Senate proposal to place caps, or ceilings,
on defense and domestic spending for the ensuing three fiscal
years. President Reagan and Senate Republican budget leaders
collaborated to devise the so-called Rose Garden Plan, which
included a 7 percent cap on defense spending, a 2 percent cap
on domestic discretionary spending, and a proposal to close
several tax loopholes in order to raise revenues. The plan reduced defense spending by $41 billion and domestic spending
by $43 billion.

Meanwhile, the House approved George Miller's pay-as-
you-go budget resolution. The pay-as-you-go budget stipulated
that any new spending increases would be funded only if com-
parable revenues were raised to pay for those increases. The
plan was designed in part to force the White House to commit
to a tax increase if it wished to increase defense spending. The
committee's first budget resolution included a three-year $182
billion deficit-reduction package, with $95.6 billion coming
from cuts in defense spending, $15 billion in domestic spend-
ing reductions, and $49.8 billion in revenue increases.

As the conference talks began, Speaker O'Neill stubbornly
opposed both the Senate defense figure and the idea of placing
uneven caps on defense and domestic spending increases.
O'Neill announced, "It looks to me that the Senate is more
intent on getting a hefty defense bill for the president than cutting the deficit." He also pointed out, "we absolutely will

not go along" with the Senate's plan for placing caps on spending.[45] O'Neill's position was backed by strong party unity in the House, as only twenty-nine Democrats voted against the pay-as-you-go budget on the House floor. Conversely, Senate Republicans struggled to pass the Rose Garden Plan. In fact, a Democratic alternative to the Senate Budget Committee's first budget resolution was tabled by a vote of 49–49.

The opposing sides remained in deadlock until Congress was forced to pass a debt-limit increase bill on June 28. (The debt limit is the ceiling on the total federal debt. If Congress fails to meet the ceiling or increase the debt limit before authorized deadlines specified by Congress, the government defaults on its obligations.) The conferees agreed to a partial deficit-reduction package totaling $63 billion, with $50 billion coming from new revenues and $13 billion from domestic spending cuts. The Speaker won a victory in the settlement, as the conferees agreed to drop the caps provision from the reconciliation bill. Nevertheless, the defense component to the deficit-reduction package remained unresolved, meaning that Congress still had not approved a first budget resolution.

After two months of stalemate, Speaker O'Neill and Senate majority leader Howard Baker (R-Tenn.) met in private sessions to seek a compromise to the defense issue. Baker offered to reduce the authorization for the MX missile as part of a deficit-reduction package, if O'Neill could assure him the Democrats would not seek further spending reductions in the conference for the defense appropriations bill. On September 20, the two leaders compromised on the defense issue. The conference budget included a 5 percent real increase in defense spending for fiscal 1985, with $2.5 billion allocated for the MX. But only $1 billion could be spent in 1984, the remaining $1.5 billion would not be voted until after the Easter recess in April 1985. With this issue settled, the conferees quickly reached a final agreement on the fiscal 1985 first budget resolution.

CONFERENCE SETTLEMENT ON FIRST BUDGET RESOLUTION, 1985. The conference fight over the fiscal 1986 first budget resolution dragged on for over two months after the House passed its first budget resolution on May 23. Conferees were deadlocked over the House's lower defense figure and over the Senate's provision that froze COLAs for social security at the current rate of inflation. The president and the Speaker spearheaded a partisan confrontation over national priorities. President Reagan deemed the House-passed first budget resolution unacceptable because of the defense estimate. Speaker O'Neill announced, "I am bitterly opposed [to a cap on the COLAs for social security] and I will so notify and instruct my conferees."[46]

Two weeks into the conference deliberations, Senate conferees offered to eliminate the COLA cap on social security, in exchange for a $59 billion revenue increase through unspecified taxes. But Reagan rejected a tax increase of any kind, arguing that it would damage prospects for tax reform. Finally, on July 9, President Reagan invited Speaker O'Neill, Majority Leader Wright, House Minority Leader Michel, Senate Majority Leader Dole, and Senate Minority Leader Robert Byrd (D-W.Va.) to the White House for a cocktail reception and a chance to discuss the issues deadlocking the conference on the first budget resolution. Reagan asked O'Neill if he could go along with the cap on the COLAs. Speaker O'Neill recalls responding, "I can't go along with this reduction on the COLAs. You can be assured that it's never going to go through the House."[47] Much to the surprise of the Senate Republican leaders, Reagan then decided to drop the reduction on the COLAs. In addition to repealing COLA caps, the two leaders agreed to a higher defense figure, no tax increases, and a promise to reduce other domestic programs as a framework for conference negotiations.

This framework was unacceptable to many Senate Republicans and House Democrats, however. In the House, Democrats complained about the domestic spending reductions necessary to meet the terms of the Reagan-O'Neill framework. Meanwhile, Senate Republicans were angry with the president for conceding the cap on social security COLAs. When the president met with congressional leaders on July 9, Domenici was operating under the assumption that the president firmly supported the caps. During the conference sessions that preceded the White House meeting, Senate Budget Committee chairman Domenici had offered to eliminate the COLAs only under the condition that deficit reduction could be achieved through higher revenues. After the president conceded the social security caps, Senate budget leaders demanded $28 billion in domestic spending cuts from the House as a prerequisite for continuing the conference meetings.

Two and a half months of struggle finally ended on August 1 after two evenings of private meetings between Budget Committee chairmen Gray and Domenici and ranking Budget Committee members Latta and Lawton Chiles (D-Fla.). The group settled on a deficit-reduction package similar to the framework agreed to by O'Neill and Reagan. The plan included reconciliation instructions calling for $55 billion in spending reductions in discretionary programs, but no changes in social security and no tax increases. The conference report passed the House with bipartisan support by a vote of 309–119.

The Speaker as Budget Process Manager

A budget resolution consists of recommendations about how much money should be authorized and appropriated for government programs and how much revenue should be raised through taxes. Yet, important as it is for Congress to pass an annual budget resolution, the truly difficult choices are decided after the resolution is approved. The irony is that long debates over budget priorities crowd out time for considering appropriations and tax bills—the bills that matter most in terms of how much money the government actually spends and how much it raises in revenues. For example, when Congress votes to reduce spending in a set of reconciliation instructions attached to a budget resolution, the differences over national priorities are displaced by conflicts over spending cuts for separate programs. The separate committees confront the problem of deciding, literally, who gets what. As Robert Reis-chauer, then a senior vice-president of the Urban Institute, once said, "Retrenchment is an unnatural act for Congress."[48] As unnatural as it might be, Congress has tried to reduce the deficit (in some way, shape, or form) every year since 1980.

When an institution tries to perform an unnatural function there is likely to be some friction in the process. In the case of the congressional budget process, dealing with the deficit has produced logjams and breakdowns in meeting specified deadlines; disputes over which committees are responsible for which programs; non-compliance with the terms of budget res-olutions; and numerous questions about procedures and sched-uling. If Congress is to have a budget process, someone must make the necessary day-to-day decisions to keep the process moving. The Rules Committee is in charge of interpreting ac-tions that violate the Budget Act, and Budget Committee staff personnel track the progress of spending and authorization bills at the committee and floor stages of the legislative process. But neither Rules nor Budget has the institutional authority to per-form the necessary tasks to coordinate the recommendations of the first budget resolution with the most difficult problems re-garding committee action on separate authorization, appropri-ations, and tax bills.

As budget decisions became more difficult to make, the Speaker was called upon to smooth over rough spots, clear away logjams, and reduce friction. Yet O'Neill's role as process man-ager conflicted with his commitment to Democratic programs. In his relations with committees involved in cutting spending for traditional Democratic programs and especially in his rela-tions with President Reagan, O'Neill resisted efforts to reduce spending and preferred to protect policy goals and Democratic House seats.

Managing the Reconciliation Process

The reconciliation process can break down at a number of points. First, the committees may not be able make the specific legislative changes instructed by the first budget resolution before the reports are due back to the Budget Committee. Second, the committees may think the Budget Committee's instructions are too specific, dictating not only the total amount of spending cuts expected of them in order to meet the budget resolution targets, but the actual programs that should be cut. The committees insist that it is their job, not the Budget Committee's, to make specific changes in the legislation under their jurisdictions. Third, some committees make changes in programs that are under the jurisdiction of other committees.[49] The committees often call upon the Speaker to resolve these problems.

Despite the Speaker's efforts, however, the House has struggled to meet the demands of reconciliation. The committees typically fell short of the Budget Committee's deadline for reporting specific legislative changes instructed in the first budget resolution. In 1982, 1983, and 1985, the House Budget Committee had to extend the deadline for the committees to report spending cuts back to the Budget Committee. Furthermore, committee reports regularly recommended higher spending levels than the instructions called for. In such cases, the Rules Committee can send the report back to the committee for revision, allow the Budget Committee to make the necessary revisions in order to meet the instructions, or simply waive the committee report and have the Budget Committee accept it as reported.

The committees are not entirely to blame for the failure of Congress to meet the demands of reconciliation, however. The problems associated with making difficult choices on specific changes in legislative programs also stem from debates over major priorities. Speaker O'Neill's strong position on traditional Democratic programs hindered the reconciliation process in some ways. As process manager, the Speaker's role is to facilitate the implementation of reconciliation procedures. But O'Neill's objective as opposition party leader was to prevent reconciliation decisions that cut further into traditional liberal programs: "We want to stop the course of the [Reagan] administration. We're trying to stop them from turning back the clock." O'Neill was confronted with the problem of having to encourage the committees to make cuts that he personally opposed. The roles of process manager and opposition party leader were in conflict. Speaker O'Neill explained the dilemma: "With reconciliation [managing the process] would mean bringing in the chairmen of the various committees and saying, 'Listen, you don't want to do it and I don't like it, but we have to compromise it out.'"[50]

Final approval of reconciliation bills also involved the Speaker in relations with the president. Most of the reconciliation instructions included tax increases, an issue President Reagan was not normally prepared to negotiate. Since the president must sign all revenue bills, Speaker O'Neill thought House Democrats should wait for Reagan's endorsement before sponsoring tax increases.

Deficit-reduction talks between Congress and the president broke down more often than they succeeded. Congress failed to pass reconciliation bills in 1983 and 1985 and passed only parts of the originally expected savings for reconciliation in 1984 and 1986. Some of that failure can be traced to the disagreement over priorities, rather than to the committees' inability to meet the demands of deficit reduction.[51] With Reagan and O'Neill firmly entrenched on taxes and social security, and Reagan opposing defense cuts, there was little room for negotiating deficit-reduction settlements.

The two leaders were inclined to defend their priorities and distance themselves from each other, rather than cooperate and compromise. Beginning in 1984, Reagan repeatedly requested a balanced budget amendment and line-item veto, two mechanisms that would limit Congress's role in the budget process. He also periodically blamed Congress for overspending. For example, when deficit-reduction meetings failed in 1983 Reagan announced, "We do not face large deficits because Americans aren't taxed enough; we face those deficits because Congress still spends too much."[52] O'Neill, on the other hand, was concerned with protecting Democratic seats and limiting the damage that deficit reduction could have on traditional Democratic programs. With the two leaders firmly opposed on major priorities, there were few programs left for Congress to cut, making it difficult for committees to meet the demands of reconciliation.

Managing the Appropriations Process

When Congress fails to pass a reconciliation bill it fails in its attempt to reduce the budget deficit. The government keeps running, even if the deficit continues to grow, but it operates in the red. Reducing the deficit is a preference for better fiscal management, not a necessity. The only necessary act Congress must perform before the beginning of every fiscal year (October 1) is to pass thirteen appropriations bills, or an omnibus continuing resolution that packages the separate bills. Passing appropriations bills is a long and difficult process. It begins with weeks of hearings in the appropriations subcommittees, continues with more debate on the House floor and in conferences with the Senate, and ends only if the president decides to sign, rather than veto the bill or bills.

The appropriations process became even more difficult as a result of restrictions on spending, delays in the budget process, and partisan debate over national priorities. In the context of deficit politics, the Speaker began to play a more active role in the appropriations process, lending support to the Appropriations Committee. The Speaker made important decisions on scheduling appropriations bills for floor consideration and, under extreme circumstances, negotiated agreements on continuing resolutions.

The appropriations subcommittees begin hearings on the thirteen appropriations bills before the House passes its first budget resolution for the upcoming fiscal year. But according to the Budget Act, the appropriations bills should not be scheduled for floor consideration until after the first budget resolution passes both the House and the Senate. The objective of this provision is to ensure that the Appropriations

Committee marks its bills in accordance with the overall targets and estimates of functional categories in the first budget resolution. Since the House and Senate were deadlocked over final agreement on the conference version of the budget resolution throughout this period, Congress invariably failed to meet the Budget Act's May 15 deadline for passing the first budget resolution. In order to expedite the appropriations process, Speaker O'Neill instructed the Rules Committee, in some cases, to draft a rule waiving the Budget Act's restriction on scheduling the appropriations bills before Congress passed the first budget resolution. The rule allowed Appropriations Committee chairman Jamie Whitten to send appropriations bills to the floor before Congress passed a budget resolution.

Speaker O'Neill's decision to schedule appropriations ahead of the May 15 deadline indicated his concern for keeping the process moving. The House has a constitutional responsibility to pass appropriations bills and the Speaker, as budget process manager, assumes much of that responsibility. Managing the budget process in a period of deficit politics required him to be more flexible with the provisions of the Budget Act. One of O'Neill's staff aides explained the purpose of scheduling the appropriations bills early:

The reason for failure to come to grips with the budget resolution was good and sufficient for not having a budget resolution perhaps. But the government couldn't run out of money, and it took a certain amount of time to process the appropriations bills. . . . [O'Neill] would give the Appropriations Committee the rope to go with the House-passed numbers if there wasn't a final budget because it had its job [to do] and that was one of the only ways it could do it.[53]

There were also partisan and political reasons for moving ahead with the appropriations process. One way to expedite the conference agreement on the first budget resolution was to pressure Senate budget leaders. An Appropriations Committee staff person observed, "The Speaker wanted to figure out a way to put pressure on Domenici on the Senate side to get off dead center and have some faithful discussions on the budget resolution." A key Budget Committee staff person agreed: "We wanted to see what the Senate Republicans had, first, so we could know how to fashion what we had, to achieve a realignment of the priorities. . . . So it was really an attempt to put pressure on them to come up with something so that we knew what we were actually dealing with."[54]

In addition to positioning the House Budget Committee against the Senate, the Speaker's announcement to move ahead with appropriations bills enabled him to defend the House and the Democratic party from attacks by President Reagan. In 1983, Reagan criticized the House for sending him continuing resolutions to sign at the end of the year, rather than submitting separate appropriations bills. In the spring of 1983, O'Neill argued that Reagan "has unfairly criticized the House for failing to pass appropriations on schedule." On April 21, Speaker O'Neill announced a schedule for passing all thirteen bills before the start of fiscal 1984. The Speaker sent a notice to all members on May 24, 1983, stating:

The leadership intends to do everything in its power to properly complete the appropriations schedule on time, in order that a continuing resolution will not be required. . . . Although the leadership cannot control the Senate's inaction or presidential vetoes, it is important that Senate Republicans and the president not have the House to blame for foot-dragging on appropriations.[55]

As O'Neill expected, the constitutional system of checks and balances slowed down the appropriations process. While the Speaker scheduled appropriations bills that included spending increases for social welfare and health programs afforded by the fiscal 1984 first budget resolution, President Reagan stood ready to veto any bills that he thought were too expensive. By August 1983, O'Neill recognized that his plan for a fast-track appropriations process was being undermined by Reagan's veto threats. He admitted, "There's no sense of going through the routine of sending things over there that you know are going to get vetoed."[56]

During O'Neill's speakership, Congress consistently relied on continuing resolutions to fund government programs. The year-end rush to complete a continuing resolution added to the

high drama of budget politics. Debate over the continuing resolutions refueled the partisan and institutional debate over the
nation's priorities. President Reagan would only sign the continuing resolution if its defense appropriation was high enough.
In the most difficult cases, the Speaker was called upon to negotiate a settlement with Senate leaders and the president.

In 1983, the government nearly shut down as a result of a
dispute over the fiscal 1984 continuing resolution. But House
and Senate leaders convened over a three-day Veterans Day
holiday to resolve a controversy over defense and social spending. O'Neill used the emergency situation to pass a $98.7 mil-
lion social welfare package. The package originally totaled $1
billion as an amendment offered by Majority Leader Jim Wright
to the House-passed continuing resolution. Before the weekend
of negotiations ended, it was pared down to one-tenth its original estimate. But Speaker O'Neill was pleased with the results
of the bargain nonetheless: "We showed them that we had a
definite means of being able to stop the further cutting of the
safety net."[57]

In 1984, some government departments did actually shut
down. The president refused to sign a continuing resolution;
he said the House wanted too much for a public works bill and
not enough for defense spending. With the 1984 presidential
election only one month away, Reagan sent home five hundred
thousand federal government employees saying, "You can lay
this right on the majority party in the House of Representatives." The Speaker disputed President Reagan's claim by
pointing out that the House had passed a budget resolution by
April, a continuing resolution by September 25, and more appropriations bills than the Senate during the year. O'Neill
called Reagan's veto a "Hollywood publicity stunt." In his
view, the president "stopped the government today not for
the purposes of good public policy, but for purposes of
melodrama." Once the rhetoric died down, the Speaker offered
to drop all funding for the water projects. This proposal facilitated an agreement and resolved another logjam in the budget
process. The Speaker was called upon to negotiate on the

House side. *Congressional Quarterly* reporter Dale Tate observed, "with that offer, the impasse on the continuing resolution was broken."[58]

Summary

In this chapter I have assessed the Speaker's role as process manager and opposition party leader from 1982 to 1986. Conditions dictated that the Speaker take on a broader range of functions in the budget process. As the process was used as a mechanism to control spending in a condition of deficit politics, the Speaker was called upon to mediate conflicts in order to keep the process moving. His influence was needed at times to break stalemates over continuing resolutions, and he was generally responsible for facilitating the reconciliation process. O'Neill's role as process manager was triggered by the problems that arose as the process moved along, and his role varied from one year to the next.

The Speaker's responsibilities as process manager often conflicted with his role as opposition party leader. Speaker O'Neill was more concerned with protecting and promoting the priorities of the House Democratic party than with trying to make the process run smoothly. In the role of opposition party leader, O'Neill's personal preferences and individual qualities were better suited to preventing the Republican leaders from cutting Democratic programs than to advancing initiatives for his own party. The distinct character of O'Neill's middleman style and his role as party spokesman contrasts sharply with the style and role played by his successor—Jim Wright.

6

Speaker Wright: Activist Leadership

in the Hundredth Congress

In the wake of Jim Wright's election to the speakership in December 1986, Democratic caucus chairman Richard Gephardt announced, "The Reagan era is ending. This is our time to lead. The long days of playing defense are over." Favorable conditions supported Gephardt's expectations of active leadership in the upcoming Hundredth Congress. Large deficits constricted policy options; the Democrats regained majority control of the Senate in the 1986 elections; House Democrats continued to display unprecedented levels of party cohesion; and President Reagan suffered politically from the Iran-Contra scandal and his "lame-duck" status.[1] Journalist Richard Cohen concurred with Gephardt, citing a "leadership vacuum" in Washington. Political scientist Barbara Sinclair later noted that the conditions were suited for "strong, policy-oriented leadership."[2]

Favorable conditions only provide leaders with opportunities, however. Leadership in any context depends partly on the qualities of the individual leader. To be sure, House Democrats anticipated that Speaker Wright would pursue a leadership style different from O'Neill's. Leon Panetta stated, "Tip let consensus flow to the top, while Jim has strong views and will be more aggressive in participating in the legislative process." Robert Matsui (D-Calif.) observed, "Wright will be a real hands-on Speaker—day to day, hour to hour. To some extent, he'll be a micro-manager of the process."[3]

Wright's roles as opposition party leader and budget process manager included the same tasks performed by O'Neill. But Wright performed those tasks in quite a different manner. While O'Neill's primary objective was to protect and ultimately try to rebuild traditional Democratic programs, Wright's objective was to propose new solutions to prevailing public problems. A damage-control strategy finds the Speaker digging in his heels and defending his party against attacks by members of the opposing party, whereas an activist strategy finds the Speaker aggressively exercising power to achieve his policy objectives. One further distinction is worth noting here. While O'Neill followed a cautious middleman style of leadership that included responding to the expressed or implied expectations of the party membership, Wright's activist style involved acting before he consulted party members, and then bargaining to achieve his policy goals.

The success of an activist style depends on the nature of the leader's tasks and the prevailing conditions under which the leader is operating. Wright's activist style and budgetary experience were important assets in the process of formulating the budget resolution during the first quarter of 1987. Wright worked closely with Budget Committee Democrats to initiate his personal budget priorities for fiscal year 1988.[4] These priorities included an $18 billion increase in tax revenues, a $23 billion cut in President Reagan's fiscal 1988 defense budget, and $1.45 billion in new spending for a number of domestic programs. With the impending GRH deficit target in place, the lame-duck status of the president, and the restoration of a Democratic majority in the Senate, there was a growing expectation among Democrats that Congress should act decisively on the budget issue. Wright clearly took advantage of the opportunity to initiate a Democratic agenda.

Wright's ability to build and maintain support for his budget priorities was limited to the Budget Committee and the House floor, however. The House-passed fiscal 1988 first budget resolution was modified substantially as it proceeded through the later stages of the budget process. As the decision-making arena expanded—to include a conference with the Senate and relations with the president—the Speaker's priorities were exposed to more complex demands. Before Wright's first year had ended, members were questioning his ambitious policy goals and the hard driving style he employed to achieve them. Wright would be reminded of the limits to strong centralized leadership, when the House voted down a reconciliation bill containing many of his priorities. Thus, at later stages of the budget process, Wright was in a far weaker position to advance his personal priorities. Members changed their expectations of the way in which the Speaker should perform the roles of opposition party leader and process manager. Wright was expected to define limitations on agreements, protect Democratic priorities, mediate intra-party conflicts, and facilitate the process.

In this chapter I assess the interactive effects of the conditions of the time and Wright's personal qualities on his leadership in the Hundredth Congress. Wright's actions conformed with the expectations that members and other observers had of him. He was a policy activist—anxious to fill the apparent "leadership vacuum," tackle the deficit problem, and "micromanage" nearly every stage of the budget process.[5]

Jim Wright: An Activist Speaker

The major distinction between O'Neill and Wright is that O'Neill acted as a party spokesman in performing his role as opposition party leader, whereas Wright was a policy activist. Congressman Vic Fazio defines the term *activist* as it applied to Wright: "As Speaker, he is a man with a lot of interests who wants to use the influence of his office to pursue his own agenda."[6] An activist is a more hands-on party leader than a party spokesman. For example, while O'Neill relied on staff to work out the details of his budget priorities and communicate them to the Budget Committee, Wright was more personally involved with the committee's daily operation. The spokesman is a cautious representative of the party's interests, while the activist is a risk taker. The tax issue is a clear illustration of the differences between the two styles. While O'Neill refrained from promoting tax increases, Wright openly announced the need to increase taxes for high-income earners as a way to reduce the deficit.

Wright openly expressed his philosophy of leadership in defense of his proposal to raise taxes: "Democrats have to demonstrate that we can govern, and tell the hard truth when it's necessary." In Wright's view, "The House should develop a program of action . . . rather than leaving the making of policy to a fragmented group of 21 committees without any cohesion. There has to be a sense of coordinated policy, a cohesive pattern to what the institution does." As an activist, Wright wanted to enact a great deal of legislation in a short time frame: "My two biggest competitors are the clock and the calendar. There are so many things I would like to do."[7]

COMMITTEE ASSIGNMENTS. A Speaker's leadership style is reflected in his criteria for making committee appointments. While Speaker O'Neill preferred competent, loyal partisans, he sought to balance the ideological composition of the Budget Committee with the ideological makeup of the House Democratic party. No less partisan, perhaps, Wright's activist style was noticeable in his preference for appointing personal allies to the Budget Committee.[8] Although the evidence is limited by the scarcity of open appointments to the Budget Committee in 1987, it seems Wright took every chance to appoint members who would facilitate his budget priorities.

When the Steering and Policy Committee and Democratic caucus met to organize the House in December 1986, Speaker Wright had few opportunities to shape the Budget Committee to his liking. Only four Democrats left the Budget Committee that year, and one of them was Speaker Wright himself, who was replaced automatically by majority leader Tom Foley. Two

other members who left the committee in 1986 were Bill
Hefner of Appropriations and Tom Downey of Ways and
Means. Since Appropriations and Ways and Means informally
designate the members who will represent them on the Budget
Committee, it appeared that only one open seat was left to be
filled by the Steering and Policy Committee. After freshmen
Democrats complained about the limited opportunities for major committee assignments, however, Wright decided to add a
seat for each party, and he promised that the additional Democratic spot would be reserved for a freshman.

A total of five new Democrats joined the Budget Commit-
tee in 1987—Foley, Richard Durbin (D-Ill.), Mike Espy (D-
Miss.), Frank Guarini (D-N.J.), and Jim Oberstar (D-Minn.).
Durbin from Appropriations and Guarini from Ways and
Means filled the two positions from the money committees.
This leaves the appointments of Espy and Oberstar the only
cases that might reveal Wright's criteria for Budget Committee
appointments.

Espy was selected over his principal opponent Benjamin
Cardin (D-Md.) to represent freshmen Democrats on the House
Budget Committee. Wright helped Espy defeat incumbent Republican Webb Franklin (R-Miss.) in the 1986 election to represent the rural second district of Mississippi. Farming had
fallen on hard times in Mississippi, and Espy exploited the situation by criticizing Franklin's legislative record on agricultural
issues. Espy also promised voters that Wright would assign
him to the Agriculture Committee, an appointment that would
allow him to address the agricultural problems in his district.[9]
Thus, although Espy had no previous legislative record in the
House, his appointment to the Budget Committee could well
have been related to his personal connection with Wright.

The senior appointment on the Budget Committee for the
Hundredth Congress was typically competitive: twelve Democrats contended for one open seat in 1986. Oberstar, a member of the Public Works Committee, had a close association
with Speaker Wright, which helped him win the assignment.
Oberstar's profile in *Politics in America* states, "Speaker Jim

Wright was an ally of Oberstar on Public Works in earlier days, and when Wright took control of the House in 1987, he not only helped the Minnesota Democrat obtain his Budget [Committee] place, but personally appointed him to the Steering and Policy Committee."[10]

Hence, there is some evidence to show that Espy and Oberstar were personal allies of Speaker Wright. When asked if it were true that Wright selected members to the Budget Committee who would support his personal priorities, one Steering and Policy Committee staff person said, "Let's just say he was pleased with the selections."[11] Wright's preferences for Budget Committee assignments fitted well with his activist approach to leadership. A Speaker concerned with advancing his priorities would most likely use the prerogatives of the office to strengthen his position on the Budget Committee.

SETTING BUDGET PRIORITIES IN THE HOUSE. At his first press conference in December 1986, Speaker Wright boldly proposed to freeze tax rates for people in high-income groups at the rates they paid prior to the passage of the Tax Reform Act of 1986.[12] With the threat of automatic spending under the GRH law firmly on the minds of most Washington politicians, Wright's freeze proposal might not have seemed so bold after all. Increased revenues procured by the tax proposal would lower the deficit and relieve members of having to vote on a package of across-the-board spending cuts. House Budget Committee chairman Bill Gray held this view: "When members look at how difficult it is to get from [an estimated fiscal 1987 deficit of] $160 billion to $108 billion they may be in the mood to do revenues. The train wreck of Gramm-Rudman is going to hit."[13]

While some conditions favored Wright's tax proposal, however, others did not. First, advocating higher taxes is a politically sensitive position, perhaps even more so during this period. President Reagan continued to earn public approval for his no-tax-increase pledge. The most recent Democratic presidential nominee, Walter Mondale, suffered an embarrassing electoral defeat, the breadth of which was undoubtedly exacerbated by his idea of raising taxes to finance the deficit. Second, Congress had just completed tax reform in 1986, and Wright's proposal directly challenged part of the new tax law. Third, the conventional wisdom concerning the budget during the Reagan years was that Americans acknowledged the deficit problem, but they were unwilling to accept the difficult choices necessary to cut the deficit.[14]

The uncertainties underlying Wright's tax proposal were reflected in the mixed response coming from House Democrats. Wright won the support of the Democrats who believed that O'Neill had been too cautious in regard to the tax issue. Mike Lowry, one of the Budget Committee Democrats who sponsored tax increases in 1986, noted, "Half the fights I had with Tip were over that very issue [tax revenues]. There's a tremendous core in the Democratic Caucus—maybe two-thirds—who wanted to move forward and be aggressive, but we could never do it because Tip just plain said, 'no.' " But Leon Panetta, another Budget Committee Democrat, was less certain about Democratic support for Wright's tax proposal: "I've always felt we had to do revenues as part of a comprehensive [deficit-reduction] package, but my concern is, I'm not sure that Democrats as a whole have arrived at that point." One of Speaker Wright's closest staff persons clarified Panetta's view:

In the beginning, taxes were something most members weren't too easy talking about, because they thought they were going to get lambasted no matter what they did on taxes. . . . In whip meetings, the Speaker would be very forward about raising taxes and it would be a free-for-all. Members said they didn't think it was right, or that we didn't have the votes, or we couldn't craft a package that was large enough at all, and we were just going to get beat up.[15]

Another problem with proposing a tax freeze and calculating new revenues into the first budget resolution was that eventually the president must sign the tax bill. Regardless of Reagan's lame-duck status, without the president's signature a tax increase was not feasible. Reagan's threats to veto tax increases concerned the chairmen of the congressional tax-writing committees. The day Wright announced his plan to increase taxes, House Ways and Means Committee chairman Dan Rostenkowski was dubious about raising taxes. Senate Finance Committee chairman Lloyd Bentson (D-Texas) was opposed to the idea: "It would be a political impossibility to pass a tax increase of any kind without the active support of the president and I've seen no sign that his opposition to that has lessened." Bentson's suspicions were confirmed by Treasury secretary James A. Baker III, "[Wright's proposal] is nothing more than a general tax increase. It would break a compact that Congress and the executive branch have made with the American people in the tax reform bill. We would be totally and unalterably opposed to that."[16]

As the spring wore on and the House Budget Committee deliberated over the fiscal 1988 first budget resolution, the chances of raising taxes hardly improved. On March 2, Speaker Wright repeated his idea of imposing more taxes on high-income groups during a speech to the National League of Cities. Although Rostenkowski said the Ways and Means Committee would try to fulfill the recommendations of the Budget Committee, he remained skeptical: "How are we going to do it without Ronald Reagan?" Shortly after Wright made his pitch for more taxes, Reagan bluntly answered Rostenkowski by saying, "There will be no tax rate increase in the 100th Congress."[17]

President Reagan's staunch opposition to raising taxes was one of the principal reasons Speaker O'Neill had refrained from advocating a tax increase. O'Neill believed that a proposal to increase taxes would damage the electoral prospects of House Democrats because Reagan would certainly veto the proposal and criticize the "tax-and-spend" Democrats. As House Budget Committee Democrats began to mark up the specific components of the fiscal 1988 first budget resolution, columnist Tom Wicker described Speaker Wright's dilemma on the tax issue: "Jim Wright's problem, and that of other Democratic leaders in the House and Senate, is that they must

either risk Mr. Reagan's denunciation and veto of a tax increase; or labor under his potent charges that their failure to
meet the arbitrary Gramm-Rudman deficit target confirms
them as 'big spenders,' he always said they were." Wicker also
argued that if Wright's tax-freeze plan was rejected in the
House or vetoed by the president, it would cause problems for
the Democratic nominee in the 1988 presidential election.[18]
The new Speaker recognized this dilemma and apparently was
willing to take the chance that a proposed tax increase would
not harm the electoral prospects of Democratic candidates. He
believed that the Gramm-Rudman deficit ceilings provided a
buffer for Democrats against Republican criticism. Wright's
job then was to sell his idea to the Democratic caucus.

In addition to convincing House Democrats of the necessity to raise taxes, Wright also had to persuade Budget Committee Democrats to accept the other components of his plan.
At the beginning of the Hundredth Congress, Wright sent to
the Budget Committee a list of specific priorities he expected
the committee to use as a framework for drafting the first budget resolution (see table 19). Although these initiatives included
only incremental spending increases, any increase in spending
seemed controversial given the constraints imposed by the
GRH deficit target. Budget Committee Democrats would have
to sacrifice their own spending priorities or, even worse, propose spending cuts in existing programs in order to afford the
Speaker's budget. Budget Committee member Jim Slattery (D-
Kan.) observed, "It's going to be very difficult to get $9 billion
out of defense."[19]

The critical point here is that, although some conditions
were favorable for the Speaker to define and initiate Democratic
priorities, the specific aspects of Wright's budget proposals
were controversial. Under almost any conditions, the establishing of budget priorities is a difficult task for any Speaker, and in
this case, it was not clear initially whether the conditions favored Wright's agenda or not. Hence, we need to look beyond
the conditions in order to determine how Wright built support
for his budget priorities.

TABLE 19
Wright's Budget Priorities for Fiscal 1988 Budget Resolution

$18 billion in new taxes
$9 billion reduction in defense spending
$9 billion reduction in non-military spending
$1.45 billion increases in the following areas: Welfare reform, Catastrophic health care for the elderly, Assistance to homeless and impoverished children, AIDs research, Drug prevention, Job training, and U.S. trade

Sources: Personal interviews with members and Budget Committee staff; and Jeffrey H. Birnbaum, "House Panel finds Defense Spending Can't Be Cut Easily," *Wall Street Journal*, March 11, 1987, p. 6.

ACTIVIST LEADERSHIP. When people on Capitol Hill talk about the Speaker's role in the budget process as performed by Jim Wright, they normally begin by describing his previous experience on the Budget Committee. Wright was the only Democrat ever to serve on the Budget Committee from the first day of its operation. As one staff person put it, "Wright was on the Budget Committee when the budget was being tested. He has more knowledge [than O'Neill] of the nuts and bolts and the institutional memory of what went on." Wright brought his budgetary experience to the speakership. One of his closest aides commented:

Jim Wright was a member of the Budget Committee since it started. He introduced amendments, negotiated with the chairman, helped with whip counts and implementation of passage on the floor. He was an extremely active member. The Speaker did not change all that much by going off the committee, in terms of his interest in and commitment to the budget process as a substantive policy instrument. . . . He makes numerous requests for materials, packages that material, sends it out to members, colleagues, and activists in the field. He is an unrelenting activist in the budget process, constantly aware of (almost to the utmost detail of) what the Budget Committee is doing.[20]

Wright aggressively pushed his priorities on the Budget Committee in many different ways: through members, Steering and Policy Committee staff, Budget Committee staff, and himself. Wright spoke at several Budget Committee Democratic caucus meetings, stressing the urgency and importance of enacting his budget priorities.

Wright combined his budget expertise with a leadership style very different from that of O'Neill. As one Budget Committee staff person observed, "O'Neill's operational style was to let consensus form and leverage it into actions. Jim Wright's operational style was to define the issues and the outcomes and then sell them to the membership." Another close observer compared Wright to O'Neill in terms of their perspectives on the budget: "O'Neill wasn't as activist a Speaker as Jim Wright is. Wright became intensely personally involved." Or, as another Budget Committee staff person put it, "Rarely did we see anything resembling Wright's activist posture under O'Neill. This Speaker [Wright] wants to set in motion his agenda, and he thinks this is the committee to do it."[21] In contrast to Wright, O'Neill never submitted a list of priorities to the Budget Committee, never issued specific instructions directly to the Democratic Budget Committee caucus, and never sponsored a tax increase. O'Neill lacked the budgetary expertise and was too concerned with consulting the membership to play an activist role in defining the committee's agenda.

What effect did Wright's budget policy expertise and activist style have on the Budget Committee? The Budget Committee had begun to take the form of a leadership committee before Wright became Speaker. The members undoubtedly accepted the fact that the Speaker's intervention in some of the committee's business was both necessary and beneficial. Nevertheless, although Budget Committee members generally cooperate with the leadership, most of them have their own ideas about solving the deficit problem. One staff member described the central problem with developing a coherent deficit-reduction plan on the Budget Committee: "The new crop of members think it is their sole duty to fix the deficit problem and are thoroughly convinced that there must be a building somewhere in Washington D.C. entitled 'Bureau of Fraud, Waste, and Abuse,' and if we find out where it is located and padlock the front door, everything will be perfect."[22]

Ultimately, Wright convinced enough Democrats that a tax increase was better than across-the-board spending cuts. In doing so, he acted upon the opportunity presented by the conditions. But it was still not easy. As one close observer noted, "It was a difficult period, because Democrats weren't sure they were ready to be open about taxes, but he brought them along."[23] Wright brought along Budget Committee Democrats by working closely with Chairman Gray and through persistent direct negotiations with the committee. His leadership style required knowledge in budget policy, confidence in discussing budgetary issues with Budget Committee Democrats, and a willingness to participate actively in formulating the budget resolution.

In short, Budget Committee Democrats supported Wright's position on taxes for three reasons. First, the reality of the GRH deficit-reduction target constrained the members' choices and produced a situation conducive to discipline and fiscal responsibility. Second, the members respected Wright because he was the Speaker, and respecting the Speaker's position had become the norm on the Budget Committee. Third, Wright's activist style and budgetary expertise enabled him to make sense of the choices confronting members and to bargain with them.

Wright also needed the cooperation of Budget Committee Democrats to initiate his list of budget priorities. The Speaker's priorities were debated in Democratic Budget Committee caucus meetings prior to the formal markup of the fiscal 1988 first budget resolution. The Democrats held four weeks of private meetings in which no consensus emerged regarding the details of the budget resolution. When the Budget Committee met in formal session to vote on the components of the fiscal 1988 first budget resolution, Committee Democrats were still divided over the amount of money that should be allotted to defense spending. The issue was settled when Committee Democrats voted 13–8 in favor of an amendment to reduce Reagan's defense budget by $23 billion, or $8 billion below the current rate of spending.

Speaker Wright alleviated the difficulty of drafting a budget resolution under the constraints of the GRH law by recommending to Chairman Gray that the Budget Committee use the OMB's economic assumptions to estimate the aggregate totals of the budget resolution (total spending, revenue, and deficit levels for the budget resolution). The Budget Committee normally uses the CBO's economic assumptions, which are less optimistic than the OMB's (see table 20). But Speaker Wright wanted the Budget Committee's first budget resolution to be judged on the same terms as the president's budget. A Budget Committee staff person explained the logic of using the OMB's assumptions:

Obviously, the more favorable your economic assumptions the less difficulty you have in meeting deficit reduction. The administration always, whether it's Democratic or Republican, has generally been interested in favorable economic assumptions. Well, given these troubled times, [Wright] saw no reason why we shouldn't go ahead and use the economic assumptions of the administration, which were more favorable.[24]

Using the OMB's assumptions enabled the committee to show a lower deficit figure and allowed members to recommend higher spending levels for their budget priorities.

TABLE 20
Comparison of OMB and CBO Economic Assumptions, Fiscal Years 1987–88 (in percentages)

Economic Indicator	OMB Assumptions		CBO Assumptions	
	FY 87	*FY 88*	*FY 87*	*FY 88*
GNP growth	+ 3.9	+ 3.7	+ 3.5	+ 2.0
Inflation[a]	+ 3.8	+ 3.6	+ 4.5	+ 4.4
Interest rate[b]	+ 3.4	+ 5.6	+ 5.6	+ 5.7

Source: House Budget Committee reported in "Budget Moves to Full House Amid Partisan Flak," *Congressional Quarterly Weekly Report*, April 4, 1987, p. 610.
[a]Inflation rate measured by Consumer Price Index.
[b]Interest rate on ninety-day Treasury bills.

In addition to recommending that the Budget Committee use the OMB's economic assumptions for the fiscal 1988 first budget resolution, Wright worked vigorously to build support among Committee Democrats for his priorities. Two accounts of Wright's relationship with the Budget Committee capture his activist leadership style at the start of the Hundredth Congress. One of Wright's closest staff persons explained:

Wright pushed early with a very specific agenda about what we ought to be doing. . . . It was a difficult debate in the Budget Committee over how much we could afford for these programs vis-à-vis other programs, which other members wanted to protect, like Space and Science and Foreign Affairs. . . . Other members were saying, "Where's the money for my stuff? If we do everything the Speaker wants to do, there won't be any room left to do anything else." I remember long debates into the night. Then we'd usually end up having a meeting with the Speaker to battle it out again, and the Speaker would reemphasize that he wanted these things in the budget. . . . We ended up carving out significant reserves in the budget resolution for all of those programs. Without having that happen, I'm not sure he would have succeeded at all.

A Budget Committee staff person relayed his perception of Wright's style:

Essentially, the members grumbled, because they were faced with a lot of choices. I mean these were not an issue of "All right, we've got two things the Speaker wants and the rest is open game." No. The members were faced with a lot of choices . . . that they had to make in putting together a budget resolution. And those choices reflected [Wright's] priorities. . . . He essentially took, with his guidance, about 60 percent of the decisions off the board. They could debate them for a while, but ultimately the Speaker was going to continue to push those items. Then it became an issue of "All right, how do we tough the remaining 40 percent?" And then [Wright] essentially said to folks, "Where you need me to referee in that 40 percent, I will do so. If you need me, come talk to me."

In comparing Wright with O'Neill, this staff person went on to say what many other members and staff personnel have said:

"We never saw that level of involvement from Tip O'Neill. Essentially his position was, 'Listen, you are the chairman, you are the committee, you work it out.' "[25]

Wright's success in gathering support for his budget priorities rested on two factors: his budget expertise and his persistent activism. Among Budget Committee Democrats, Wright was able to claim legitimacy on a party issue by using his personal skills and the weight of the Speaker's office. By demonstrating policy expertise and consorting with members to work out their differences, Wright eventually was able to build support for his priorities on the Budget Committee.

Problems with Maintaining Partisan Support beyond the Budget Committee

When the budget resolution reached the floor, Speaker Wright's budget resolution benefited from partisan politics and a deficit-driven agenda. Party unity scores peaked by 1987 (see figure 3). Meanwhile, Reagan's congressional support declined substantially (see figure 6). The uncertainty of passing budget resolutions, which was a trademark of politics on the House floor during the 1970s and early 1980s, had virtually disappeared by 1987. With the GRH deficit ceilings in place, the Rules Committee received so few requests to amend the first budget resolution that it opened the floor for amendments and substitutes. After Budget Committee Republicans claimed that the Democrats precluded them from the process of drafting the first budget resolution, ranking Republican Delbert Latta decided that, for the first time ever, he would not offer an alternative budget. He complained, "If we're just going to get Republican votes, there's no reason to offer one."[26] The substitute budget resolution of Republican William Dannemeyer (R-Calif.) was soundly rejected 47–369. A Black caucus substitute was also defeated by a wide margin, 56–362. Budget Committee Chairman Gray attempted to embarrass President

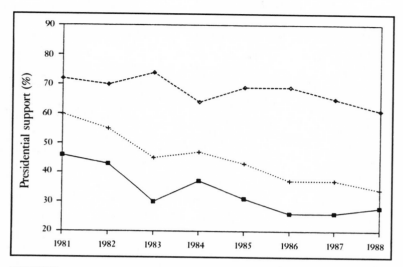

FIGURE 6. *Presidential support for Reagan, 1981–88.* —+— = *House Southern Democrats;* —■— = *House Democrats;* —◇— = *House Republicans.* Data from *Congressional Quarterly Almanac,* 1975–88.

Reagan by proposing his budget as a substitute to the Budget Committee plan. Reagan's budget was defeated 27–394.

In this context, Speaker Wright's budget package, consisting of an $18 billion increase in revenues and a list of spending priorities for fiscal 1988, was assured smooth passage on the floor. The House approved the budget resolution by a nearly straight party-line vote of 230–192—only nineteen Democrats voted "nay," and Republicans voted unanimously against the budget. The conflicting priorities between Reagan and Wright were clearly indicated by the differences in the budgetary allocations for defense, agriculture, commerce and housing credit, transportation, community and regional development, education and social services, health, and income security (see table 21).

After the House passed the Budget Committee's first budget resolution, however, the Speaker confronted the usual roadblocks and setbacks that characterized budgetary poli-

TABLE 21
Comparison of Major Budget Functions for Fiscal 1988 Budget: President Reagan vs. House Budget Committee (HBC) (billions of dollars in budget authority)

Function	Reagan's Budget	HBC Budget	Difference
National defense	312.0	288.7	23.3
Agriculture	22.2	29.5	7.3
Commerce and housing credit	8.8	12.7	3.9
Transportation	24.6	28.35	3.75
Community and regional development	5.3	7.6	2.3
Education, employment, and social services	28.8	36.45	6.65
Health	41.4	45.7	4.3
Income security	160.2	168.6	8.4

Source: House Budget Committee, reprinted in Elizabeth Wehr, "House Adopts Democrats-Only FY '88 Budget," *Congressional Quarterly Weekly Report*, April 11, 1987, pp. 657–61.

tics during the 1980s. Wright continued to pursue an activist leadership style, but conditions changed as the year progressed and Wright's budget confronted resistance from the Senate and the president. Even members of the House majority party began to question Wright's hard driving style and ambitious policy goals. Before year's end, Wright's priorities were substantially modified at several points in the budget process: (1) the conference with the Senate over the first budget resolution; (2) in meetings to revise the GRH targets; (3) during passage of the reconciliation bill; and (4) in summit meetings between congressional leaders and White House officials. Before his first year ended, Wright had experienced the limitations to activist leadership in the House.

Conference Stage: Fiscal 1988 Budget Resolution

Even though the Democrats regained a majority in the Senate in 1986, the House and the Senate continued to have trouble settling their differences over the first budget resolution. The conference debate revealed divisions within the Democratic party over national priorities and how to pay for them. Vic Fazio described the deadlock: "There is a real, honest clash between every branch of the Democratic Party—the futurists versus the New Dealers; the technocrats, the defense people, versus the people who want to feed kids."[27]

In 1987, the Senate approved a first budget resolution with $301.5 billion for defense, about $13 billion more than the House. Several House Budget Committee Democrats—including Butler Derrick, George Miller, and Marty Russo (D-Ill.)—objected to settling on a higher defense figure for the first budget resolution. They argued that the spending levels for domestic programs estimated in the first budget resolution would be trimmed further along in the budget process. And a higher defense budget would pressure Congress to cut domestic programs even more than expected by the end of the year.[28] Consequently, on June 4, liberal Democrats on the House Budget Committee rejected a compromise plan reached by House and Senate Democratic party leaders that would have decreased defense below the Senate mark by only $1.5 billion. Russo explained the liberals' reason for rejecting the defense figure offered by the leaders: "It's not a Democratic priority."[29]

About one week later, Senate negotiators refused a proposal by liberal House Democrats to split the difference between the original defense figures in the House's and the Senate's first budget resolutions. At that point, Chairman Gray relinquished hope for a compromise between House and Senate Democrats: "It appears that there is no need for further meetings. Each house will have to govern under different guidelines."[30]

The conference debate finally ended when House Budget Committee Chairman Gray and Senate Budget Committee chairman Lawton Chiles (D-Fla.) met privately and worked out a compromise with the assistance of Speaker Wright and Majority Leader Byrd. As process manager, Speaker Wright played an important role in mediating the differences to break the deadlock. The leaders agreed to a higher defense budget under the assumption that the president would sign a tax increase of $19.3 billion. With the tax increase, defense outlays would be $289.5 billion, and without the tax increase defense outlays would be $283.6 billion for fiscal 1988.

Generating support for the plan was difficult—yet another signal that the solid Democratic party cohesion demonstrated on the first budget resolution was beginning to crack. It was reported that Wright had to pressure many House Budget Committee liberal Democrats to support the defense agreement.[31] Miller grudgingly pledged his support for the conference budget: "The test is not whether we can govern, but whether we can govern badly. If we increase taxes and we're not reducing the deficit, that's not what [Democrats] should be taking to the public."[32] The conference version of the fiscal 1988 first budget resolution finally passed the House on June 23 by a vote of 215–201, over two months past the deadline of April 15. The final vote indicated that party unity had begun to weaken, as thirty-four Democrats voted against the conference report, compared with the nineteen who voted against the House's original version of the first budget resolution.

Despite the growing differences among House Democrats, the conference report reflected the agreement by leaders in both chambers that the first budget resolution should be used to coax Reagan to decide between his top priorities—lower taxes or higher defense spending. The central message of the conference bill was that if Reagan wanted a higher defense budget, he would have to agree to a tax increase. Yet, as Congress passed its fiscal 1988 first budget resolution, Reagan showed no signs of budging on taxes. During a meeting with Senate Republicans he held up an oversized pencil inscribed "VETO" and told them, "Using taxes to cure deficits is like using leeches to cure anemia. We're not going to counter one evil with another."[33] Needless to say, any chance of settling on a meaningful deficit-reduction agreement required the president's cooperation. Thus, continuing efforts toward finding a solution to deficit problems focused on strategies of compelling Reagan to compromise on his pledge not to increase taxes.

The Politics of Deficit Reduction

The politics of deficit reduction took on a slightly different tone in 1987 partly as a result of Wright's leadership style. Much like O'Neill, Wright's role as opposition party leader involved defining the limits of compromise. But Wright's activist style included a more aggressive approach to the deficit problem. Unlike O'Neill, Wright was willing to force the tax issue on Reagan by proposing a tax increase. By directly confronting the deficit problem, Wright set up a showdown with Reagan. The battle was played out on two fronts: (1) revising the GRH law, a procedural mechanism employed to structure Reagan's choices for reducing the deficit, and (2) a budget summit meeting between White House officials and congressional leaders that was born out of necessity rather than sincere cooperation.

REVISING GRAMM-RUDMAN-HOLLINGS. House and Senate budget leaders began to consider revising the GRH deficit-reduction law while the reconciliation process was underway. Senator Gramm wanted to extend the deficit-reduction timetable for balancing the budget and amend the original law in order to restore the automatic trigger for spending cuts that was ruled unconstitutional in July 1986.[34] The principal negotiators for the House Democratic party were majority leader Tom Foley and Ways and Means chairman Dan Rostenkowski. Foley and Rostenkowski agreed with Speaker Wright that the ultimate objective of the Gramm-Rudman talks was to position the congressional budget for what appeared to be an inevitable showdown over taxes between Wright and Reagan. The Speaker wanted to ensure that the GRH law forced Reagan either to change his mind and sign a tax increase bill or accept the consequences of an automatic reduction in defense spending.

Speaker Wright remained at arm's length from the actual conference meetings on GRH since there was general agreement that the law would be revised. But the impact of his previous efforts to lead the party were clearly evident as the conferees met to decide the fate of GRH. Rostenkowski observed, "If Jim Wright was not as strong as he has been with respect to raising revenues . . . We wouldn't be talking about it now."[35] Hence, the next move for the Democrats in trying to enact a tax bill was to structure the automatic cuts provision so that Reagan had to choose between his two major priorities, low taxes and high defense spending.

Rostenkowski made certain that any revisions to the original deficit-reduction schedule would not undermine this objective. If the revised deficit target for fiscal 1988 was raised to nearly the current deficit level, then only a small amount of savings would be needed through the automatic cuts in order to meet the new target. Hence, if the deficit-reduction target was raised too high, Reagan could avoid a tax increase and simply order the automatic cuts without sacrificing a substantial reduction in defense. In Rostenkowski's opinion, the Democrats had come too far and risked too much already to let the president off the hook.

The House passed the conference version of the revised GRH law on September 23, 1987. The new law reestablished the automatic trigger by giving the OMB rather than the General Accounting Office (GAO) final authority to determine the automatic cuts. The sequester order was to be issued by the president, in the event that the real deficit level breached the deficit ceiling established by the GRH law. The number of programs subject to sequestration was further reduced under the revised GRH law. About two-thirds of the entire budget was now exempt from automatic cuts. The law also revised the annual deficit-reduction schedule (see table 22).

For fiscal 1988, the revised deficit ceiling was $144 billion. According to reports on the current deficit level, as of September 1987, Congress would have to reduce the deficit by $23 billion by October 20 in order to meet the fiscal 1988 ceiling and avoid a sequester order. If Congress failed to meet that deadline, the first report on the automatic cuts would take effect. If the president and Congress did not enact the necessary legislation to reduce the deficit by November 20, the automatic cuts

TABLE 22
Comparison of Original Gramm-Rudman Deficit-Reduction Schedule with Revised Schedule (in billions)

Fiscal Year	Annual Deficit Ceiling	
	Original Plan	Revised Plan
1986	171.9	—
1987	144.0	—
1988	108.0	144.0
1989	72.0	136.0
1990	36.0	100.0
1991	0.0	64.0
1992	—	28.0
1993	—	0.0

Source: Compiled by author from Elizabeth Wehr, "Congress Clears Gramm-Rudman Fix," *Congressional Quarterly Weekly Report*, September 26, 1987, p. 2311.

became permanent. For all practical purposes, under the new GRH law, President Reagan either had to sign a reconciliation bill including higher taxes or accept as much as a 10.4 percent reduction in defense spending. Even though the White House disliked the situation created by the GRH revisions, the president signed the bill, recognizing the adverse political consequences of vetoing a bill that proposed to balance the budget. Thus, Rostenkowski had succeeded in forcing Reagan to choose between his top priorities.

THE 1987 RECONCILIATION BILL. With the new deficit ceiling set and the automatic cuts pending, the Budget Committee revised its reconciliation package for fiscal 1988. The original reconciliation bill called for a $19.3 billion tax increase and $17.7 billion in spending cuts for a total deficit-reduction package of $37 billion. Under the new Gramm-Rudman ceiling set at $144 billion, Congress needed only a $23 billion reconciliation bill with $12 billion to come from tax revenue increases.[36] On October 15, when the Ways and Means Committee reported a $12.3 billion tax bill to the

Budget Committee as part of the reconciliation package, Rostenkowski predicted, "I'll bet you [President Reagan] will sign this bill when it reaches his desk."[37] But for the moment at least, Reagan maintained his opposition to a tax increase despite the impending threat of an automatic cut in defense.

Reagan changed his mind on October 19, when the Dow Jones industrial average plummeted 508 points, or 22.6 percent of its paper value in one day. In comparison, on the infamous Black Tuesday of October 28, 1929, that triggered the Great Depression, the market declined only 12.8 percent in dollar value. Politicians and economists blamed the federal deficit and the United States trade debt as the two most likely reasons for the sharp decline in the market. The partisan mood in Washington abated temporarily with the urgent need to devise a solution to the deficit problem. Rostenkowski observed, "I expect that there will be dozens of theories about the cause of yesterday's market drop. No matter how it is explained, or by whom, one factor will be present in every analysis—the need to reduce the federal deficit." The day following the crash, Speaker Wright invited President Reagan "to join with the bipartisan leadership of Congress in convening an economic summit, without crippling preconditions, to deal with America's long-term structural problems."[38] Reagan announced he was willing to bargain and would put everything on the table except social security.

As the summit meetings began on October 26, the House was scheduled to vote on the revised reconciliation package for fiscal 1988. But the reconciliation bill that incorporated Wright's budget plan was haunted by past problems of Democratic party disunity. The source of dissatisfaction among Southern Democrats was a welfare program attached to the reconciliation bill. The so-called Downey package extended Medicaid coverage, revised the food stamps program, established a work program for long-term welfare dependents, and required states to extend eligibility for the Aid to Families with Dependent Children (AFDC) program to two-parent families in cases where the primary wage earner was unemployed.[39] The total welfare package would cost the federal government $148 million in fiscal 1988 and $1.7 billion over three years. The Downey package was drafted in accord with the welfare provisions approved as part of the fiscal 1988 first budget resolution.

Southern Democrats disliked this mix of tax revenues and additional welfare spending because parts of the Downey package required the states to increase welfare expenditures. Buddy MacKay (D-Fla.) described the problem with the reconciliation bill: "It's got two lightening rod issues [taxes and welfare]; both of which are career threatening in the South. . . . We [the Southern states] really are poor, and the states have got to put up some money [to make the Downey plan work]. It's easier to be a liberal if you are from Connecticut."[40] Wright attempted to compensate the Southern Democrats for the welfare plan by adding $3 billion in defense spending to a continuing appropriations bill for fiscal 1988.[41]

The compromise failed to rescue Speaker Wright from suffering his first major defeat of the year, however. On the morning of October 29, forty-eight Democrats (thirty-two from the South) aligned with Republicans to defeat the rule on the reconciliation bill by a vote of 203–217. The Democratic coalition forged in the spring to support Wright's budget had fallen apart at the worst possible moment, just after the nation's economy had reached the brink of crisis (the reconciliation bill was taken to the floor only ten days after the stock market crashed). Wright had been warned in advance that the Downey package would cause problems for both conservative and liberal Democrats. But he had promised Rostenkowski, Augustus F. Hawkins (D-Calif.), and a number of other sponsors of the welfare plan, that it would be included in the reconciliation bill.[42] Several liberal Democrats voted against the reconciliation bill in protest of a decision by Wright to appease Southern Democrats on the defense appropriation. Dan Glickman (D-Kan.) commented on the Speaker's failure to judge correctly the preferences of House Democrats: "It was a good lesson for the leadership. When there is grumbling from the membership, it needs to be listened to. The antennae need to be out a little higher."[43]

Nonetheless, the feisty Speaker pushed ahead. Immediately after the vote on the rule, Minority Leader Michel requested that the House take several days to formulate a bipartisan substitute reconciliation bill. In spite of Michel's plea, Speaker Wright asked the Rules Committee to convene at 12:45 P.M. the same afternoon and draft another rule for the reconciliation bill. On Wright's instructions, Rules stripped the welfare provision, as well as a number of other points of dispute, from the original bill. Wright announced that the new reconciliation bill should be called up for reconsideration that very same day. The Speaker said that, if the House did not act quickly, "it puts total initiative in the hands of the executive branch of Government over something the Constitution declared was the primary business of the House of Representatives."[44]

But House rules prohibit reconsideration of a rule on the same day it is defeated. So Wright used his parliamentary powers to circumvent any discrepancies in the timing of the new rule. Despite protests by Republican leaders, the Rules Committee met to revise the rule on the reconciliation bill, and the House reconvened the same afternoon. In order to consider the revised reconciliation bill, Wright ended the legislative day and, within a few minutes, proceeded to start a new legislative day.[45]

The new rule for considering the revised reconciliation bill passed easily by a vote of 238–182, with only thirteen Democrats dissenting. But when the bill itself was voted on, it appeared that Speaker Wright's parliamentary sleight of hand had backfired. With no time remaining on the House clock for passing the reconciliation bill, the vote was 205–206. Wright delayed announcement of the final results on the vote until Jim Chapman (D-Texas) returned to the floor to change his vote, making the final tally 206–205. Wright quickly declared that the reconciliation bill was passed. House Republicans booed Wright and shouted that they had been cheated.

Wright justified his actions by arguing that it was necessary for the House to pass a reconciliation bill to serve as a bench mark for the budget summit talks, which had begun earlier that week. The Speaker also added it was well within the rules for members to change their votes: "It has always been to this occupant of the Chair's knowledge a policy of the Chair to honor the desire of any Member in the Chamber to change his vote and if no other Members desired to vote or to change their votes all time has expired. On this vote the yeas are 206 and the nays are 205."[46]

While Wright's parliamentary tactics were well within the bounds of his formal powers as presiding officer, there was considerable disdain among Republicans and Democrats for his aggressive leadership style. Vin Weber (R-Minn.) took the occasion to compare Wright with his predecessor Tip O'Neill: "It's now really sunk in. This Speaker may be less ideological, but he is considerably more partisan in a fairly ruthless way." Bob Carr (D-Mich.) pointed out, "The honeymoon definitely is over." Amid the turmoil, Wright decided to postpone floor consideration of a continuing appropriations bill that was reported out of the Appropriations Committee on the same day the reconciliation bill was voted on. Perhaps the most important point, however, is that the first budget resolution passed by the Congress in June had changed significantly by the time the reconciliation bill passed on October 29. The tax increase was lowered by $7 billion, a higher defense figure was estimated into the bill, and the welfare provision was dropped. As Marty Russo observed, the final product of the reconciliation bill was a "totally different animal."[47]

The limitations on Wright's ability to sustain support for his carefully crafted budget package were clear enough. As the budget progressed through the process, it was amended to meet the particular interests of House Democrats rather than satisfy the Speaker's priorities.

THE BUDGET SUMMIT AND ITS AFTERMATH. The fate of the House-passed reconciliation bill was decided in budget summit meetings with White House officials and congressional budget leaders. A mood of distrust and suspicion, typical of deficit politics, pervaded the summit meetings. The two sides were not brought together in the spirit of bipartisan cooperation; rather, they were forced together under emergency economic conditions. The stock market crash set off an alarm, warning the president and Congress that something must be done to reduce the federal deficit. Yet considerable differences between Republicans and Democrats remained over how to achieve that objective. The situation demanded a modicum of agreement on deficit reduction, but the conflicting priorities of the two sides were too strong to yield a long-term deficit-reduction agreement.

The group of principal negotiators on the White House side of the summit meetings included Treasury secretary James Baker, White House chief of staff Howard Baker, national security adviser Frank Carlucci, OMB director James C. Miller III, and assistant for White House legislative affairs William Ball. Majority Leader Foley, the chief negotiator for the House, was joined by Appropriations Committee chairman Jamie Whitten, Budget Committee chairman Bill Gray, and Ways and Means Committee chairman Dan Rostenkowski. Republicans on the House side included minority whip Trent Lott (R-Miss.) and ranking members Silvio Conte (R-Mass.) from Appropriations, Delbert Latta from Budget, and John Duncan (R-Tenn.) from Ways and Means. Senate Democratic negotiators included ranking Democrat on Appropriations Bennett Johnston (D-La.), Finance Committee chairman Lloyd Bentsen, and Budget Committee chairman Lawton Chiles. Senate Republicans included Minority Leader Dole and ranking minority members Mark Hatfield (R-Ore.) from Appropriations, Bob Packwood (R-Ore.) from Finance, and Pete Domenici from Budget.

Speaker Wright disagreed in principle with the idea of holding a summit with the White House. But he called for the meetings in the hope that they would force Reagan to sign a tax increase bill. One of Wright's closest staff persons noted, "The objective of the summit was to get a tax increase. But, institutionally, [Wright] doesn't like the idea of a couple of members representing the whole body. . . . He's just not in favor of it."[48] Although Wright did not participate directly in the meetings, Foley kept the Speaker informed of any proposals for deficit reduction being considered throughout the meetings, and Wright took part in defining the provisions for compromise that the House Democratic party could accept.

Pressed by the demands of the situation, the summit meetings ended with a settlement on November 20, the date set for issuing a sequester order for automatic cuts as specified under the Gramm-Rudman law. The summit produced a two-year deficit-reduction plan for fiscal years 1988 and 1989 that included tax increases and spending reductions totaling $76 billion. The package would reduce the deficit by $33 billion in fiscal 1988 and $42.7 billion in fiscal 1989, with $9.1 billion coming from new revenues the first year and $14 billion the following year. Nevertheless, participants from both parties were disappointed that the agreement failed to resolve long-term deficit problems. Panetta observed, "The summit agreement does not in a major way approach the deficit issue." Lott called the summit agreement "a nameless child nobody will claim."[49]

The problems that burdened the summit resembled those that had dominated budget politics throughout the 1980s: deadlock over priorities, intense partisanship, and an institutional struggle over the role of Congress and the president. Neither the Republican White House nor the Democratic Congress wanted to compromise its highest priorities. At one point, Rostenkowski walked out of the summit meetings because of the administration's hard line on taxes. After the meetings ended, Buddy MacKay, an early advocate of having a White House–congressional budget summit, admitted that he had been naive in thinking that the two parties could agree on a meaningful deficit-reduction package. MacKay said, "It was a bipartisan mechanism attended by the most partisan people in both parties." Speaker Wright complained that the summit blurred the lines between the two parties and compromised the constitutional roles of the two branches. He argued, "We didn't invite the administration up here to write legislation."[50]

Even though the summit established a framework for reducing the deficit for fiscal years 1988–89, Congress still needed to pass a reconciliation bill and an omnibus appropriations bill. Neither task would be completed easily, given the general disenchantment over the summit agreement. The Speaker and the extended majority party leadership played a critical role in carrying out the instructions issued by the summit agreement. Speaker Wright arbitrated a dispute between House and Senate conferees over funding levels for Medicare and Medicaid. The House proposal for Medicaid to assist poor women and children was nearly four times higher than the Senate's proposal. Ignoring Reagan's threat to veto the House's Medicaid provision, Henry Waxman (D-Calif.), chairman of the health subcommittee of the House Energy and Commerce Committee, argued that Congress was absolutely not bound by the summit agreement.[51] After meeting with party leaders, Waxman conceded his position and complied with the guidelines of the agreement.

The Speaker also mediated differences between the president and Congress and between the two chambers over several provisions in the omnibus appropriations bill. House and Senate leaders negotiated a compromise on spending for Nicaraguan Contra aid. The House leadership also decided to drop the so-called fairness doctrine, a regulation of the Federal Communications Commission that required broadcasters to air both sides of all public issues. Before the leadership intervened, Reagan threatened to veto the appropriations bill if it included the fairness doctrine.[52]

By the time all of the discrepancies over spending levels were worked out, the president signed a 30-pound, 2,100-page, $603.9 billion omnibus appropriations bill that packaged all thirteen separate appropriations bills for fiscal 1988. It was the second consecutive year and the third time in history that all regular appropriations were packaged in a single appropriations bill. The president expressed his distaste for omnibus bills: "While I must agree with these bills at this time, wrapping up the entire legislative business of our country into two thousand page bills on the eve of Christmas is no way to do business. The normal legislative process should have produced 13 separate appropriations bills."[53]

Wright's First Year in Retrospect

Speaker's Wright's first year in office began with a flurry of legislative successes. With Reagan crippled by the Iran-Contra situation, Wright took advantage of strong party unity to initiate an agenda for the Hundredth Congress through the first budget resolution. His experience in budget policy and his activist leadership style complemented the current conditions, which called for activist leadership, although the situation offered no guarantee that Wright's priorities would be accepted by the party.

The struggle to pass a reconciliation bill in October, however, and concessions made to Reagan on the final reconciliation and omnibus appropriations bills exemplified the limitations of sustaining party leadership. Speaker Wright had to rely on Republican support in order to gain approval for the two final omnibus bills. The omnibus appropriations bill passed 209–208, with Democrats voting 116–128 and Republicans voting 93–80. The reconciliation bill passed 237–181, with Democrats voting 193–51 and Republicans voting 44–130. Speaker Wright was successful in getting the president to sign a tax increase as part of the final reconciliation bill. But that concession came after the market crash, and only $9 billion in total revenues were earned from the tax increase—half the original amount recommended in the House-passed fiscal 1988 first budget resolution.

The long arduous struggle over the fiscal 1988 budget took a toll on House members. Not only did the participants in the summit negotiations complain about the frustration that accompanied the stalemate, but many members disliked the summit as a way of making important budgetary decisions. Marvin Leath described the sentiment of many House members: "You work all year in your committee and then you end up with three-quarters of the government run by a half-dozen people locked up in a room for three or four weeks. I resent that."[54]

The resentment voiced by Leath and experienced by many House members, combined with Reagan's criticism of the legislative process, was translated into a set of expectations for the following legislative session. The expectations were to have a more orderly budget process and to pass thirteen individual appropriations bills before the start of the upcoming fiscal year.

The 1988 Appropriations Process

The frustration members expressed over omnibus appropriations bills in December 1987 continued into January 1988. Three Democrats representing different ideological perspectives of the party—liberal George Miller, moderate Buddy MacKay, and conservative Charles Stenholm—drafted and sent a letter to Speaker Wright stressing the importance of passing all thirteen separate appropriations before the fiscal year began on October 1. Miller described the purpose of the letter: "We should formally inform the House leadership in the upcoming session that support for a catchall CR [continuing resolution] within our caucus is very unlikely."[55] The forty-nine Democrats who signed the letter warned that they would vote against a year-ending omnibus appropriations bill.

President Reagan expressed similar sentiments in his nationally televised 1988 State of the Union message to Congress. During the speech, Reagan lifted each of the omnibus bills he had signed in December 1987 and remarked, "Congress shouldn't send another one of these. No, and if you do, I will not sign it." Clearly, according to Majority Leader Foley, the mood was set for Congress to implement a timely appropriations process: "There is not a strong pull in an election year to take on a bitter debate over budget issues. The pull will be toward cooperation, conciliation, and speed."[56]

Speaker Wright's activist leadership style complemented the context and the expectations identified by the president and the House Democrats. Wright was instrumental in moving the appropriations process along so that Congress could achieve the goal of passing all thirteen appropriations bills on time. In February 1988, Wright met with all the subcommittee chairmen of the Appropriations Committee to stress the urgency of moving quickly on their appropriations bills. One Appropriations Committee staff person described Wright's approach: "[In] February, Speaker Wright met with our subcommittee chairmen and started beating that cadence. You know, beating those drums. [Telling the chairmen], 'Let's get those hearings done, mark up your bills. On May 15 you guys can go ahead even without the budget resolution and start passing those bills, we'll make adjustments later if we have to.' "[57]

Since the summit agreement established the framework for the fiscal 1989 budget, the first budget resolution was not a very important document in terms of either setting priorities or positioning the House Democratic party. The Budget Committee concentrated mainly on dividing up the additional $148.1 billion for discretionary spending that was granted under the terms of the summit. But even the important decisions on new expenditures fell under the jurisdiction of the Appropriations Committee. Although Budget Committee members quarrelled over what programs deserved the larger slices of the budget pie, the debate was settled quickly in the House. The House passed the Budget Committee's version of the first budget resolution on March 26 with bipartisan support.

The conference proceedings for the first budget resolution lasted six weeks, however, as conferees haggled over what little discretionary spending was left under the summit agreement. Because of the conference deadlock, Speaker Wright ordered the Appropriations Committee to mark the individual appropriations bills according to the House-passed first budget resolution and to prepare them for floor consideration. Speaker O'Neill had made the same decision several times in the 1980s.

Wright was simply continuing in the same vein. With the broad budget totals and spending limitations already settled, furthermore, there was no need to wait for conference approval of the first budget resolution.

Passing all the separate appropriations bills on time required more than getting an early jump on the process. Wright skillfully exercised the powers of the Speaker's office, in order to meet the expectations of the president and the House members. He used the Rules Committee even more aggressively than O'Neill had done, to schedule spending bills so that the appropriations process moved swiftly. Rules Committee chairman Claude Pepper pointed out, "Wright has acted more upon the assumption that the Rules Committee is a branch of the leadership than Speaker O'Neill."[58]

Wright's hands-on approach to the Rules Committee was an important element in the successful completion of the separate appropriations bills in 1988. Since appropriations bills are privileged under the rules of the House, the Appropriations Committee can request a rule from the Rules Committee to schedule the bills for floor consideration at any time. Nevertheless, the process of issuing the rule for debate can be obstructed by points of order made against the contents of an appropriations bill. The Rules Committee can waive points of order against appropriations bills and usually does so at the request of the majority party leadership. In 1988, as an appropriations staff person put it:

We virtually had carte blanche from Speaker Wright on appropriations bills. . . . When we reported a bill out of committee, we would go to the leadership and say, "We reported it today and we're going to the Rules Committee and want [it] to be on the floor the following Tuesday." And the answer would be, "No problem." I can't think of one occasion when we wanted to schedule one of those thirteen appropriations bills and were told "no."

In some cases, this staff person also noted, Speaker Wright pushed the Rules Committee to extraordinary lengths in order to implement the appropriations process:

Interestingly too, in order to meet this schedule, sometimes we had to have the Rules Committee meet on a Friday. And a Friday session of the Rules Committee is generally unheard of. But the leadership was so committed to getting our bills on the floor, they'd tell the Rules Committee, "You are an arm of the leadership, we want to hold a meeting on Friday or Monday in order to grant a rule so that we can have an appropriations bill on the floor on Tuesday."

Wright did more than respond to the scheduling requests of the Appropriations Committee. As one of Wright's staff persons observed, the Speaker pushed the committee: "It wasn't easy getting all the appropriations bills done on time. From my perspective, there was only one reason that happened and that was Jim Wright. He wouldn't let it alone. He wouldn't let Jamie Whitten alone, or anyone alone. He was going to do it, and he was going to do it on time, even if there was pain, and there was a lot of pain."[59]

As the October 1 deadline for passing the appropriations bills approached, Speaker Wright became heavily involved in mediating conflicts over spending levels for specific programs, in order to move along the appropriations bills. On September 22, Wright met with seven subcommittee chairmen of the Appropriations Committee who were deadlocked with their Senate counterparts over conference agreements. Julian Dixon (D-Calif.), chairman of the Appropriations Subcommittee on the District of Columbia, explained the purpose of the meeting: "The Speaker made it clear he wanted all the bills out of conference and on the floor by next week." Appropriations Committee chairman Jamie Whitten observed, "[Wright] is anxious to get them out. We're all anxious to get them out."[60]

Wright arbitrated a dispute between House and Senate conferees on the transportation appropriations bill. President Reagan promised to veto the bill if it included certain airline labor provisions adopted by the Senate. Wright averted a likely presidential veto by informing House conferees to drop the provision and by persuading Senate Majority Leader Byrd to schedule the airline labor provisions separately from the appropriations bill.

The most salient problem in the appropriations process involved a conflict between President Reagan and the Armed Services Committee. On August 3, Reagan vetoed an authorization bill that contained arms control policies limiting the number of submarines and a provision prohibiting the Pentagon from shifting funds for the Strategic Defense Initiative (SDI) program to other defense programs. Following the veto, Defense secretary Frank Carlucci and Armed Services Committee chairmen Sam Nunn (D-Ga.) of the Senate and Les Aspin (D-Wis.) of the House met to negotiate a compromise on the authorization bill. In order to keep the appropriations process moving, Wright held a meeting of members from the Defense Subcommittee of the Appropriations Committee and from the Armed Services Committee, to arrange a deal whereby the defense appropriations bill would go to the floor while the differences over the defense authorization bill were being worked out. As it turned out, Carlucci, Nunn, and Aspin reached a satisfactory agreement on the authorization bill, and the defense appropriations bill passed in the closing hours of the last legislative day before the fiscal year began. In order to meet the October 1 deadline, the House agreed to two final Senate-passed amendments to a $282 billion defense appropriations bill.

Summary

Speaker Wright's style as opposition party leader and process manager contrasts sharply with that of O'Neill. Wright's approach to Budget Committee assignments was based more on fulfilling his personally defined agenda than on balancing the ideological composition of the Budget Committee with that of the party membership. Wright was more active in setting specific priorities of the Budget Committee's first budget resolution. He used the Rules Committee more aggressively than O'Neill in scheduling appropriations bills. These distinctions highlight the importance of individual leadership qualities. An individual leader's policy expertise and conception of leadership make a big difference in how the Speaker's role is performed.

Wright's activist style was particularly well suited for setting the party's priorities in the early months of 1987 and for facilitating the appropriations process in 1988. In the former case, he took advantage of favorable conditions to define a specific set of priorities. In the later case, the budget summit agreement set the context for Congress to pass thirteen separate appropriations bills, and Wright's persistent leadership style was critical in meeting that objective.

But activist leadership—characterized by setting forth a clear agenda and working tenaciously to achieve the fundamental components of that agenda—is not always successful. Activist leaders are impatient, and more likely to act aggressively when conditions call for cautious deliberation. The breakdown of Democratic party unity on the omnibus reconciliation and appropriations bills in the final days of 1987 clearly demonstrates the limitations of activist leadership in the House. Wright failed to listen carefully enough to Democratic opinions on the Downey welfare provision, and he offended many Democrats when he dropped the provision from the 1987 omnibus reconciliation bill. Although Wright's proposal to increase taxes was partially approved under emergency conditions, the politics of deficit reduction revealed the limitations of the Speaker's capacity to sustain support for his priorities through the entire budget cycle.

As conditions changed, Wright's budgetary preferences were subordinated to the practical concerns of managing the budget process. In response to the 209–208 vote on the fiscal 1988 appropriations bill in which a majority of House Republicans voted "yea" and a majority of House Democrats voted "nay," Wright admitted, "In the final analysis, government becomes the art of the possible."[61] Wright was reflecting on the realities of the Speaker's role in the budget process.

While members tolerate activist leadership at times, they expect the Speaker to subordinate his preferences when institutional and party-related problems demand his attention. These include passing a budget that represents the party's interests and enforcing budgetary decisions so that Congress can maintain a budget process. When the Speaker's personal preferences conflict with his role in the budget process, those preferences must necessarily give way to broader institutional or party goals.

7

Leadership in the Post-Reform House:

Patterns and Paradoxes

W_{hen} *Speaker Albert* addressed the House in May 1975, pleading with members to support the first budget resolution sponsored by the new Budget Committee, he could scarcely have imagined the actions that would be taken by Speaker Wright twelve years later. Albert concentrated on nurturing the budget process, a role that served modest purposes—"to pass a budget resolution and do it on time." Despite his party's opposition to a Republican president, the Speaker dared not "comment on the amendments pending or prospective," or "make a brief for any particular provision or position," let alone attempt to initiate budget priorities. Could we imagine Albert delaying final decision on a roll call vote for a major bill, after time had already expired on the House clock, until a member returned to the floor to change his vote and reverse the outcome? One could reasonably surmise that neither Albert's conception of leadership nor the prevailing conditions encouraged the activist policy leadership Wright displayed in the Hundredth Congress. Yet Wright's preferences were not always shared by House Democrats. As his dramatic first year in office came to a close, the majority party splintered, and Republican votes were needed to approve the 1987 omnibus reconciliation and appropriations bills.

How could the development of the speakership from Albert to Wright include a significant expansion of influence in policy-making on the one hand and clear limitations to leadership on the other? The answer involves a mixture of individual and contextual factors, both short-term and long-term. Short-term conditions shape the problems and opportunities of the day, whereas enduring conditions place limitations on leaders. Within these constraints, leadership style may vary with respect to individual qualities; thus, Wright's style sharply distinguished him from O'Neill. Yet, both Speakers confronted similar dilemmas in attempting to lead the majority party and the House. They shared the realization that leadership is a complex configuration of individual and contextual elements.

The Speaker's role in the budget process exhibits several contrary tendencies: continuity and change, conflict and compatibility, and growing influence over policy decisions accompanied by limitations to policy leadership. Prevailing problems require the Speaker to continue performing traditional leadership tasks, while changing conditions demand new functions. Since roles develop quite apart from individual factors, they may conflict or be compatible with individual preferences and qualities. Leaders must respond to conditions and adapt their individual qualities and preferences to new roles. Finally, short-term opportunities to affect budget decisions emerge in the foreground of enduring constraints to policy leadership.

In order to evaluate these paradoxes, I should first review the Speaker's roles and identify the conditions under which they developed. Then I will consider the implications of individual factors for understanding leadership and assess the multiple relationships between leaders and members.

Change and Continuity in the Speaker's Role

One aim of this book is to describe how the Speaker's role in the budget process changed in response to problems and opportunities of the post-reform period. A second objective is to explain more precisely why those changes occurred. The analysis leads us to address several questions. First, how do the Speaker's post-reform roles in the budget process compare with his pre-reform roles as the chief leader of the majority party and institutional leader of the House? Second, how did the Speaker's particular roles in the budget process evolve during the post-reform era itself? Finally, what specific conditions produced changes in the Speaker's role?

Both continuity and change are present in the Speaker's roles from the pre-reform to the post-reform period, and within the post-reform period itself. While the Speaker retains traditional coalition-building, party-maintenance, and presiding-officer functions throughout the post-reform era, with the passage of the Budget Act he began to perform new tasks particular to problems in the budget process. His role expanded further during the 1980s to include policy-oriented tasks both inside and outside the House, tasks that were uncommon to pre-reform Speakers. (By "pre-reform Speakers" here I mean as far back as the demise of Speaker Cannon in 1910.) Thus, a review of the evolution of the Speaker's roles in the budget process indicates that the functions that define the Speaker's roles might be classified in three categories: (1) simple applications of traditional tasks to the area of budget policy; (2) new tasks that deal particularly with budgeting, but that are similar to traditional party and institutional leader roles; and (3) altogether new tasks that were uncharacteristic of the Speaker's pre-reform roles.

During the 1970s, the Speaker's roles in the budget process (those of nurturer and process manager) included traditional tasks associated with his roles as institutional and majority party leader. Thus, while the Budget Act demanded new tasks particular to budgeting, in principle they were almost natural applications of the Speaker's roles as presiding officer and party leader. In the nurturer role, the Speaker carried out basic supportive tasks for the new budget process: educating key players about new procedures, organizing committees, and reducing fears that the new process posed a threat to the committees' powers.

As process manager, the Speaker was involved in coalition building and mediating committee conflicts, two essential tasks for maintaining the budget process. These functions were not extraordinary for the Speaker; they generally marked an application of traditional tasks to a new policy issue. Yet, the demands of managing the process under fiscal constraints did spawn a different relationship between the Speaker and the Rules Committee. As early as 1980, the Rules Committee began to limit the number of floor amendments to the Budget Committee's first budget resolution.[1] The Speaker also intervened directly with Rules on the reconciliation bill later that year. These were examples of how the Speaker could use new powers over rules to execute the role of process manager.

The most prominent changes in the Speaker's role came in the 1980s, however. The Speaker became involved in policy-making at the committee stage and in negotiating budget agreements with the president and the Senate leaders. The Speaker's participation in and influence over policy outcomes varied with short-term conditions and individual factors. Yet, the Speaker's input into the substance of budget policy marked a clear change from his pre-reform roles. At least since the downfall of Speaker Cannon in 1910, Speakers typically left policy decisions to the discretion of committees.

The Speaker's involvement in policy-making emanates partly from the nature of budget policy itself. Since the Budget Committee's budget resolution attempts to articulate the priorities of the majority party, it offers an opportunity for party leaders to become more involved in policy-making. The Speaker is probably less likely to become involved in other policy areas. Still, the Speaker did not actively engage in policy-oriented tasks until the 1980s, years after the Budget Act was enacted. This development suggests that, although the new process offered the potential for policy leadership, the Speaker's policy-making role emerged with changes in political and policy conditions, not solely by way of institutional reform.

Recall the conditions that produce changes in the Speaker's role in the budget process. Institutional conditions stemmed mostly from reforms that strengthened the Speaker's organizational powers, the Budget Act itself, and later the deficit-reduction provisions of the GRH law. Important political conditions include party unity, electoral outcomes, and partisan control of the White House and Congress. The key policy factors consist of economic trends, budget priorities, and the deficit. Some of these factors have direct, independent effects on the Speaker's roles; others are intertwined.

It seems that institutional reforms—changes in the Speaker's powers and the Budget Act—had the least direct effect on the development of the Speaker's roles in the budget process. Reforms that broadened the Speaker's powers—Rules Committee appointments and the creation of the Steering and Policy Committee—affected his roles in the budget process. But these resources have more to do with how the Speaker performs his roles than with how those roles develop, and I shall address their effects in the following section on leadership style. Meanwhile, the Budget Act prescribed no specific role for the Speaker. With the exception of the nurturer role, which stemmed partly from the ambiguity of the Budget Act, the Speaker's roles were responses to problems and opportunities related to changes in political and policy-related conditions.

This is not to say that budget reforms were unimportant, but their effects on the Speaker's role in the budget process were indirect. Working interactively with political and policy-related factors, the provisions of the Budget Act and the GRH law did influence the Speaker's roles in important ways. For example, large deficits inspired the use of reconciliation, which in turn led to a variety of conflicts between committees and the membership. These conflicts created a greater demand for the Speaker's intervention in mediating committee disputes. The deficit also encouraged the deficit-reduction schedule and sequestration mechanism of the GRH law. The deficit ceiling for fiscal 1988 formed the backdrop for Speaker Wright's tax initiative in 1987.

The deficit also had direct effects on the development of the Speaker's role. The deficit contributed to the growing centralization of decision making in the House and expanded the Speaker's role to include policy-oriented tasks during the 1980s. Deficits create conflicts over priorities, limit opportunities for new spending initiatives, and in some cases lead to negotiations among party leaders. Thus, deficits contribute to opportunities for policy leadership but also create problems for managing the budget process.

Partisan control of Congress and the presidency also affects the Speaker's capacity to engage in policy leadership. When the president is of the opposite party, the Speaker is recognized as the most prominent leader of his party. He is more likely to participate in developing budget priorities and negotiating with other party leaders on behalf of his party. But divided government is only one contributing factor to policy leadership. For, even though Speaker Albert was leader of the party opposite President Ford, he played no role in formulating budget policy. Party unity and the margin of House seats held by the majority party also affect the Speaker's policy-making capacity.[2] The Speaker is poorly situated to initiate priorities if his party is divided or holds only a slim margin of seats over the minority party, or in both these cases. These problems require the Speaker to focus mainly on coalition-building, rather than on policy-oriented tasks. On the other hand, when the party is more unified, the Speaker is apt to turn more attention to policy tasks.

Although short-term conditions may create opportunities for the Speaker to participate in policy-making, there are enduring constraints on policy leadership. The Speaker has become a more prominent actor in policy-making, but institutional fragmentation, the norm of representation, and presidential powers continue to limit the most activist opposition party leader from exercising policy leadership.

Hence, if the most significant changes in the Speaker's role have been a more influential and active involvement in policy-making and in mediating conflicts, then the deficit, electoral changes, and party unity are the most important factors in role development. Large deficits created more problems with internal management, while strong party unity and divided government stimulated more opportunities for policy leadership. These tasks were not anticipated by institutional reforms, though they may have been helped by them. Finally, despite the centralizing features of House politics in the 1980s, enduring characteristics of the political system limit the Speaker's capacity to exercise policy leadership.

The growing number and variety of the Speaker's functions beg the question of which roles are most important. Is the Speaker of the post-reform House concerned more with institutional tasks or with party priorities? The answer seems to rest, again, on the problems and opportunities underlying policy decisions. During the 1970s, though the Speaker surely was interested in the party's budgetary preferences, he was expected to deal primarily with institutional problems and procedural concerns. The Speaker's emphasis was on managerial tasks—keeping the process running and managing conflict.

Yet, once concerns for maintaining the process gave way to policy objectives, and once budgeting became an ad hoc and partisan affair, the Speaker often subordinated procedural guidelines to policy and party objectives. Thus, the Speaker's role as opposition party leader took precedence over the role of process manager. Time and again, O'Neill ignored the formal budget timetable if necessary in order to halt Reagan's efforts to cut domestic spending. The Speaker's emphasis on policy and partisan goals was furthered after 1982 when the problem of passing budget resolutions was mitigated by higher levels of party cohesion among House Democrats. The Speaker continued to play an important part in maintaining party unity, but with the reduced uncertainty of passing budget resolutions, his emphasis shifted to policy-oriented functions.

In short, the House will always rely on the Speaker for certain tasks related to the Speaker's formally recognized positions as presiding officer and leader of the majority party. Yet, amid the continuity of these roles, the problems and opportunities of the post-reform period encouraged new functions that demanded the Speaker's attention. The evidence supports the proposition set forth in my introductory chapter, that leadership roles, defined in terms of functions, are more fluid than might be thought.

Leadership Style: Context and Individual Factors

Related to but different from the question of how leader roles develop is how they are performed. This study supports the proposition that conditions play a significant part in shaping the constraints on leadership style. It also confirms the view that leaders must attend to the expectations of party members. Yet, my study indicates that these generalizations must be qualified to accommodate a leader's individual qualities and preferences and the complex relationships between the Speaker and the members. My findings indicate that both contextual factors and individual qualities contribute to an explanation of leadership style. Furthermore, though leaders attend to the goals of party members, leader preferences are important in defining leader-follower relationships. Leadership cannot always be defined in terms of member expectations, it often involves interaction between the preferences of leaders and followers. Let us consider each of these points in more detail.

The comparison between O'Neill and Wright offers an instructive example of how individual factors affect leadership style. Both leaders performed the opposition party leader role under roughly similar conditions. Three critical contextual factors that permitted policy leadership—divided government, high party unity, and deficit constraints—were in place by 1983. Short-term factors varied slightly, but not enough to alter the comparison between the two leaders' styles following a midterm election. O'Neill's position in 1983 was bolstered by a larger gain of House seats than Wright had in 1987. President Reagan was in a weak public position in both years, though for different reasons. O'Neill's case for increasing expenditures for social programs was enhanced by what appeared to be a total failure of Reagan's economic policy during the first quarter of 1983. Wright's position was strengthened by the Iran-Contra scandal. It is impossible to tell whether a president's relations with Congress are weakened more by recession and a failed economic policy than by an event like Irangate. The only other relevant short-term factor was party control in the Senate, regained by the Democrats in 1986, a change that may or may not have helped Wright.[3]

Since conditions were similar, a contextual view of leadership would predict that Wright and O'Neill would pursue similar styles. This was the view professed by political scientist Steven Smith, who anticipated that, "Beyond obvious cosmetic differences, I do not expect Jim Wright's basic leadership style to differ greatly from Tip O'Neill's." Perhaps Smith was correct in saying that the styles do not differ greatly. But then again, how much is "greatly"? The statement implies that it is not enough to matter.[4]

This study shows that the two leaders' styles differed significantly (if not greatly), and that the differences are due primarily to each leader's policy expertise and conception of leadership. Consider the evidence. O'Neill issued a questionnaire to members to find out their views before endorsing budget priorities; Wright moved out ahead of the Democratic caucus to initiate an agenda for the Hundredth Congress. O'Neill treated the whip meeting as a way to learn about party members' views on the budget; Wright used it as a forum for pushing his agenda. O'Neill relied on staff to oversee policy developments on the Budget Committee; Wright personally intervened on committee business. These are just a few ways in which Wright's use of the Speaker's powers differed from O'Neill's. The differences may not be great, but they reflect distinct styles that cannot be explained by contextual analysis alone.

The contrast between O'Neill and Wright offers several important conclusions about the effects of individual factors on leadership. First, leaders have more autonomy in defining leadership style than the contextualist view of leadership permits. To be sure, conditions place limitations on leadership and encourage certain styles, but they can not dictate how leaders must act. Leaders decide, within a given set of constraints, how to perform their roles. Thus Wright could pursue an activist style while O'Neill did not, though both Speakers operated under similar conditions.

Second, not all congressional leaders pursue a middleman approach—mediating the various preferences within the party. We assume that leaders must act as middlemen because of the structure of the congressional party. But the comparison between O'Neill and Wright indicates that leaders are not destined to pursue that approach. Speaker O'Neill conformed to a middleman style; Wright did not. Rather than accommodate party members and let an agenda develop, Wright sought to define the party's interests.

Third, individual factors help to explain how leaders are likely to adapt to different conditions and the expectations their roles demand. A Speaker with budget policy expertise will adapt more easily to a condition that encourages a policy-oriented leadership—he is likely to be more assertive in initiating specific policy proposals. A cautious Speaker is more apt to be criticized by members of his party when he fails to respond to a situation suited for policy leadership. On the other hand, an activist Speaker may act hastily in a situation that calls for a deliberate approach. The course of action a leader takes depends on how the individual adapts to the situation at hand, and the expectations expressed by members.

Relationships between Leaders and Followers

A final point raised by this study is that the relationships between leaders and followers are not dictated by member preferences alone. Undoubtedly, leaders must be responsive to the expectations of House members. A Speaker who ignores the clear and consistent policy preferences or political goals of the House membership is bound to meet resistance. But consider the numerous cases in which member preferences are unclear or inconsistent, or in which the leader deliberately attempts to advance his own preferences. In these situations, the relationships between the Speaker and the majority are not easily defined by member expectations. The relationships are interactive with respect to the preferences of leaders and followers and can take a variety of forms.

Interactive relationships are important, not only because they reflect a complex view of leadership but because they affect the performance of leadership roles. Let us consider four scenarios introduced in Chapter 1 with reference to examples cited throughout the book. These four scenarios are: (1) a leader expresses disagreement with members' preferences but sets personal preferences aside to serve a broader institutional or party role. (2) Member preferences are unclear or divided, in which case the leader lacks sufficient information to respond to member expectations. (3) The leader defines preferences ahead of members and then attempts to build support for them. (4) The leader deliberately ignores the preferences of members and suffers defeat, an action that might eventually culminate in reforms to limit the leader's powers.

The first scenario is closest to a relationship in which the leader responds directly to the preferences of the followers. But it differs somewhat because here we find the leader at least expressing disagreement, if not resistance, before performing the role expected of him. We might call this a grin-and-bear-it situation, one that creates a conflict between a leader's preferences and the roles he is expected to perform. This case came up in 1980, as Speaker O'Neill reluctantly went about the job of managing the budget process despite the House Democrats' vote to cut spending for programs he personally supported. The extent to which this situation affects budget decisions will vary with the leader and the strength of the majority. In this case, O'Neill basically removed himself from most of the early decisions in the process—an act that may or may not have affected the progress of the budget resolution. (From the beginning, O'Neill denounced the summit agreement and later voiced disapproval of the first conference report on the first budget resolution. But the extent to which his ambivalence disrupted the process is almost impossible to determine.) He realized his responsibility to the House, however, and after the second conference report was settled, he played an important active role in building support for the budget resolution.

The second scenario—member preferences are unclear or divided—is also difficult to define in terms of what the members expect of the leader. Here we find that the leader's preferences are important to the party's strategy, but they must compete with those of a variety of other actors. Sharp intraparty divisions may significantly weaken the Speaker's influence and hinder the majority from acting decisively. This scenario is quite common to the Speaker of a divided majority party, but the most extreme effects were registered in 1981. House Democrats were divided and held only a small margin of seats over Republicans. Initially, Speaker O'Neill yielded to the moderate-conservative sentiment of the party, much as he had in 1980. But Reagan's electoral momentum, popularity, and skillful White House staff upset Democratic plans for a conservative budget alternative and forged a winning coalition of Boll Weevil Democrats and Republicans. Once the reconciliation process began, Speaker O'Neill's role as party leader conflicted with his role as process manager. O'Neill was expected to manage the reconciliation process, which included spending cuts that neither he nor his party's majority supported. The effects were manifest: the leadership's strategy for dealing with reconciliation was riddled with confusion; conflict developed between committee chairmen and the House membership; and the House was forced to abdicate its lawmaking function.

The third possible scenario emerges when a leader initiates his own preferences ahead of the members and lobbies them for support. Speaker O'Neill never pursued this type of relationship with House Democrats. His participatory, middle-man style encouraged members to express their preferences, and for the leader to consider them before deciding how to act. Speaker Wright, on the other hand, forged a leader-initiated relationship with House Democrats during the first few months of his speakership. Wright initiated a bold set of budget priorities prior to consulting members and then personally appealed for support from party whips, committee chairmen, and members of the Budget Committee. Wright's style indicates that, given the right conditions and the right leader, the relationship between the Speaker and party members can be premised on the leader's preferences, rather than on those of party members.

The final scenario is when a leader ignores members' preferences and loses their support in pursuit of his own priorities. If this relationship persists, members might pass reforms to curtail the leader's powers.[5] Speaker Wright's actions on the 1987 reconciliation bill provide an example of a leader ignoring, or at least miscalculating, the preferences of fellow Democrats. Some observers have argued that Wright's behavior reflected a broader problem with his leadership style, which culminated in ethics violations and his eventual resignation from the House. According to this view, Wright violated the limits to House leadership.[6] Yet, his actions on the reconciliation bill did not have drastic consequences. Wright was reminded of the limits to strong party leadership in the House, but members did not enact reforms to curb the Speaker's powers as a result of the Speaker's actions.[7]

These four scenarios and the interactive effects of conditions and individual factors reveal important insights into congressional leadership. A complex institution, affected by internal and external conditions and involving a variety of actors with multiple goals, is unlikely to furnish static roles for leaders and simple relationships between leaders and members. Although all Speakers are expected to perform certain functions in the legislature, we should not expect the functions performed by the Speaker in the roles of institutional and party leader to remain stagnant. And we should not expect different Speakers to respond similarly under similar conditions. Bounded by the limitations posed by the enduring characteristics of the political system, the Speaker's roles and style are likely to vary with individual factors and conditions that shape the problems and opportunities of House politics.

Notes
Index

Notes

1. Problems and Opportunities: The Origins of Leadership

1. The critical nature of budget policy is defined nicely by Joseph White and Aaron Wildavsky, *The Deficit and the Public Interest* (Berkeley: University of California Press, 1989), preface. For a measure of the increasing congressional workload devoted to budgetary bills, see Allen Schick's collection of time-series data on budget-related roll call votes from 1955 to 1988, in Norman J. Ornstein, Thomas E. Mann, and Michael J. Malbin, *Vital Statistics on Congress, 1989–90* (Washington: Congressional Quarterly Press, 1990), p. 183. For a discussion of the centralization of leadership, see Roger H. Davidson, "The New Centralization on Capitol Hill," *The Review of Politics*, vol. 49 (1988), pp. 345–64; and Lawrence C. Dodd and Bruce I. Oppenheimer, "Consolidating Power in the House: The Rise of a New Oligarchy," in Lawrence C. Dodd and Bruce I. Oppenheimer, eds., *Congress Reconsidered*, 4th ed. (Washington: Congressional Quarterly Press, 1989).

2. For these and other problems with the budget process, see Allen Schick, ed., *Crisis in the Budget Process* (Washington: American Enterprise Institute, 1986); and Allen Schick, *The Capacity to Budget* (Washington: The Urban Institute Press, 1990), chap. 1. For a contrary view, see John B. Gilmour, *Reconcilable Differences?* (Berkeley: University of California Press, 1990).

3. Barbara Sinclair, *Majority Leadership in the U.S. House* (Baltimore: Johns Hopkins University Press, 1983).

4. A sample of this literature would include, most recently, John M. Barry, *The Ambition and the Power: The Fall of Jim Wright* (New York: Viking Press, 1989); Tip O'Neill, *Man of the House* (New York: Random House, 1987); Christopher Matthews, *Hardball* (New York: Summit Books, 1988); and Hedrick Smith, *The Power Game* (New

York: Random House, 1988). Some of these studies account for the effects of broader contextual factors more than others.

5. The most pronounced accounts of this view would include Joseph Cooper and David W. Brady, "Institutional Context and Leadership Style: The House from Cannon to Rayburn," *American Political Science Review*, vol. 75 (1981), pp. 411–25; Charles O. Jones, "House Leadership in an Age of Reform," in Frank H. Mackaman, ed., *Understanding Congressional Leadership* (Washington: Congressional Quarterly Press, 1981); and Sinclair, *Majority Leadership*.

6. For a discussion of the problems associated with individual variables and behavioral political science, and an attempt to resolve them, see Lewis J. Edinger, "Political Science and Political Biography: Reflections on the Study of Leadership," *Journal of Politics*, vol. 26 (1964), pp. 423–39.

7. For studies of party leadership, see Randall Ripley, *Majority Party Leadership in Congress* (Boston: Little, Brown and Company, 1969), and *Party Leaders in the House of Representatives* (Boston: Little, Brown and Company, 1967); Robert L. Peabody, *Leadership in Congress: Stability, Succession and Change* (Boston: Little, Brown and Company, 1976); Ronald M. Peters, Jr., *The American Speakership* (Baltimore: Johns Hopkins University Press, 1990); and David W. Rohde, *Parties and Leaders in the Postreform House* (Chicago: University of Chicago Press, 1991). A number of studies of committee leadership also take this view, including John F. Manley, "Wilbur Mills: A Study of Congressional Leadership," *American Political Science Review*, vol. 63 (1969), pp. 442–64; John E. Owens, "Extreme Advocacy Leadership in the Pre-Reform House: Wright Patman and the House Banking and Currency Committee," *British Journal of Political Science*, vol. 15 (1985), pp. 187–205; and Randall Strahan, *New Ways and Means* (Chapel Hill: University of North Carolina Press, 1990), chap. 5.

8. Peters, *The American Speakership*, p. 273.

9. Or, "Rightly or wrongly, leaders must attend to their majorities," as Charles O. Jones puts it ("Joseph G. Cannon and Howard W. Smith: An Essay on the Limits of Leadership in the House of Representatives," *Journal of Politics*, vol. 30 [1968], p. 617). See also David W. Rohde and Kenneth A. Shepsle, "Leaders and Followers in the House of Representatives: Reflections on Woodrow Wilson's *Congressional Government*," *Congress and the Presidency*, vol. 14 (1987), pp. 111–33; and Barbara Sinclair, "Strong Party Leadership in a Weak Party Era—The Evolution of Party Leadership in the Modern

House," paper presented at the conference "Back to the Future: The United States Congress in the Twenty-first Century" held in Norman, Oklahoma, 1990. The most comprehensive study of leader-follower relationships per se is by James MacGregor Burns, *Leadership* (New York: Harper and Row, 1978).

10. This case might vary only slightly from the straightforward view that a leader must respond to followers, depending on the extent of discretion assumed by the leader in the leader-follower relationship. At least in the most extreme case (the "principal-agent" model), a leader is absolutely bound to the expectations of followers. In the principal-agent case, the leader's preferences would be unimportant to the extent that the leader presumably would never voice any preferences. Thus, there would be no disagreement to begin with between the leader and the followers.

11. This is essentially the point made by Jones in "Joseph G. Cannon and Howard W. Smith."

12. See Lance T. LeLoup, *The Fiscal Congress* (Westport, Connecticut: Greenwood Press, 1980), pp. 7–8; Joel Havemann, *Congress and the Budget* (Bloomington: Indiana University Press, 1978), pp. 22–24; and Dennis S. Ippolito, *Congressional Spending* (Ithaca, New York: Cornell University Press, 1981), p. 49.

13. These functions include national defense, international affairs, science and space, energy, natural resources, agriculture, commerce and housing, transportation, community development, education and social services, health, Medicare, income security, social security, veterans' benefits, justice, general government, and general fiscal assistance.

14. For a discussion of the reconciliation process, see Allen Schick, *Reconciliation and the Congressional Budget Process* (Washington: American Enterprise Institute, 1981).

15. For more on this point, see Naomi Caiden, "The Politics of Subtraction," in Allen Schick, ed., *Making Economic Policy in Congress* (Washington: American Enterprise Institute, 1983), p. 104; Roger H. Davidson, "The Congressional Budget: How Much Change? How Much Reform?" in W. Thomas Wander, F. Ted Hebert, and Gary W. Copeland, eds., *Congressional Budgeting: Politics, Process and Power* (Baltimore: Johns Hopkins University Press, 1984), p. 163. For a review of some of these innovations, see Walter J. Oleszek, *Congressional Procedures and the Policy Process*, 2d ed. (Washington: Congressional Quarterly Press, 1984), pp. 63–66; Allen Schick, "The Evolution of

Congressional Budgeting," in Schick, *Crisis in the Budget Process;* and Schick, *The Capacity to Budget,* chap. 6.

16. For studies documenting the historical roles of the Speaker of the House, see especially Mary Parker Follett, *The Speaker of the House of Representatives* (New York: Longmans, Green and Company, 1896); George B. Galloway, *History of the House of Representatives* (New York: Thomas Y. Crowell Company, 1961), pp. 101–9; and Peters, *The American Speakership.*

17. For a discussion of party functions, see Ripley, *Party Leaders in the House,* chap. 3, and *Majority Party Leadership in Congress,* pp. 5–7. For the Speaker as the opposition party leader, see Ripley, *Party Leaders in the House,* p. 18.

18. For a summary of the Speaker's powers during this period, see Follett, *The Speaker of the House,* pp. 298–301; and Peters, *The American Speakership,* pp. 62–91. For a description of the events leading to Cannon's downfall, see William Rea Gwinn, *Uncle Joe: Archfoe of Insurgency* (New York: Bookman Associates, 1957), chap. 6; and George R. Brown, *The Leadership of Congress* (Indianapolis: Bobbs-Merrill, 1922), pp. 152–54. Brown argues that Cannon's downfall was only part of a wider reform movement against centralized power, one that eventually undermined the party nominating system (Brown, *The Leadership of Congress,* pp. 22, 115, 119, and 138). But see Jones, who argues that Cannon's decline was a direct consequence of excessive abuse of the Speaker's powers, indicating the limits to centralized leadership in a representative body (Jones, "Joseph G. Cannon and Howard W. Smith," pp. 619–34).

19. The primary leader of the Democratic caucus was Oscar Underwood (D-Ala.), the majority floor leader and chairman of both the Ways and Means Committee and the Committee on Committees. See Brown, *The Leadership of Congress,* pp. 176–78, 185; Richard Bolling, *Power in the House* (New York: E. P. Dutton and Company, 1968), p. 94; and Ripley, *Majority Party Leadership in Congress,* pp. 52, 62.

20. Chang-wei Ch'iu, *The Speaker of the House of Representatives* (New York: Columbia University Press, 1928), pp. 315–16.

21. For a summary statement of this point, see Barbara Sinclair, "Congressional Leadership: A Review Essay and a Research Agenda," in John J. Kornacki, ed., *Leading Congress: New Styles, New Strategies* (Washington: Congressional Quarterly Inc., 1990), p. 113. For assessments of the middleman style of leadership see, for example, David Truman, *The Congressional Party: A Case Study* (New York: John Wiley

& Sons, 1959), p. 205; Samuel C. Patterson, "Legislative Leadership and Political Ideology," *Public Opinion Quarterly*, vol. 27 (1963), pp. 399–410; Jones, "Joseph G. Cannon and Howard W. Smith"; and Aage R. Clausen and Clyde Wilcox, "Policy Partisanship in Legislative Recruitment and Behavior," *Legislative Studies Quarterly*, vol. 12 (1987), pp. 243–63.

22. Unlike policy expertise and conception of leadership, policy preferences do not affect leadership style per se. But, as we shall see, preferences are important in defining role conflicts, particularly when a Speaker is expected to perform a role that is incompatible with his preferences.

23. For treatment of role conflicts facing members of Congress, see Roger H. Davidson, *The Role of the Congressman* (New York: Pegasus, 1969), pp. 188–90. For a discussion of role conflicts involving leaders, see John C. Wahlke, Heinz Eulau, William Buchanan, and LeRoy C. Ferguson, *The Legislative System* (New York: John Wiley & Sons, 1962), pp. 182–83.

24. Allen Schick, *Congress and Money* (Washington: The Urban Institute, 1980), p. 6. For other discussions of the concept of integration, see Richard F. Fenno, "The House Appropriations Committee: The Problem of Integration,"*American Political Science Review*, vol. 56 (1962), p. 310; Davidson, *The Role of the Congressman*, p. 19; Joseph Cooper, "Congress in Organizational Perspective," in Lawrence C. Dodd and Bruce I. Oppenheimer, eds., *Congress Reconsidered* (New York: Praeger Publishers, 1977), pp. 143–45; Jones, "House Leadership in an Age of Reform," p. 122; and James L. Sundquist, *The Decline and Resurgence of Congress* (Washington: The Brookings Institution, 1981), p. 427.

25. Randall Ripley, *Congress: Process and Policy*, 3d ed. (New York: W. W. Norton and Company, 1983), p. 4.

26. For a discussion of how conditions during the Hundredth Congress were conducive to policy-oriented leadership, see Barbara Sinclair, "House Majority Party Leadership in the Late 1980s," in Dodd and Oppenheimer, *Congress Reconsidered*, 4th ed. For the effects of homogenous preferences on party leadership, see Rohde and Shepsle, "Leaders and Followers in the House of Representatives," pp. 111–33. See also David W. Rohde, "Agenda Change and Partisan Resurgence in the House of Representatives," paper presented at the conference "Back to the Future: The United States Congress in the Twenty-first Century," held in Norman, Oklahoma, 1990.

27. See Peters, *The American Speakership*, chaps. 4, 5.

28. I include impressions based on thirty-three open-ended interviews with members and staff, mostly from the House Budget Committee and Steering and Policy Committee. I distinguished those interviewees who chose to remain anonymous by assigning each an interview number. The names of those people who granted me permission to quote them directly are cited in the text.

2. The Reforms of the 1970s

1. See Charles O. Jones, "How Reform Changes Congress," in Susan Welch and John G. Peters, eds., *Legislative Reform and Public Policy* (New York: Praeger Publishers, 1977), p. 20.

2. Jones, "House Leadership in an Age of Reform," p. 119.

3. For discussions of how external events and internal pressures led to reform, see Leroy N. Rieselbach, *Congressional Reform* (Washington: Congressional Quarterly Press, 1986), chap. 1; and Roger H. Davidson and Walter J. Oleszek, "Adaptation and Consolidation: Structural Innovation in the U.S. House of Representatives," *Legislative Studies Quarterly*, vol. 1 (1976), pp. 37–65. On the issue of how internal and external pressures apply to the Budget Act of 1974, see W. Thomas Wander, "The Politics of Congressional Budget Reform," in Wander, Hebert, and Copeland, *Congressional Budgeting*, pp. 3–30.

4. For an analysis of the effects of these changes, see Steven S. Smith, *Call to Order* (Washington: The Brookings Institution, 1989).

5. Jones, "House Leadership in an Age of Reform," p. 119.

6. For a discussion and analysis of multiple referral, see Roger H. Davidson, Walter J. Oleszek, and Thomas Kephart, "One Bill, Many Committees: Multiple Referrals in the U.S. House of Representatives," *Legislative Studies Quarterly*, vol. 12 (1988), pp. 3–27.

7. Steven S. Smith and Bruce A. Ray, "The Impact of Congressional Reform: House Democratic Committee Assignments," *Congress and the Presidency*, vol. 10 (1983), p. 224.

8. Jones, "House Leadership in an Age of Reform," p. 126.

9. Aaron Wildavsky, *The Politics of the Budgetary Process* (Boston: Little, Brown and Company, 1964). For a discussion of presidential budgeting from 1921 to 1975, see Louis Fisher, *Presidential Spending Power* (Princeton: Princeton University Press, 1975), chap. 2.

10. Allen Schick, "The Distributive Congress," in Schick, *Making Economic Policy in Congress.*

11. This description of the appropriations process relies on Richard F. Fenno, *The Power of the Purse* (Boston: Little, Brown and Company, 1966), and "The House Appropriations Committee," pp. 310–24.

12. For a detailed description of the Ways and Means Committee prior to the reforms of the 1970s, see John F. Manley, *The Politics of Finance* (Boston: Little, Brown and Company, 1970).

13. Schick, *Congress and Money*, chap. 2. See also Gilmour, *Reconcilable Differences?* chap. 1.

14. Jones, "How Reform Changes Congress," p. 20; and John W. Ellwood and James A. Thurber, "The Politics of the Congressional Budget Process Re-examined," in Lawrence C. Dodd and Bruce I. Oppenheimer, eds., *Congress Reconsidered*, 2d ed. (Washington: Congressional Quarterly Press, 1981), p. 247.

15. Ellwood and Thurber, "Politics of the Congressional Budget Process," pp. 247–51. See also Wander, "The Politics of Congressional Budget Reform."

16. Schick, *Congress and Money*, p. 52.

17. Two of Albert's closest staff persons commented on Albert's role in balancing the diverse interests on the budget reform bill. But neither could recount the details of many meetings with committee chairmen. For more evidence on this point, as it relates to Albert's role in securing passage of the anti-impoundment section of the Budget Act, see Peters, *The American Speakership*, pp. 180–83.

18. For a description of the different types of backdoor spending, see Schick, *Congress and Money*, pp. 215–17.

19. This discussion of reform relies on Wander, "The Politics of Congressional Budget Reform," pp. 17–19 (17).

20. Ibid., p. 17. For an excellent description of the conflicts between the Ways and Means Committee and the Appropriations Committee prior to the reform, see Schick, *Congress and Money*, chap. 2.

21. Schick, *Congress and Money*, p. 80. For an explanation of why the representatives of the appropriations committees consented to recommendations that favored the tax committees, see ibid., pp. 58–59. See also House Committee on Rules, *Hearing to Improve Congressional Control over Budgetary Outlays and Receipt Totals*, 93d Cong., 1st sess. (Government Printing Office, 1973), p. 48.

22. Wander, "The Politics of Congressional Budget Reform," pp. 19, 20; and Schick, *Congress and Money*, p. 60.

23. House Committee on Rules, *Hearing*, p. 44.

24. Quotations from Schick, *Congress and Money*, pp. 61–62.

25. House Committee on Rules, *Hearing*, pp. 151–54.

26. Ibid., p. 96.

27. These amendments dealt with the time period between committee reports to the Budget Committee and floor consideration of the budget resolution. See Schick, *Congress and Money*, p. 65.

28. The president's revisions include any tax expenditures and five-year projections for future costs of government programs.

29. The translation of the budget functions (that is, budget priorities) to program estimates is called a crosswalk procedure. This procedure is necessary because the budget functions are aggregates of separate legislative programs; the authorization and appropriations committees deal with the separate programs themselves, not the broad functional categories of the budget resolution.

30. Reconciliation procedures could be used for budget authority in the upcoming fiscal year, or for budget authority granted in previous years but taking effect in the upcoming fiscal year or subsequent years, or for both.

31. House Committee on Rules, *Hearing*, pp. 86, 114.

32. Ibid., p. 328.

33. All quotations by Peabody from ibid., p. 338; for Peabody's entire testimony, see pp. 336–42.

34. Ibid., pp. 343–45 (343).

35. Ibid., p. 103.

36. Schick, *Congress and Money*, p. 80; Roger H. Davidson, "The Congressional Budget: How Much Change? How Much Reform?" in Wander, Hebert, and Copeland, *Congressional Budgeting*, p. 163. For a more updated discussion of the changes in the process, see Rudolph G. Penner and Alan J. Abramson, *Broken Purse Strings: Congressional Budgeting 1974 to 1988* (Washington: The Urban Institute Press, 1988), pp. 75–79.

37. Schick, *Congress and Money*, pp. 80–81.

3. From Nurturer to Process Manager: The Speaker's Roles, 1975–80

1. Interview with Bolling, February 8, 1989.

2. Allen Schick notes the importance of party leadership in the reconciliation process in *Reconciliation*, p. 40.

3. For a more detailed discussion of how reconciliation creates conflicts between committees and the House majority, see Gilmour, *Reconcilable Differences?* chaps. 3, 4.

4. O'Neill quoted in Mercer Cross, "Carter and Congress: Fragile Friendship," *Congressional Quarterly Weekly Report*, February 26, 1977, pp. 361-62.

5. See Barbara Sinclair, "Coping with Uncertainty: Building Coalitions in the House and Senate," in Thomas E. Mann and Norman J. Ornstein, eds., *The New Congress* (Washington: American Enterprise Institute, 1981). See also Stanley Bach and Steven S. Smith, *Managing Uncertainty in the House of Representatives* (Washington: The Brookings Institution, 1988).

6. For partisan voting alignments and ideological divisions among Democrats during this period, see Schick, *Congress and Money*, pp. 239-45. A useful indicator of the ideological heterogeneity of House Democrats compared with House Republicans is the standard deviation, or measure of dispersion, around the mean ideological scores for each party. In the Ninety-fourth Congress, the mean conservative coalition opposition score for House Democrats was 56.15 and the standard deviation was 26.85, while the Republican mean was 18.55 and the standard deviation was 16.65. Likewise in the Ninety-fifth Congress, the mean for House Democrats was 55.47 with a standard deviation of 26.45, while for the Republicans the mean was 17.88 with a standard deviation of 16.72. Thus ideology among House Democrats was more dispersed than among House Republicans.

7. See LeLoup, *The Fiscal Congress*, p. 34; and Ippolito, *Congressional Spending*, p. 201.

8. Matt Pinkus, "Albert: From a Cabin in the Cotton Patch to Congress," *Congressional Quarterly Weekly Report*, June 12, 1976, p. 1492. For a discussion of how leaders attempt to manage change, see Roger H. Davidson, "Congressional Leaders as Agents of Change," in Mackaman, *Understanding Congressional Leadership*.

9. Conable quoted in "Congress Will Have to Change Its Ways," *Congressional Quarterly Weekly Report*, January 18, 1975, p. 135.

10. Elder Witt and Tom Arrandale, "Overestimating the Capability of Congress," ibid., June 28, 1975, pp. 1343-46.

11. "Freshmen Meet Albert," ibid., June 21, 1975, p. 1295.

12. Judy Gardner, "Committees Open Hearings on 1977 Budget," ibid., February 7, 1976, p. 264.

13. Interview with Bolling, February 8, 1989.

14. Interview with Adams, March 3, 1989.

15. Ibid.

16. *Congressional Record*, May 1, 1975, p. 12767.

17. Interview with Adams, March 3, 1989.

18. Interview with Albert, February 2, 1989.

19. See Nelson W. Polsby, "Two Strategies of Influence: Choosing a Majority Leader, 1962," in Nelson W. Polsby and Robert L. Peabody, eds., *New Perspectives on the House of Representatives* (Chicago: Rand McNally, 1969). See also Peters, *The American Speakership*, pp. 155–58.

20. Interview with Bolling, February 8, 1989; interview with Adams, March 3, 1989.

21. John J. Rhodes, *The Futile System* (McClean, Virginia: EPM Publications, 1976), pp. 32–33. For a concise statement of O'Neill's governing philosophy, see O'Neill, *Man of the House*, pp. 376–78.

22. Democrat quoted in Bruce F. Freed, "Albert Retirement Promises Leadership Fight," *Congressional Quarterly Weekly Report*, June 12, 1976, p. 1491; O'Neill quoted in Barry Hager, "O'Neill: A Popular, Skilled Party Loyalist," ibid., December 11, 1976, p. 3296.

23. O'Neill, *Man of the House*, p. 274. The quotation comes from Thomas P. Southwick, "House Changes Complicate O'Neill's Vow to Become 'A Strong Speaker,' " *Congressional Quarterly Weekly Report*, December 25, 1976, p. 3365.

24. O'Neill quoted in Hager, "O'Neill," p. 3296; interview with O'Neill, February 14, 1989; O'Neill, *Man of the House*, p. 285.

25. Interview with anonymous staff person (1).

26. Interview with anonymous staff person (2).

27. Barbara Sinclair, "The Speaker's Task Forces in the Post-Reform House of Representatives," *American Political Science Review*, vol. 75 (1981), pp. 391–410.

28. For an assessment of these two functions in particular, see Barbara Sinclair, *Majority Leadership*. For a more extensive list of functions, see Ripley, *Majority Party Leadership in Congress*.

29. See Sinclair, *Majority Leadership*, chap. 6.

30. O'Neill quoted in Irwin B. Arieff, "House, Senate Chiefs Attempt to Lead a Changed Congress," *Congressional Quarterly Weekly Report*, September 13, 1980, p. 2696.

31. See Bach and Smith, *Managing Uncertainty in the House*, and Smith, *Call to Order*.

32. *Congressional Record*, May 9, 1979, p. 2931.

33. For a discussion of the majority party leadership's use of the strategy of inclusion (that is, including many Democrats to participate in the legislative process), see Sinclair, "The Speaker's Task Forces."

34. Jimmy Carter, *Public Papers of United States Presidents: Jimmy Carter, 1977* (Washington: Government Printing Office, 1978), p. 619.

35. Giaimo quoted in Judy Gardner, "Budget Targets: Back to the Drawing Board," *Congressional Quarterly Weekly Report*, April 30, 1977, p. 777.

36. Ibid.

37. Judy Gardner and Thomas P. Southwick, "Budget Process Survives Second House Test," ibid., May 7, 1977, p. 843.

38. Wright quoted in ibid., p. 842.

39. Bevill quoted in Ann Cooper, "House Democratic Whips: Counting, Coaxing, and Cajoling," ibid., May 27, 1978, p. 1304.

40. Jimmy Carter, *Public Papers of United States Presidents: Jimmy Carter, 1978* (Washington: Government Printing Office, 1979), p. 96.

41. O'Neill quoted in Alan Berlow, "Coalitions Forming in Congress to Fight for Restoration of Social Program Spending," *Congressional Quarterly Weekly Report*, January 27, 1979, p. 126.

42. Sinclair, *Majority Leadership*, p. 176.

43. Ibid., p. 177.

44. Mineta quoted in Christopher R. Conte, "Democratic Coalition Nears Budget Test," *Congressional Quarterly Weekly Report*, May 5, 1979, p. 815.

45. Giaimo quoted in Gail Gregg, "Senate, House Plan Votes on Spending Limit," ibid., March 8, 1980, p. 642.

46. The new economic assumptions, which predicted a higher inflation rate and lower unemployment, were favorable to the goal of a balanced budget. By expecting higher inflation (11.75 percent instead of 10.4 percent), the budget estimated higher revenues earned from higher wages. By projecting a lower unemployment rate (lower than the original estimate of 7.5 percent), the budget deficit was reduced, as more people were expected to pay taxes and fewer people would receive unemployment insurance.

47. O'Neill quoted in Gail Gregg, "Balanced Budget Drive Wins Broad Support on Capitol Hill," *Congressional Quarterly Weekly Report*, March 8, 1980, p. 641.

48. O'Neill quoted in Christopher R. Conte, "House Bogs Down in Budget Amendments," ibid., May 12, 1979, p. 879; Giaimo

quoted in Gail Gregg, "Balanced Budget Moves toward House Show-down: Senate Action Planned," ibid., April 26, 1980, p. 1076. For more on this point, see Ippolito, *Congressional Spending*, p. 92.

49. Bauman quoted in Gail Gregg, "Amendments to Be Limited in House Budget Debate," *Congressional Quarterly Weekly Report*, April 19, 1980, p. 1057.

50. Rules Chairman Bolling defined the problem: "We have to devise a technique whereby those who wish to use the budget process as a means of making political points are limited to making those points on macro issues" (quoted in Conte, "House Bogs Down in Budget Amendments," p. 879).

51. Sinclair, *Majority Leadership*, p. 183.

52. Gail Gregg, "House Budget Plan Survives Floor Challenges from Left and Right," *Congressional Quarterly Weekly Report*, May 3, 1980, p. 1166.

53. Gray quoted in Irwin B. Arieff, "6 Liberal Democrats Found Themselves on the Outside during Budget Markup," ibid., March 29, 1980, p. 847.

54. O'Neill quoted in Gail Gregg, "House Outlook Grim for Budget Conference," ibid., May 24, 1980, p. 1980.

55. O'Neill quoted in Gail Gregg, "House Sends Budget Back to Conference," ibid., May 31, 1980, p. 1459; Giaimo quoted in Gail Gregg, "Budget Impasse Continues as Spending Pressures Mount," ibid., June 7, 1980, p. 1541.

56. Sinclair, *Majority Leadership*, pp. 186, 187. For this account of events on the passage of the conference report, I rely primarily on pp. 186–88.

57. Schick, *Congress and Money*, pp. 361, 200.

58. The fiscal 1976 second budget resolution, passed in December 1975, is an exception to this general observation. Yet 1975 was the first year after the Budget Act was passed, and it was considered a trial run for the new budget process.

59. Schick, *Congress and Money*, p. 361.

60. For more on assumed legislative savings, see Gilmour, *Reconcilable Differences?* pp. 105–7.

61. Panetta quoted in Christopher R. Conte, "Congress' Resolve to Curb Spending Faces First Test," *Congressional Quarterly Weekly Report*, March 31, 1979, p. 586.

62. *Congressional Record*, May 3, 1979, pp. 9678–79.

63. For a discussion of these two cases, see Schick, *Congress and Money*, pp. 387–88.

64. *Congressional Record*, June 5, 1979, p. 13331.

65. Giaimo quoted in "Budget Conference Divided," *Congressional Quarterly Weekly Report*, October 20, 1979, p. 2316.

66. Giaimo quoted in Gail Gregg, "Key Lawmakers Urge Caps on Spending and Taxes," ibid., December 8, 1979, p. 2762. Following this rationale, in December 1979, Giaimo introduced a bill drafted by Jim Jones (D-Okla.) that would limit federal spending to 27.5 percent of the GNP by fiscal year 1983.

67. Harrison Donnelly, "Uncontrollable U.S. Spending Limits Hill Power of the Purse," ibid., January 19, 1980, pp. 117–24.

68. For more on entitlements, see R. Kent Weaver, "Controlling Entitlements," in John E. Chubb and Paul E. Peterson, eds., *The New Direction in American Politics* (Washington: The Brookings Institution, 1985); and Aaron Wildavsky, *The New Politics of the Budgetary Process* (Glenview, Illinois: Scott Foresman and Company, 1988), chaps. 7, 8. Weaver points out, however, that there are exceptions to the general view that entitlements can only be reduced by changing laws. He also shows that, after a period of expansion from 1965 to 1974, the growth in spending for entitlements stabilized from 1975 to 1984 (Weaver, "Controlling Entitlements").

69. Panetta quoted in Donnelly, "Uncontrollable U.S. Spending Limits Hill Power of the Purse," p. 124.

70. Giaimo quoted in Gail Gregg, "Senate, House Plan Votes on Spending Limit," *Congressional Quarterly Weekly Report*, March 8, 1980, p. 644.

71. *Congressional Record*, May 7, 1980, p. 10153.

72. Udall quoted in Gail Gregg, "House Votes Balanced Budget, Senate Stalls," *Congressional Quarterly Weekly Report*, May 10, 1980, p. 1228.

73. Obey quoted in Arieff, "6 Liberal Democrats Found Themselves on the Outside during Budget Markup," p. 846.

74. Gregg, "House Votes Balanced Budget, Senate Stalls," p. 1229. The eight House committees were Armed Services, Education and Labor, Commerce, Post Office, Public Works, Small Business, Veterans, and Ways and Means.

75. Giaimo quoted in Timothy B. Clark and Richard E. Cohen, "Balancing the Budget: A Test for Congress—Can It Resist the Pressures to Spend?" *National Journal*, April 12, 1980, p. 592.

76. Gail Gregg, "Storm Brewing over Budget Reconciliation," *Congressional Quarterly Weekly Report*, June 21, 1980, p. 1714.

77. Giaimo quoted in ibid.; O'Neill quoted in ibid., p. 1715.

78. Sinclair, *Majority Leadership*, p. 188.

79. Harrison Donnelly, "Reconciliation Bill Cleared for House Floor Action," *Congressional Quarterly Weekly Report*, August 30, 1980, p. 2625.

80. Sinclair, *Majority Leadership*, p. 189.

81. For Bolling's speech, see *Congressional Record*, September 4, 1980, p. 24192.

82. Sinclair, *Majority Leadership*, p. 190.

4. The Speaker under Stress: Budget Politics in 1981

1. O'Neill, *Man of the House*, p. 346.

2. *Mandate* is defined here in terms of four characteristics: (1) a clear message in the presidential campaign; (2) electoral success of the president's party in Congress; (3) electoral results that exceed public expectations; and (4) a president who runs along with his party in the general election. Charles O. Jones, "Ronald Reagan and the U.S. Congress: Visible-Hand Politics," in Charles O. Jones, ed., *The Reagan Legacy: Promise and Performance* (Chatham, New Jersey: Chatham House, 1988), pp. 32–34.

3. O'Neill, *Man of the House*, p. 346.

4. See William Schneider, "The November 4 Vote for President: What Did It Mean?" in Austin Ranney, ed., *The American Elections of 1980* (Washington: American Enterprise Institute, 1981), pp. 227–33.

5. Christopher Buchanan, "Youth Is on the Right in House Freshman Class," *Congressional Quarterly Weekly Report*, January 3, 1981, p. 3. See also Thomas E. Mann and Norman J. Ornstein, "The Republican Surge in Congress," in Ranney, *American Elections of 1980*, p. 296.

6. The House narrowly rejected the Holt substitute amendment in 1978 by a vote of 197–203, and in 1979 by a vote of 198–218.

7. The CDF quoted in Irwin B. Arieff, "Hill Democrats, Republicans Organize for 97th Congress," *Congressional Quarterly Weekly Report*, November 29, 1980, p. 3432.

8. David A. Stockman, *The Triumph of Politics* (New York: Harper and Row, 1986), p. 159.

9. For evidence supporting this thesis, see Paul R. Abramson, John H. Aldrich, and David W. Rohde, *Change and Continuity in the 1980 Elections* (Washington: Congressional Quarterly Press, 1982), pp.

119–57; Kathleen A. Frankovic, "Public Opinion Trends," in Gerald Pomper, ed., *The Election of 1980* (Chatham, New Jersey: Chatham House, 1981), p. 113; Gregory B. Markus, "Political Attitudes during an Election Year: A Report on the 1980 NES Panel Study," *American Political Science Review*, vol. 76 (1982), p. 560; and Wilson Carey McWilliams, "The Meaning of the Election," in Pomper, *Election of 1980*, p. 170.

10. Interview with O'Neill, February 14, 1989. For another version of the same point, see O'Neill, *Man of the House*, p. 337.

11. O'Neill quoted in Irwin B. Arieff, "Reagan Courts Legislators in Visit to Hill," *Congressional Quarterly Weekly Report*, November 22, 1980, p. 3393.

12. Warren E. Miller and J. Merrill Shanks, "Policy Directions and Presidential Leadership: Alternative Explanations of the 1980 Presidential Election," *British Journal of Political Science*, vol. 12 (1982), p. 352; Charles O. Jones, "A New President, a Different Congress, a Maturing Agenda," in Lester M. Salamon and Michael S. Lund, eds., *The Reagan Presidency and the Governing of America* (Washington: The Urban Institute, 1984), p. 263.

13. For Reagan's fiscal 1982 budget message see Ronald Reagan, *Public Papers of United States Presidents: Ronald Reagan, 1981* (Washington: Government Printing Office, 1982), pp. 222–24.

14. This point was made in my interviews with Jones and with his staff personnel. To clarify his position, Jones publicly announced that a three-year plan would be "devastating to the budget and would bring chaos to the financial market" (quoted in Gail Gregg, "Final Carter Budget Sets Challenge for Reagan," *Congressional Quarterly Weekly Report*, January 17, 1981, p. 125).

15. Jones quoted in Gail Gregg, "Beleaguered Budget Process Faces New Pressures in 1981," ibid., January 10, 1981, p. 66.

16. Downey and Pickle quoted in Dale Tate, "Congress Shapes Strategy for Reagan Economic Plan," ibid., February 28, 1981, p. 377; Jones quoted in Gail Gregg, "Reagan Proposes Dramatic Reduction in Federal Role," ibid., March 14, 1981, p. 443.

17. Steven S. Smith, "Budget Battles of 1981: The Role of the Majority Party Leadership," in Allan P. Sindler, ed., *American Politics and Public Policy* (Washington: Congressional Quarterly Press, 1982), p. 52; O'Neill quoted in Gail Gregg, "Democrats Score on Budget in House and Senate Panels," *Congressional Quarterly Weekly Report*, April 11, 1981, p. 619.

18. Regan and Stockman quoted in Richard E. Cohen, "Budget Battles Take to the Trenches—But Who Ever Said It Would Be Easy?" *National Journal*, April 13, 1981, p. 647.

19. Jones quoted in Gregg, "Democrats Score on Budget in House and Senate Panels," p. 619; Belew quoted in Richard E. Cohen, "The 'Fun and Games' Are Over—Now Congress Has to Enact the Cuts," *National Journal*, May 16, 1981, pp. 888–89.

20. See Barbara Sinclair, *Majority Leadership*, p. 193.

21. Stockman quoted in William Greider, "The Education of David Stockman," *Atlantic Monthly* (December 1981), p. 44.

22. For the White House lobbying strategy, see Hedrick Smith, "Taking Charge of Congress," *New York Times Magazine*, August 9, 1981, pp. 17–18; and Steven J. Wayne, "Congressional Liaison in the Reagan White House: A Preliminary Assessment of the First Year," in Norman J. Ornstein, ed., *President and Congress: Assessing Reagan's First Year* (Washington: American Enterprise Institute, 1982).

23. Reagan, *Public Papers . . . Ronald Reagan, 1981*, p. 394.

24. O'Neill quoted in Irwin B. Arieff, "Budget Fight Shows O'Neill's Fragile Grasp," *Congressional Quarterly Weekly Report*, May 9, 1981, p. 786; Jones quoted in Dale Tate and Gail Gregg, "Congress Set for Showdown on First Budget Resolution," ibid., May 2, 1981, p. 743.

25. For O'Neill's speech, see *Congressional Record*, May 7, 1981, pp. 9014–16.

26. Sinclair, *Majority Leadership*, p. 196; Reagan, *Public Papers . . . Ronald Reagan, 1981*, p. 419.

27. Miller quoted in Dale Tate, "House Provides President a Victory on the 1982 Budget," *Congressional Quarterly Weekly Report*, May 9, 1981, p. 785.

28. O'Neill, *Man of the House*, p. 344.

29. On O'Neill's strategy, see Smith, "Budget Battles of 1981," pp. 51–52; and Sinclair, *Majority Leadership*, pp. 192–93.

30. Gramm quoted in Irwin B. Arieff, "Maverick Negotiates 'Bipartisan Budget,'" *Congressional Quarterly Weekly Report*, April 18, 1981, p. 672).

31. Sinclair, *Majority Leadership*, pp. 194, 193.

32. Measured in terms of opposition to the conservative coalition, the average liberal rating among Budget Committee Democrats declined from 66 percent in the Ninety-sixth Congress to 48 percent in the Ninety-seventh.

33. See Smith, "Budget Battles of 1981," p. 57.

34. The attempted assassination of Reagan on March 30, 1981, contributed to his popularity at this time. For discussion of how this event affected public opinion, see James W. Ceaser, "The Reagan Presidency and American Public Opinion," in Jones, *The Reagan Legacy*, p. 184.

35. Hefner quoted in Arieff, "Budget Fight Shows O'Neill's Fragile Grasp," p. 786.

36. Interview with anonymous staff person (4). This combination of factors essentially concurs with the conclusion drawn by Sinclair in *Majority Leadership*, p. 213.

37. For discussion of alternative leadership strategies in dealing with reconciliation, see Sinclair, *Majority Leadership*, pp. 197–98; and Smith, "Budget Battles of 1981," pp. 60–65.

38. Udall quoted in Dale Tate, "Reconciliation Breeds Tumult as Committees Tackle Cuts," *Congressional Quarterly Weekly Report*, May 23, 1981, p. 890; Perkins quoted in Dale Tate, "Reconciliation Changes Still Face Tough Hill Battles," ibid., June 13, 1981, p. 1029, and in Tate, "Reconciliation Breeds Tumult as Committees Tackle Cuts," p. 891.

39. Interview with anonymous staff person (5).

40. Interview with anonymous staff person (6).

41. Interview with anonymous staff person (7).

42. Interview with anonymous staff person (5).

43. Interview with anonymous staff person (7).

44. O'Neill quoted in Tate, "Reconciliation Breeds Tumult as Committees Tackle Cuts," p. 891; Perkins quoted in Tate, "Reconciliation Changes Still Face Tough Hill Battles," p. 1029; Jones quoted in Tate, "Reconciliation Breeds Tumult as Committees Tackle Cuts," p. 891.

45. For a detailed discussion of how the debate over the rule was settled, see Sinclair, *Majority Leadership*, pp. 200–204.

46. Reagan, *Public Papers . . . Ronald Reagan, 1981*, p. 519.

47. O'Neill and Reagan quoted in Smith, "Taking Charge of Congress," p. 16.

48. In May 1981, the Senate voted 96–0 to reject an attempt by the administration to raise the age requirement for social security benefits.

49. Stockman, *The Triumph of Politics*, p. 219.

50. *Congressional Record*, June 25, 1981, p. 14078.

51. O'Neill quoted in Dale Tate and Andy Plattner, "House Ratifies Savings Plan in Stunning Reagan Victory," *Congressional Quarterly Weekly Report*, June 27, 1981, p. 1128.

52. Stockman, *The Triumph of Politics*, p. 218. Stockman points out that White House chief of staff James Baker and congressional liaison Max Friedersdorf also thought Gramm-Latta II had no chance of passing until the Democratic leadership opened up the rule for amendments.

53. Hedrick Smith listed some of the "sweeteners" offered by the White House to southern Democrats—"sugar price support legislation, more funds for Medicaid, Conrail, energy subsidies for the poor, a slow-down on mandatory conversion for coal to industrial boilers in oil-producing states" (Smith, "Taking Charge of Congress," p. 17); Jones quoted in Tate and Plattner, "House Ratifies Spending Plan in Stunning Reagan Victory," p. 1128; Breaux quoted in Smith, "Taking Charge of Congress," p. 17.

54. Quoted in Sinclair, *Majority Leadership*, p. 212.

55. For Stockman's account of how the reconciliation bill was formulated, see Stockman, *The Triumph of Politics*, pp. 205–23.

56. Reagan, *Public Papers . . . Ronald Reagan, 1981*, pp. 563–64.

57. Reagan quoted in Dale Tate, "Tax Cut Compromise Barred as Committee Markups Near," *Congressional Quarterly Weekly Report*, April 18, 1981, p. 670; O'Neill quoted in Gail Gregg, "Reagan Proposes Dramatic Reduction in Federal Role," ibid., March 14, 1981, p. 445.

58. For Ways and Means treatment of the tax bill, see Strahan, *New Ways and Means*, pp. 124–29.

59. Rostenkowski and Bush quoted in Tate, "Tax Cut Compromise Barred as Committee Markups Near," p. 670.

60. See Stockman, *The Triumph of Politics*, p. 169.

61. Smith, "Budget Battles of 1981," pp. 68–69.

62. O'Neill quoted in Irwin B. Arieff, "Conservative Southerners Are Enjoying Their Wooing as Key to Tax Bill Success," *Congressional Quarterly Weekly Report*, June 13, 1981, p. 1024.

63. Smith, "Taking Charge of Congress"; and Elizabeth Wehr, "White House's Lobbying Apparatus Produces Impressive Tax Vote Victory," *Congressional Quarterly Weekly Report*, August 1, 1981, pp. 1372–73.

64. O'Neill quoted in Pamela Fessler, "Tax Cut Passed by Solid Margin in House, Senate," *Congressional Quarterly Weekly Report*, Au-

gust 1, 1981, p. 1374; Baker quoted in Wehr, "White House's Lobbying Apparatus Produces Impressive Tax Vote Victory," p. 1372.

65. O'Neill and Garn quoted in Dale Tate, "New Reagan Budget Cuts Face Stiff Fight," *Congressional Quarterly Weekly Report*, September 26, 1981, p. 1819.

66. See Dale Tate, "Hill GOP Seeks Alternatives to Reagan Budget Cut Plans," ibid., October 10, 1981, p. 1943.

67. For example, on October 6, 1981, the House approved an appropriation for the departments of Labor, Health and Human Services, and Education that exceeded Reagan's budgetary request by $4 billion. Allen Schick, "How the Budget Was Won and Lost," in Ornstein, *President and Congress*, pp. 25–27.

68. Irwin B. Arieff, "'Gypsy Moths' Poised to Fly against Reagan's New Cuts, Charge Pledges Are Broken," *Congressional Quarterly Weekly Report*, October 10, 1981, p. 1950–52.

69. For a detailed discussion of the divisiveness within the Reagan administration, see Stockman, *The Triumph of Politics*, pp. 288–325.

70. Stockman quoted in Greider, "The Education of David Stockman," p. 38.

71. O'Neill quoted in Dale Tate and Pamela Fessler, "GOP Senators Assume Budget Leadership," *Congressional Quarterly Weekly Report*, November 14, 1981, p. 2217.

72. Domenici, Latta, and Panetta quoted in Dale Tate, "Dispute over Tax Increases Stalls Action on 1982 Budget," ibid., November 7, 1981, p. 2165.

73. O'Neill quoted in Dale Tate, "One Spending Crunch Ends, Another Looms," ibid., November 28, 1981, p. 2052; Reagan quoted in Tate and Fessler, "GOP Senators Assume Budget Leadership," p. 2216.

74. O'Neill, *Man of the House*, p. 344; interview with anonymous member (12); O'Neill, *Man of the House*, p. 345.

75. Lance T. LeLoup, "After the Blitz: Reagan and the U.S. Congressional Budget Process," *Legislative Studies Quarterly*, vol. 7 (1982), pp. 324–30, 332–36; and Jones, "A New President, a Different Congress, a Maturing Agenda," pp. 261–87.

76. Schick, "How the Budget Was Won and Lost," p. 26.

77. Wayne, "Congressional Liaison in the Reagan White House: A Preliminary Assessment of the First Year," pp. 49–65.

78. Barbara Sinclair, "Agenda Control and Policy Success: Ronald Reagan and the 97th Congress," *Legislative Studies Quarterly*, vol. 10 (1985), pp. 291–312.

79. Darrell M. West, *Congress and Economic Policymaking* (Pittsburgh: University of Pittsburgh Press, 1987), pp. 37–64.

5. Speaker O'Neill: Opposition Party Leader and Process Manager, 1982–86

1. Schick, "The Distributive Congress," in Schick, *Making Economic Policy in Congress*, pp. 257–72. A distributive policy condition serves all interests, whereas in a redistributive condition, resources are transferred from one interest to another.

2. Louis Fisher, "The Budget Act of 1984: A Further Loss of Spending Control," in Wander, Hebert, and Copeland, *Congressional Budgeting*, pp. 180–83; and Wildavsky, *New Politics of the Budgetary Process*, p. 219.

3. Caiden, "The Politics of Subtraction," p. 104.

4. See also Schick, "The Evolution of Congressional Budgeting," p. 35; and John W. Ellwood, "The Great Exception: The Congressional Budget Process in an Age of Decentralization," in Lawrence C. Dodd and Bruce I. Oppenheimer, eds., *Congress Reconsidered*, 3d ed. (Washington: Congressional Quarterly Press, 1985), p. 337.

5. Rohde and Shepsle, "Leaders and Followers in the House of Representatives," pp. 111–33.

6. The quotations in the previous three paragraphs are from an interview with anonymous staff person (3).

7. Interview with anonymous staff person (4).

8. Interview with Jones, February 13, 1989.

9. All of O'Neill's quotations in the previous two paragraphs are from an interview with O'Neill, February 14, 1989.

10. Latta quoted in Martin Tolchin, "Democratic Leadership Seeks Role in Reagan's Forthcoming Budget," *New York Times*, January 13, 1982, p. A17.

11. The Atari Democrats include many members from the Class of 1974, like Dick Gephardt, Leon Panetta, and Tim Wirth. See Alan Ehrenhalt, "'Human Need' Bloc Emerges in Budget Debate," *Congressional Quarterly Weekly Report*, February 12, 1983, p. 359.

12. The president proposed a three-year deficit-reduction plan totaling $239 billion. For Reagan's budget message, see Ronald Reagan, *Public Papers of United States Presidents: Ronald Reagan, 1982* (Washington: Government Printing Office, 1983), pp. 126–29.

13. O'Neill quoted in Dale Tate, "Congress Balks at '83 Budget with Cuts and High Deficits," *Congressional Quarterly Weekly Report*, February 13, 1982, p. 223, and in Irwin Arieff, "Democrats Air a Bleak 'State of the Union,' " ibid., January 30, 1982, p. 154.

14. O'Neill quoted in Dale Tate, "Leaders Press Quest for Budget Alternative," ibid., March 13, 1982, p. 560.

15. Stockman, *The Triumph of Politics*, p. 353. For a more detailed account of the Gang of Seventeen meetings, see White and Wildavsky, *The Deficit and the Public Interest*, pp. 234–38.

16. Reagan, O'Neill, Jones, and Domenici quoted in Dale Tate, "Keys to Budget Compromise Emerge from Leaders' Talks," *Congressional Quarterly Weekly Report*, April 10, 1982, p. 787–88.

17. Reagan and O'Neill quoted in Dale Tate, "Budget Talks Reflect Unique Political and Economic Brew," ibid., April 24, 1982, p. 903.

18. Smith, *The Power Game*, p. 531. For a description of the meeting, see pp. 529–32.

19. O'Neill was referring to the cut in the COLA for social security payments that Stockman referred to as "an essential ingredient of the compromised plan" (Stockman, *The Triumph of Politics*, p. 354). For this exchange between Reagan and O'Neill, see ibid. and also Smith, *The Power Game*, p. 531.

20. Interview with O'Neill, February 14, 1989. The last two quotations in the paragraph, by O'Neill and by Laxalt, are from Dale Tate, "Budget Battle Erupts on Hill as Compromise Talks Fizzle," *Congressional Quarterly Weekly Report*, May 1, 1982, p. 969.

21. Interview with anonymous staff person (3).

22. For further discussion of the King of the Mountain rule for the fiscal 1983 first budget resolution, see Bach and Smith, *Managing Uncertainty in the House*, p. 77.

23. *Congressional Record*, May 27, 1982, p. 12502.

24. Jones and O'Neill's reference to a "true Democratic budget" quoted in Andy Plattner, "Muddy Tracks of House Votes Offer Few Clues," *Congressional Quarterly Weekly Report*, June 5, 1982, p. 1327; Jones' second quotation in this paragraph is from Dale Tate, "Representative Jones: Beleaguered Budget Chairman," ibid., June 19, 1982, p. 1449.

25. O'Neill quoted in Dale Tate, "Congress Faces Uphill Battle to Achieve Budgeted Savings," ibid., June 26, 1982, p. 1507.

26. For a good discussion of the formulation and enactment of TEFRA, see White and Wildavsky, *The Deficit and the Public Interest*, pp. 249–58.

27. O'Neill quoted in Dale Tate, "Elections '82: Referendum on Reaganomics?" *Congressional Quarterly Weekly Report*, October 23, 1982, p. 2719. Reagan advanced a stay-the-course theme in the 1982 congressional elections, emphasizing that Reaganomics would take time to repair the fiscal disaster created by Democratic policies that had been enacted long before he was elected.

28. Alan Ehrenhalt, "Lasting Election Effects Likely in House," ibid., November 6, 1982, p. 2779; Miller quoted in Dale Tate, "Pragmatism Is the Watchword as House Budget Committee Heads into 1984 Fiscal Storm," ibid., March 5, 1983, p. 462.

29. Interview with O'Neill, February 14, 1989. For a discussion of the limitations of the Speaker's influence on the Steering and Policy Committee, see Smith and Ray, "The Impact of Congressional Reform," pp. 219–40.

30. See Ehrenhalt, "'Human Need' Bloc Emerges in Budget Debate," p. 359.

31. This point was made in several interviews with Budget Committee members and staff personnel. Chairman Jones mentions elsewhere that the Budget Committee was "somewhat stacked against me" in 1983 (quoted in Dale Tate, "Budget Committee Chairman Jim Jones . . . Will He Come In from the Cold?" *Congressional Quarterly Weekly Report*, March 17, 1984, p. 597).

32. O'Neill, *Man of the House*, p. 349.

33. O'Neill quoted in Tate, "Pragmatism Is the Watchword as House Budget Committee Heads into 1984 Fiscal Storm," p. 463; Wright quoted in Dale Tate, "House Approves $936 Billion Budget for '84," *Congressional Quarterly Weekly Report*, March 26, 1983, p. 602.

34. Information about the staff's role in drafting the budget resolution is from an interview with an anonymous Budget Committee staff person involved in the spell-down session.

35. O'Neill quoted in Tate, "House Approves $936 Billion Budget for '84," p. 601.

36. As part of that effort, Gephardt organized a weekend retreat to Sulfur Springs, West Virginia, during the first weekend in March 1985, which was attended by 135 Democrats. Gephardt also worked

with Senator Sam Nunn and Virginia governor Chuck Robb to set up a Democratic Leadership Council consisting of forty governors, senators, and representatives, who met to discuss policy proposals that would bring the Democratic party closer to the mainstream of America.

37. O'Neill quoted in Diane Granat, "Democratic and GOP Leaders Named for the 99th Congress," *Congressional Quarterly Weekly Report*, December 8, 1984, p. 3053, and in Diane Granat, "Junior Democrats Gain a Louder Voice . . . Leadership Panels Will Serve as Forum," ibid., December 8, 1984, p. 3054.

38. Interview with O'Neill, February 14, 1989.

39. Diane Granat, "Congress Goes to Work under Budget Cloud," *Congressional Quarterly Weekly Report*, January 18, 1986, p. 103.

40. Reagan quoted in Elizabeth Wehr, "Budget Impasse Shows No Signs of Breaking," ibid., January 25, 1986, p. 137.

41. O'Neill and Gray quoted in Elizabeth Wehr and Stephan Gettinger, "Congress Falling Behind on Budget Deadlines," ibid., April 12, 1986, p. 791.

42. Anonymous member quoted in Stephan Gettinger, "The Making of the Democrats' Budget . . . a New Conservative-Liberal Coalition," ibid., May 17, 1986, p. 1081.

43. Stephan Gettinger, "House OKs Democratic Budget for Fiscal 1987," ibid., May 17, 1986, p. 1081.

44. O'Neill quoted in ibid., p. 1079.

45. O'Neill quoted in Dale Tate, "Budget Conference Meets, and Deadlocks," ibid., June 16, 1984, p. 1412, and in Dale Tate, "Hill Deficit Reductions Hinge on Conference Deliberations," ibid., June 2, 1984, p. 1295.

46. O'Neill quoted in Jacqueline Calmes, "House, with Little Difficulty, Passes '86 Budget Resolution," ibid., May 25, 1985, p. 971.

47. Interview with O'Neill, February 14, 1989.

48. House Budget Committee, *Hearing on Budget Process Review*, 97th Cong., 2d sess. (Washington: Government Printing Office, 1982), p. 37.

49. These are my observations of the problems with meeting reconciliation instructions. For a further discussion of jurisdictional conflicts, see Gary W. Copeland, "Changes in the House of Representatives after the Passage of the Budget Act of 1974," in Wander, Hebert, and Copeland, *Congressional Budgeting*, p. 63; and Gilmour, *Reconcilable Differences?* chap. 4.

50. O'Neill quoted in Diane Granat, "Legislative Business Proceeds amidst Hill's Political Battles," *Congressional Quarterly Weekly Report*, July 7, 1984, p. 1608; interview with O'Neill, February 14, 1989.

51. Insufficient majorities would be another reason for failing to pass reconciliation. Gilmour, *Reconcilable Differences?*

52. Ronald Reagan, *Public Papers of United States Presidents: Ronald Reagan, 1983* (Washington: Government Printing Office, 1984), p. 1538.

53. Interview with anonymous staff person (3).

54. Interviews with anonymous staff persons (9) and (10).

55. O'Neill quoted in Diane Granat, "Congressional Decks Cleared to Tackle '84 Appropriations," *Congressional Quarterly Weekly Report*, May 28, 1983, p. 1043.

56. O'Neill quoted in Diane Granat, "Congress Heads Home for Five-Week Recess," ibid., August 6, 1983, p. 1595.

57. O'Neill quoted in Diane Granat, "Congress Clears 1984 Continuing Resolution," ibid., November 19, 1983, pp. 2431–32.

58. Ronald Reagan, *Public Papers of United States Presidents: Ronald Reagan, 1984* (Washington: Government Printing Office, 1985), p. 1434; O'Neill quoted in Diane Granat, "Reagan Shuts Government: Democrats Object," *Congressional Quarterly Weekly Report*, October 6, 1984, p. 2420; Dale Tate, "Politics Prods Congress to Clear Money Bill," *Congressional Quarterly Weekly Report*, October 13, 1984, p. 2616.

6. Speaker Wright: Activist Leadership in the Hundredth Congress

1. Gephardt quoted in Janet Hook, "House Leadership Elections: Wright Era Begins," *Congressional Quarterly Weekly Report*, December 13, 1986, p. 3070. When the Irangate scandal became public, Reagan's approval ratings declined nearly twenty points in one month (Ceaser, "The Reagan Presidency and American Public Opinion," p. 201).

2. Richard E. Cohen, "Full Speed Ahead," *National Journal*, January 30, 1988, p. 240; Barbara Sinclair, "House Majority Party Leadership in the Late-1980s," in Dodd and Oppenheimer, *Congress Reconsidered*, 4th ed.

3. Panetta and Matsui quoted in Hook, "House Leadership Elections," p. 3070.

4. For an insider's account of how Wright's personality was reflected in his effort to initiate the party's budget priorities, see Barry, *The Ambition and the Power*, chap. 6.

5. For other descriptions of Wright's style see ibid.; Richard E. Cohen, "Quick-Starting Speaker," *National Journal*, May 30, 1987, pp. 1409–13; Richard E. Cohen, "Wright Angle," *National Journal*, October 17, 1987, p. 2633; Cohen, "Full Speed Ahead," pp. 238–44; Janet Hook, "Speaker Jim Wright Takes Charge in the House," *Congressional Quarterly Weekly Report*, July 11, 1987, pp. 1483–88; Janet Hook, "Jim Wright Takes Big Risks to Amass Power," *Congressional Quarterly Weekly Report*, March 12, 1988, pp. 623–26; Peters, *The American Speakership*, pp. 264–68, and Rohde, *Parties and Leaders in the Postreform House*, pp. 105–18.

6. Fazio quoted in Cohen, "Full Speed Ahead," p. 240.

7. Wright quoted in Elizabeth Wehr, "Wright Pushes Harder for Taxes as a Way to Cut Budget Deficit," *Congressional Quarterly Weekly Report*, March 7, 1987, p. 426, and in Hook, "Speaker Jim Wright Takes Charge in the House," pp. 1486–87.

8. Wright's preference for appointing allies was also evident in appointments to the Steering and Policy Committee and the deputy whips organization. See Hook, "Speaker Jim Wright Takes Charge in the House"; Jacqueline Calmes, "The Hill Leaders: Their Places on the Ladder," *Congressional Quarterly Weekly Report*, January 3, 1987, p. 6; and Barry, *The Ambition and the Power*, pp. 80–83.

9. Janet Hook, "House Democrats, Republicans Begin Committee Assignments," *Congressional Quarterly Weekly Report*, December 13, 1986, p. 3073. As he campaigned against Franklin, Espy "carried around in his pocket a promise from Speaker-to-be Jim Wright that if elected he would get a seat on the Agriculture Committee" (Michael Barone and Grant Ujifuser, eds., *The Almanac of American Politics* [Washington: National Journal Inc., 1987], p. 655).

10. Alan Ehrenhalt, ed., *Politics in America* (Washington: Congressional Quarterly Press, 1987), p. 807.

11. Interview with anonymous staff person (5).

12. These rates were lowered by the Tax Reform Act of 1986. The Tax Reform Act stipulated that the tax rate ceiling for the highest income bracket be reduced from 50 percent to 38.5 percent in 1987 and 33 percent in 1988.

13. Gray quoted in Stephan Gettinger, "Key Democrats Press Revenues as Means to Reduce the Deficit," *Congressional Quarterly*

Weekly Report, December 12, 1986, p. 3075. As I note further along in the chapter, GRH was revised in September 1987 to restore the automatic trigger declared unconstitutional by the Supreme Court in July 1986.

14. A Gallup poll from September 28 to October 1, 1984, revealed that only 34 percent of survey respondents were in favor of a tax increase to reduce the deficit, while 62 percent opposed the idea (see *Gallup Report* no. 229 [Princeton, New Jersey: The Gallup Poll, 1984], p. 6). A *Wall Street Journal*/NBC News survey conducted in January 1986 revealed that 31 percent of the respondents surveyed thought that the federal deficit was the most serious public problem. Yet, 86 percent opposed cutting Medicare, 69 percent opposed cutting social programs for the poor, and 56 percent opposed a tax rate increase (see Ellen Hume, "Americans See Deficit as a Disease, but They Balk at Proposed Cures," *Wall Street Journal*, February 11, 1986, p. 29).

15. Lowry and Panetta quoted in Hook, "House Leadership Elections," p. 3070; interview with anonymous staff person (5).

16. Bentson and Baker quoted in Gettinger, "Key Democrats Press Revenues as Means to Reduce the Deficit," p. 3075.

17. Rostenkowski quoted in Wehr, "Wright Pushes Harder for Taxes as a Way to Cut Budget Deficit," p. 426; Ronald Reagan, *Weekly Compilation of Presidential Documents*, vol. 23, (Washington: Government Printing Office, 1987), p. 256.

18. Tom Wicker, "The Democrats' Dilemma," *New York Times*, March 25, 1987, p. A27.

19. Slattery quoted in Jeffrey H. Birnbaum, "House Panel Finds Defense Spending Can't Be Cut Easily," *Wall Street Journal*, March 11, 1987, p. 6.

20. Interviews with anonymous staff persons (1) and (4).

21. Interviews with anonymous staff persons (10), (5), and (4).

22. Interview with anonymous staff person (1).

23. Interview with anonymous staff person (5).

24. Interview with anonymous staff person (4).

25. Interviews with anonymous staff persons (5) and (10). My interviews with members and staff produced other, remarkably similar accounts of Wright's ability to get his list of priorities into the Budget Committee's first budget resolution.

26. Latta quoted in Elizabeth Wehr, "Budget Moves to Full House amid Partisan Flak," *Congressional Quarterly Weekly Report*, April 4, 1987, p. 609.

27. Fazio quoted in Elizabeth Wehr, "Fiscal 1988 Budget Conference Remains Stalled," ibid., June 13, 1987, p. 1227.

28. See Jeffrey H. Birnbaum, "Democrats Kill Budget Proposal in Committee," *Wall Street Journal*, June 5, 1987, p. 4; and Tom Kenworthy, "House Liberals Balk at Budget Compromise," *Washington Post*, June 5, 1987, p. A4.

29. Russo quoted in Kenworthy, "House Liberals Balk at Budget Compromise," p. A4.

30. Gray quoted in Tom Kenworthy, "Senate Negotiators Reject House Defense Budget," *Washington Post*, June 11, 1987, p. A5.

31. See Tom Kenworthy, "House and Senate Democrats Finally Settle Budget Dispute," *Washington Post*, June 18, 1987, pp. A1, A8; and Elizabeth Wehr, "Democrats Agree on $1 Trillion 1988 Budget," *Congressional Quarterly Weekly Report*, June 20, 1987, p. 1298.

32. Miller quoted in Kenworthy, "House and Senate Democrats Finally Settle Budget Dispute," p. A8.

33. Reagan, *Weekly Compilation of Presidential Documents*, p. 685.

34. Gramm argued that when the annual deficit targets were originally calculated for fiscal 1986 through fiscal 1991, they had underestimated the size of deficit by about $50 billion for the first year. Consequently, the mandated deficit targets for subsequent years were unrealistically low. According to Gramm, the targets should be revised upward to accommodate the original miscalculation (see Elizabeth Wehr, "Congress Faces Backlog of Economic Decisions," *Congressional Quarterly Weekly Report*, September 5, 1987, pp 2121–22).

35. Rostenkowski quoted in Hook, "Speaker Jim Wright Takes Charge in the House," p. 1488.

36. See Elizabeth Wehr, "Democrats Snared in Gramm-Rudman Trap?" *Congressional Quarterly Weekly Report*, October 3, 1987, pp. 2394–95.

37. Rostenkowski quoted in Elizabeth Wehr, "Deficit Bill Rests on Risky $12 Billion Tax Hike," ibid., October 17, 1987, p. 2504.

38. Rostenkowski and Wright quoted in *Congressional Record*, October 20, 1987, pp. H8784, H8782.

39. For details on the Downey package, see Patrick L. Knudson, "House Will Try Again on Welfare Overhaul," *Congressional Quarterly Weekly Report*, October 31, 1987, p. 2655.

40. MacKay quoted in Elizabeth Wehr, "Southern Democrats Dislike Tax-Welfare Mix," ibid., October 17, 1987, p. 2505.

41. See Elizabeth Wehr, "Wright Finds a Vote to Pass Reconciliation Bill," ibid., October 31, 1987, 2653–55.

NOTES TO PAGES 195–207

42. See ibid., p. 2654.

43. Glickman quoted in Janet Hook, "Bitterness Lingers from House Budget Votes," ibid., November 7, 1987, p. 2712.

44. *Congressional Record*, October 29, 1987, p. H9142.

45. For an account of Wright's actions, see ibid., H9157–58.

46. Ibid., p. H9447.

47. Weber, Carr, and Russo quoted in Hook, "Bitterness Lingers from House Budget Votes," p. 2713.

48. Interview with anonymous staff person (5).

49. Panetta quoted in Janet Hook, "Congress Will Evade the Usual Budget Battles," *Congressional Quarterly Weekly Report*, February 20, 1988, p. 332; Lott quoted in Elizabeth Wehr, "Summit Deal Fails to Forestall Automatic Cuts," ibid., November 21, 1987, p. 2861.

50. MacKay and Wright quoted in Elizabeth Wehr, "As Dust Settles from Battle to Cut Deficit . . . Second Thoughts on Budget Summitry," ibid., December 26, 1987, p. 3188.

51. See Elizabeth Wehr, "Conferees Push to Finish Deficit-Reduction Bill," ibid., December 19, 1987, p. 3115.

52. See Jacqueline Calmes, "Reagan Wins Concessions in Final Funding Bill," ibid., December 26, 1987, p. 3185.

53. Reagan, *Weekly Compilation of Presidential Documents*, p. 1547.

54. Leath quoted in Janet Hook, "GOP Chafes under Restrictive Rules," *Congressional Quarterly Weekly Report*, October 10, 1987, p. 3184.

55. Miller quoted in Janet Hook, "Democrats Protest Catchall Bills," ibid., January 16, 1988, p. 126. See also Janet Hook, "House-Senate Acrimony Bedevils Democrats," ibid., February 13, 1988, p. 296.

56. Ronald Reagan, *Public Papers of the Presidents of the United States: Ronald Reagan, 1988* (Washington: Government Printing Office, 1990), p. 86; Foley quoted in Janet Hook, "Congress Will Evade the Usual Budget Battles," p. 332.

57. Interview with anonymous staff person (9).

58. Pepper quoted in Janet Hook, "GOP Chafes under Restrictive House Rules," p. 2451.

59. Interviews with anonymous staff persons (9) and (5).

60. Dixon and Whitten quoted in David Rapp, "Wright, Byrd Pushing to Finish All 13 Spending Bills by October 1," *Congressional Quarterly Weekly Report*, September 24, 1988, p. 2638.

61. Wright quoted in Cohen, "Full Speed Ahead," p. 242.

7. *Leadership in the Post-Reform House: Patterns and Paradoxes*

1. See also Bruce I. Oppenheimer, "The Changing Relationship between House Leadership and the Committee on Rules," in Mackaman, *Understanding Congressional Leadership;* and Bach and Smith, *Managing Uncertainty in the House.*

2. For a discussion of how partisanship affects House majority leadership of the opposition party, see Ripley, *Majority Party Leadership in Congress,* chap. 5.

3. Since the Democrats regained control of both chambers, Reagan's position was further weakened in 1987. But Wright still faced the possibility of competing with a Senate majority leader, fresh after six years in the minority. If the events of the budget cycle are at all meaningful, the struggle to reach a conference solution on the fiscal 1988 first budget resolution indicates that Wright's priorities met substantial resistance from Senate Democrats. Was Democratic control of the Senate an advantage or a liability for Wright? The question is debatable.

4. Steven S. Smith, "O'Neill's Legacy for the House," *The Brookings Review,* vol. 5 (1987), p. 35. Strangely enough, Smith seems to agree with me: "Personal qualities are important, especially at the margins, and margins count in legislative politics" (ibid., p. 35). But he never explores the individual factors that distinguish the styles of O'Neill and Wright.

5. This is essentially the point made by Jones in "Joseph G. Cannon and Howard W. Smith."

6. This is the central argument made by Barry, *The Ambition and the Power.* See also Peters, *The American Speakership,* pp. 273–80.

7. Enacting reforms to limit leaders' powers would seem to be a reasonable standard for determining if a leader violated the limits to leadership (at least as Jones defines those limits). His two cases of limits to leadership—Speaker Cannon and Rules Committee chairman Howard Smith—both involved reform (Jones, "Joseph G. Cannon and Howard W. Smith," p. 617).

Index

Adams, Brock, 55–58
Aid to Families with Dependent Children (AFDC), 194
Albert, Carl: and Budget Act of 1974, 231n17; individual style of, 55–59; as middleman, 31; as nurturer of budget process, 16, 53–59, 89, 209; as party leader, 47, 54, 214
Amendment process, and the budget, 62–63, 72
Anthony, Beryl, 93
Appropriations process, 4, 167–71, 202–06
Armstrong, William L., 97
Ashbrook, John, 67
Aspin, Les, 206
Atari Democrats, 137

Backdoor legislation, 33
Baker, Howard, 141, 150, 161, 198
Baker, James A., III, 122, 125, 139, 141, 179, 198
Balanced budget: and conflicting economic estimates, FY 1981, 235n46; as objective in late 1970s, 70–71, 82, 86
Balanced Budget and Deficit Control Act of 1985. See Gramm-Rudman-Hollings deficit reduction law (GRH)
Ball, William, 198
Bentsen, Lloyd, 179, 198
Bevill, Tom, 68
Black caucus, 186

BOB. See U.S. Bureau of the Budget
Bolling, Richard: as founder of the Budget Act of 1974, 42, 46, 55, 58, 72, 74, 236n50; and FY 1981 budget, 87; and Gang of Seventeen meetings, 139, 141; and lobbying against Gramm-Latta I, 113, 115–16; as House Rules Committee chairman, 139
Boll Weevils, 92, 95, 99, 148, 220
Brademas, John, 74
Breaux, John B., 118, 151
Brodhead, William, 74
Brown, Harold, 65
Buchanan, Christopher, 92
Budget Act (Congressional Budget and Impoundment Control Act) of 1974, 3–4, 9–10, 37–44, 76–78; ambiguity of, 25–26, 29, 55, 72, 213; ambiguous role of committees in, 44–45; ambiguous role of Speaker in, 44–45, 47–50, 55, 213; attempts to circumvent, 128; and executive branch, 48–50, 56, 126; formal procedures outlined in, 76–78; greater power given to Congress in, 29–45, 49; and House Rules Committee, 164; initial success of, 76–82; and new role for Speaker, 16, 19–23, 46–53, 211–13; power given to House Democrats in, 56; program functions of, 9, 227n13; and reconciliation process, 84; as revised by

Gramm-Rudman-Hollings, 3, 10;
and Speaker's role as nurturer of
budget process, 16, 46–53, 55;
timetable of, 38–40, 55, 159. *See
also* Gramm-Rudman-Hollings deficit reduction law
Budget and Accounting Act of 1921,
8, 29
Budget resolution. *See* First budget
resolution; Second budget resolution; Third budget resolution
Budget summit meeting of 1987, 191,
197–202, 207, 220
Budget task force, 1978, 67–69
Bureau of the Budget. *See* U.S. Bureau of the Budget
Burleson, Omar, 65
Burleson amendment, 65–66
Bush, George, 120
Byrd, Robert, 162, 189, 205

Caiden, Naomi, 130
Cannon, Joseph, 3, 12, 28, 228*n28*,
253*n7*
Cardin, Benjamin, 176
Carlucci, Frank, 198, 206
Carr, Bob, 197
Carter, Jimmy: balanced budget plan
of, 50, 52, 65, 68, 70–71; budget
ideas of, 128; and conflicts with
Congress over budget, 49–52, 58,
60–61, 64–67, 74–75, 77; defeat
of by Reagan, 91, 93–94; defense
spending requests of, 66, 69, 74–
75; indecisive fiscal policy of, 64–
67; job plan of, 64
Carter administration, 52, 60–61, 77
CBO. *See* Congressional Budget
Office
CDF. *See* Conservative Democratic
Forum
Chiles, Lawton, 163, 189, 198
Closed rule, 71–73, 112, 114
Coalitions, and Speaker's role, 62–64,
69, 73, 99
Coehlo, Tony, 155
Cohen, Richard, 172

COLA amendment, FY 1981 budget,
86–87
Committees. *See* U.S. Congress; U.S.
House of Representatives
Conable, Barber, 54
Congress. *See* U.S. Congress
Congressional Budget and Impound-
ment Control Act of 1974. *See*
Budget Act of 1974
Congressional Budget Office (CBO),
9, 37–38, 184
Conservative Democratic Forum
(CDF), 92
Conte, Silvio, 198
Continuing resolution, 167–71, 202

Dannemeyer, William, 186
Davidson, Roger, 44
Defense spending: in FY 1988 budget, 173, 180, 183, 187–90, 197;
increased in 1970s, 35, 52, 65–66,
68–69, 74–75; increased in 1980s,
91–92, 95–100, 104, 138, 141–42,
153–62, 197; Reagan's insistence
on, 170
Deficit: alleged underestimation of,
1986–91, 251*n34*; and Boll Weevils, 99–100; and budget conflicts
of 1970s, 16–17, 47, 51, 56, 58,
60, 65–67, 70, 78, 80, 82; and
budget conflicts of 1980s, 128,
130, 136–38, 146, 149–63; ceilings
for, FY 1986, 156; ceiling raised in
1987, 191–93; conflicting estimates
of, FY 1981, 235*n46*; detrimental
effect on budget process of, 164–
67, 172–80; and FY 1983 budget,
142, 156; and FY 1986 budget,
155–58; and Gramm-Latta I, 111;
impact on Speaker's role of, 214–
15; popular unconcern with,
250*n14*; as projected by OMB, FY
1987–88, 184–85; and Reagan's
1981 tax plan, 120, 122, 124. *See
also* Gramm-Rudman-Hollings deficit reduction law
Dellums, Ronald, 107

Democratic Leadership Council, 246n36

Democratic party: disunity of (1980s), 207, 209, 233n6, ideological divisions of (1970s), 46–54, 58–66; and liberal ratings for House Budget Committee members, 240n32; new power in House of, 54–57, 61, 63, 253n3; unity of (late 1980s), 186, 192, 201

"The Democratic Plan for Economic Recovery," 154

Democratic Steering and Policy Committee, 35

Democratic Study Group (DSG), 34–36

Derrick, Butler, 69, 189

Disaster loans, 80

Dixon, Julian, 205

Dole, Robert, 139, 146, 162, 198

Domenici, Pete, 123, 139–41, 162–63, 168, 198

Domestic and social programs: alleged inadequacy of funding for, 61, 66–69, 73–74, 80; battles over, 1983–86, 153–63; cuts in, 1981, 90–91, 95, 123; cuts in, 1982, 138; and Downey welfare amendment (1987), 194–95, 207; in FY 1984 budget, 169–70; and Gramm-Latta I, 109, 111; and Gramm-Latta II, 114–17; O'Neill's defense of, 61, 80, 101, 132–37, 143, 169–70; popular support for, 250n14. See also Aid to Families with Dependent Children; Food stamp program; Medicaid; Medicare; Welfare

Downey, Tom, 97, 176

Downey welfare amendment, 194–95, 207

DSG. See Democratic Study Group

Duberstein, Kenneth M., 139

Duncan, John, 198

Durbin, Richard, 176

Economy, and the budget: in the late 1970s, 51–52, 58, 64–70; in the 1980s, 91, 21–24, 130–38, 142, 147–50, 154; and Reagan victory, 1980, 91; supply-side theory of, 93, 119–20, 124, 136–37. See also Deficit

Ehrenhalt, Alan, 148

Entitlements, 37, 83, 237n68

Espy, Mike, 176–77

Executive branch: and Budget and Accounting Act of 1921, 8, 29; and Budget Act of 1974, 56; budget deadline for, 38; excessive power of, 1960s, 26; and Gramm-Latta II, 126; reduced power of, vis-à-vis Congress, 1970s, 48–50, 56, 58

"An Exercise in Hard Choices," 153

Fairness doctrine (FCC), 200

Fazio, Vic, 151, 158, 174, 189

First budget resolution: and Budget Act of 1974, 9–10, 20, 49; content of, 36–39; FY 1976, 57; FY 1978, 64; FY 1979, 67–68; FY 1980, 68–70; FY 1981, 70–76, 84; FY 1983, 142–46; FY 1985, 159–61; FY 1988, 173–74, 188–90; FY 1989, 203; increasing amendments to, late 1970s, 51, 63; and O'Neill, 67–76; as planning tool, 56; and Speaker's role, 59, 73, 163–64; as targets, 78, 80

Fisher, Joseph, 67

Foley, Thomas P., 72, 74, 175, 199, 202

Food stamp program, 194

Ford, Gerald, 214

Franklin, Webb, 176

Fraser, Donald, 35

Function 500, 69–70

Gang of Seventeen (1982), 139–40

GAO. See General Accounting Office

Garn, Jake, 123

General Accounting Office (GAO), 192

Gephardt, Richard, 74, 155, 172, 246n36

Gettinger, Stephan, 158

Giaimo, Robert, 61, 65–66, 70–75, 81–85
Glickman, Dan, 195
Gramm, Phil, 93, 97, 99, 103–04, 112, 191, 251n34
Gramm-Latta I, 91, 97–118
Gramm-Latta II, 110–18, 126
Gramm-Rudman-Hollings deficit reduction law (Balanced Budget and Deficit Control Act of 1985, GRH), 3, 10: and FY 1986 budget, 155–58; and 1987 budget summit, 199; and 1988 deficit target, 173, 177, 180, 183–84, 186, 188; revisions of, 10, 91, 97–118, 126, 128, 147, 191–93; and Speaker's role, 213
Grassley, Charles E., 97
Gray, Bill, 73, 157, 163, 177, 183–84, 186, 189, 198
Great Society, 59, 71, 132, 146, 155
Greider, William, 124
GRH. See Gramm-Rudman-Hollings deficit reduction law
Guarini, Frank, 176
Gypsy Moths, 115

Hansen Committee, 27
Hatfield, Mark, 198
Hawkins, Augustus F., 195
Hefner, Bill, 93, 99, 104, 176
Hefner amendment, 99, 102, 104
Hollings, Ernest, 74–75
Holt, Marjorie, 67, 92
House. See U.S. House of Representatives

Impoundment of funds, 31, 37, 231n17
Inflation, 70, 235n46
Interest rates, 51
Iran-Contra scandal, 172, 201, 217, 248n1

Johnston, Bennett, 198
Joint Commission on the Budget, 9
Joint Economic Committee, 38

Joint Study Commission on Budget Control (JSC), 32–36, 40, 79
Jones, Charles O., 26–27
Jones, Jim: conservatism of, 239n14, 246n31; and FY 1981 budget, 93–97, 99, 100–04, 111–14, 118, 120; and FY 1983 budget, 143–44, 154; and Gang of Seventeen, 139–40; and O'Neill, 134, 137
JSC. See Joint Study Commission on Budget Control

Kemp-Roth tax plan, 95, 154
King of the Mountain rule, 142

Latta, Delbert, 74–75, 87, 97, 99, 136, 163, 186, 198
Laxalt, Paul, 139–41
Leadership: combined influences on, 5–8, 13–15; and Congress, 5–8; and individual style, 5–8, 216–18; as interactive process, 5, 7–8; irrelevance of policy preferences to, 229n22; principal-agent model of, 227n10; and relation between leaders and followers, 218–22; and Speaker's role, 210–22
Leath, Marvin, 157–58, 202
Leferetti, Leo, 86
Legislative Reorganization Act of 1946, 9
Legislative Reorganization Act of 1970, 27, 62
Lew, Jack, 135
Lott, Trent, 198–99
Lowry, Mike, 151, 158, 178

MacKay, Buddy, 194, 199, 202
Madden, Ray J., 34
Mahon, David, 41
Mandate, presidential, 238n1
Martin, David, 41
Matsui, Robert, 172
Matsunaga, Spark, 40
Medicaid, 194, 200
Medicare, 200, 250n14
Meese, Edwin, 141

Michel, Robert, 113–14, 117, 123, 162, 196
Michel-Latta substitute (FY 1983 budget), 143
Miller, George, 102, 149, 151, 157, 160, 189, 202
Miller, James C., 198
Miller, Warren E., 94
Mineta, Norman, 69, 74
Moakley, Joe, 86
Mondale, Walter, 154, 177
MX missile, 161

New Deal, 59, 71, 132, 134, 138, 141, 146, 155
Nicaragua, 200
Nixon, Richard, 31, 37
Nofziger, Lyn, 100
Nunn, Sam, 206, 246n36

Oberstar, Jim, 176–77
Obey, David, 69, 73, 83–84, 93
Office of Management and Budget (OMB), 95, 112, 118, 126, 156,184–85, 192
Omnibus appropriations bill, 4, 200–02
O'Neill, Thomas P. (Tip): and agreement not to oppose Reagan for six months, 93–94, 126; and battle with Reagan's economic strategies, 119–22, 125–27, 136–42, 215; compared to Wright, 210–22; defense of domestic and social programs by, 61, 80, 101, 132–37, 143, 169–70, 215; and first budget resolutions, 67–76; and FY 1983 budget, 142–54; and Gramm-Latta I, 100–05, 111, 113; and Gramm-Latta II, 116–17; and Hefner amendment, 99; and House Budget Committee, 130–36, 147–63; ideological convictions of, 60–61, 68–70, 90; individual style of, 47, 49, 58–62, 216–18; lack of budgetary expertise of, 60–61, 129–35; as majority leader, 57, 64; as middleman, 89, 108, 129, 131, 133, 146–
47, 151, 171, 173, 182, 186, 217–18; as opposition party leader, 90–94, 101–05, 108, 128–42, 146; as party spokesman, 22, 105–10; as process manager, 16, 19, 58–62, 67–76, 168–71, 203, 219–20; and reconciliation process, 83–87; role conflict of, 18–19, 89, 108, 129–36, 139, 146, 164–67; defense of social security by, 140–42, 245n19; strong partisanship of, 59, 61, 130, 132, 136, 138–42, 159–67, 171, 173; and taxes, 119–22, 175, 179; use of whip system by, 217

Packwood, Bob, 198
Panetta, Leon, 74, 78, 82, 114, 124–25, 172, 178, 199
Pay-as-you-go budget (1985), 160–61
Peabody, Robert, 42–43
Pepper, Claude, 43–45, 204
Perkins, Carl D., 107, 109, 111
Peters, Ronald, 6
Pickle, J. J., 96
Political parties. See Democratic party; Speaker of the House; Republican party
President. See Executive branch
Program functions, of Budget Act of 1974, 9, 227n13

Ray, Bruce A., 28
Rayburn, Sam, 57
Reagan, Ronald: criticism of Congress by (1987), 202; declining support for (1982), 136–37; declining popularity of, 1986, 172–73, 178; declining popularity of, 1987, 87, 186, 202, 216–17, 253n3; and defense spending increases, 91–92, 95–100, 104, 138–42, 153–62, 170, 197; economic plan of (1982), 136–42, 147–54; election of, 91, 93–94; and FY 1981 budget, 90–95, 100; and FY 1984 budget, 169–70; and FY 1987 budget, 156–57; and FY 1988 budget,

186–87, 190–94; and Gramm-
Latta I, 97–110, 113–18; and
Gramm-Latta II, 116–18, 127,
242n53; and Iran-Contra scandal,
201, 248n1; lack of House support
(1983), 216–17; mandate of, 90–
95, 126–27, 238n1; 1981 tax plan
of, 120, 122, 124; persuasive lobbying by, 100, 119–22, 127, 162;
and request for balanced budget
amendment, 166; refusal of to raise
taxes, 119–22, 138–41, 157, 166,
177–80; and veto as enforcement
tool, 122–25, 169–70, 206
Reagan administration, 18–19, 91–92,
99, 111, 121–22
Reagan Democrats, 136
Reconciliation process: and committee
conflicts, 17; congressional resistance to, 53, 81–86, 91–93; and
FY 1983 budget, 144–46; and FY
1988 budget, 193–97, 200–01; and
Gramm-Latta I, 105–10; and
Gramm-Latta II, 110–18; O'Neill's
misgivings about, 61, 71, 145; pur-
pose of, according to Budget Act,
9–10, 39–40, 47–49, 232n30;
Speaker's role in, 47–49, 107–10,
164–67; and taxes, 144–46
Recorded teller (roll-call) vote. See
Roll-call (recorded teller) vote
Rees, Thomas, 40
Regan, Donald, 98, 124, 139
Reischauer, Robert, 164
Republican party, 233n6
Rhodes, John J., 59
Riders, to appropriations bills, 4
Ripley, Randall, 21
Robb, Charles, 246n36
Rodino, Peter, 107
Roll-call (recorded teller) vote,
27, 63
Roosevelt, Franklin D., 49
Rose Garden Plan (1984), 160–61
Rostenkowski, Dan, 119–21, 139,
179, 191–95, 198–99
Russo, Marty, 189, 197

Schick, Allen, 20, 30–31, 34,
44–45, 77
Schumer, Charles E., 158
SDI. See Strategic Defense
Initiative
Second budget resolution, 9,
39–40, 64
Senate Budget Committee, 74
Senate Finance Committee, 34
Seniority system, in Congress, 27
Sequestration process, and Gramm-
Rudman-Hollings, 10
Shanks, E. Merrill, 94
Sinclair, Barbara, 75, 85, 172
Slattery, Jim, 180
Smith, Howard, 253n7
Smith, Steven S., 28, 97, 217
Social security: assault on, 1981,
241n48, 245n19; congressional con-
trol over, 1970s, 34; and debate
over freezing COLAs, 1985, 162–
63; exempted from appropriations
decisions, 39; and FY 1976 budget, 57; and FY 1988 budget, 194;
and Gramm-Latta II, 115, 117;
O'Neill's defense of, 140–42,
245n19
Speaker of the House
———— Budgetary role of: and ambiguities of Budget Act, 44–45, 47–
50, 55, 213; and appropriations
process, 167–71; debate over, 40–
44, 91, 212–16; and first budget
resolution, 59, 73, 163–64; and
Gramm-Latta I, 107–10; and
Gramm-Rudman-Hollings, 213; as
nurturer, 16, 46–58, 77, 88–89; as
process manager, 16, 46–47, 88–
89, 90–91, 125–26, 152–54, 163–
64, 212; and reconciliation process,
47–49, 107–10, 164–67
———— And Congress: as coalition
builder, 92, 212–15; and congressional turf battles, 17; as "czar"
(1890–1910), 12; and House Budget Committee, 40–43, 81, 150–
58, 175; and House Rules

Committee, 10, 12–13, 27–29, 72, 212–13; as mediator, 110–18, 212–15

—— Leadership role of: changes in, 23–24, 56–63, 147–71, 210–16; conflicts in, 17–19, 107–10, 125–27, 171, 208, 229n22; impact of deficit on, 214–15; impact of external factors on, 213–16; impact of individual qualities on, 13–15; multiplicity of, 10–19; new powers outlined in Budget Act for, 16, 19–23, 46–53, 211–13; traditional limits on, 209, 211–12

—— As party leader: of majority party, 10–14, 17, 29, 43–44, 215; of opposition party, 16–17, 21–22, 125, 214–16; as party standard bearer, 19–23, 62, 214–15

Stenholm, Charles, 92–93, 202

Stockman, David: and attempt to cut social security COLAs, 245n19; discredited, 124; and FY 1983 budget, 150; and Gang of Seventeen (1982), 139–41; and Gramm-Latta II, 111–18; and 1981 Reagan budget, 93, 95–99; and 1981 Reagan tax plan, 120; and Phil Gramm, 103

Stock market crash, 1987, 194–95, 198, 201

Strategic Defense Initiative (SDI), 206

Supply-side economic theory, 119–20, 124, 136–37

Symms, Steven D., 97

Task force on legislative savings, 78–79

Tate, Dale, 171

Tax Equity and Fiscal Responsibility Act of 1982 (TEFRA), 145–46

Taxes: and budget summit (1987), 198–99, 201; and Congress, 33; and FY 1986 budget, 157–62; and FY 1987 budget, 156; and FY 1988 budget, 190–94, 197; increases in proposed by TEFRA (1982), 145–46; inequities of dur-ing 1970s, 35; popular opposition to raises in, 250n14; proposed cuts in, FY 1977, 64–67; Reagan's refusal to raise, 119–22, 138–42, 157–62, 166, 177–80; reductions in, first Reagan administration, 91, 95, 99, 119–22, 138–42; tied to defense expenditures, FY 1988, 190–204, 197; Wright's advocacy of raising, 175–79, 183

Tax Reform Act of 1986, 177–78, 249n12

TEFRA. See Tax Equity and Fiscal Responsibility Act of 1982

Third budget resolution, FY 1977, 64

Udall, Morris, 83, 109

Udall amendment, 83, 85

Ullman, Al, 43, 65

Underwood, Oscar, 228n19

Unemployment: and budgets of the late 1970s, 51, 64, 69–70, 235n46; Carter's plan to alleviate, 64; conflicting estimates of, FY 1981, 235n46; in 1981, 123; in 1982, 136, 143; in 1983, 147–50; and O'Neill's protection of benefits (1982), 143

U.S. Bureau of the Budget (BOB), 30

U.S. Congress: and Budget Act of 1974, 3–4, 29–45, 49, 56; characteristics of leadership in, 5–8; committee government of, 13, 78; and conflict between Senate and House (1982–86), 159; and need to reform budget process, 9, 26, 29, 31–47, 159; power of, vis-à-vis executive branch (1970s), 48–50, 56, 58; turf battles in, 17. See also Speaker of the House

U.S. Department of Health, Education, and Welfare, 67

U.S. Federal Communications Commission, 200

U.S. House of Representatives: black caucus of, 186; and campaign finance reform, 25; conflict among committees of, 17, 48; entrenched

committee system of, 20–21, 25–
29, 54; fragmentation of power in,
21–22, 25; and House Appropriations Committee, 17, 30, 33, 35,
79; and House Armed Services
Committee, 65–66, 206; and
House Committee on Committees,
12; and House Education and Labor Committee, 95; and House
Post Office and Civil Service
Committee, 84–85, 145; and
House Small Business Committee,
80; and House Steering and
Policy Committee, 12–13, 27–29,
40–41, 132–33, 150, 213, 249n8;
and House Ways and Means
Committee, 12, 27, 28, 30, 33–34,
119–21, 133
———— House Budget Committee:
ambiguities about function of, 80–
81; changing ideology among members of, 150–58; and conflicts with
House Appropriations Committee,
17; creation of, in Budget Act of
1974, 36–37, 40; impact of Wright
on, 175, 182–86; liberalism of Democrats on, 50–53, 64–69, 103–04,
240n32, 246n31; O'Neill's relation
to, 130–36, 147–63; Speaker's appointments to, 40–43, 150, 175;
term limits for members of, 41; traditional power of Speaker on, 150
———— House Rules Committee:
budget reform proposal of, 34–37;
and closed rule, 71–73; function
of, in Budget Act of 1974, 164;
limited power of in 1970s, 27–29;
1961 reform of, 13; Speaker's relation to, 10, 12–13, 27–29, 72, 204,
206, 212–13

USSR, 51

Vietnam War, 26

Wander, W. Thomas, 32, 34
War Powers Act, 49
Watergate scandal, 26, 59
Waxman, Henry, 200
Weber, Vin, 197
Weiss, Ari, 235, 141
Welfare, 207
Whip system, and budget process,
12, 67–58, 75, 217
Whitten, Jamie, 35–36, 43, 79, 84–
85, 168, 198, 205
Wicker, Tom, 179–80
Wildavsky, Aaron, 30
Williams, Pat, 151
Wright, Jim: activist style of, 173–86,
191, 203–09, 218, 221; budgetary
expertise of, 181–86; and budget
summit of 1987, 198–200; and
closed rule, 72; as coalition builder,
181–86; compared to O'Neill, 103,
210–22; elected Speaker (1986),
172; and FY 1981 budget, 74; and
FY 1983 budget, 141, 153; and FY
1986 budget, 162; and FY 1988
budget, 180, 187–91, 195–97,
201–06, 253n3; and House Steering and Policy Committee appointments, 249n8; individual style of,
216–18; as majority leader, 63, 67;
as opposition party leader, 22, 173,
191; as process manager, 16, 19,
173, 207; role conflicts of, 19; and
Senate Democrats, 253n3; tax initiatives of, 177–78, 180, 213; and
use of House Rules Committee,
204, 206

Pitt Series in Policy and Institutional Studies
Bert A. Rockman, Editor

The Acid Rain Controversy
James L. Regens and Robert W. Rycroft

Affirmative Action at Work: Law, Politics, and Ethics
Bron Raymond Taylor

Agency Merger and Bureaucratic Redesign
Karen M. Hult

The Aging: A Guide to Public Policy
Bennett M. Rich and Martha Baum

Arms for the Horn: U.S. Security Policy in Ethiopia and Somalia, 1953–1991
Jeffrey A. Lefebvre

The Atlantic Alliance and the Middle East
Joseph I. Coffey and Gianni Bonvicini, Editors

The Budget-Maximizing Bureaucrat: Appraisals and Evidence
André Blais and Stéphane Dion, Editors

Clean Air: The Policies and Politics of Pollution Control
Charles O. Jones

The Competitive City: The Political Economy of Suburbia
Mark Schneider

Conflict and Rhetoric in French Policymaking
Frank R. Baumgartner

Congress and Economic Policymaking
Darrell M. West

Congress Oversees the Bureaucracy: Studies in Legislative Supervision
Morris S. Ogul

Democracy in Japan
Takeshi Ishida and Ellis S. Krauss, Editors

Demographic Change and the American Future
R. Scott Fosler, William Alonso, Jack A. Meyer, and Rosemary Kern

Economic Decline and Political Change: Canada, Great Britain, and the United States
Harold D. Clarke, Marianne C. Stewart, and Gary Zuk, Editors

Executive Leadership in Anglo-American Systems
Colin Campbell, S.J., and Margaret Jane Wyszomirski, Editors

Extraordinary Measures: The Exercise of Prerogative Powers in the United States
Daniel P. Franklin

Foreign Policy Motivation: A General Theory and a Case Study
Richard W. Cottam

"He Shall Not Pass This Way Again": The Legacy of Justice William O. Douglas
Stephen L. Wasby, Editor

History and Context in Comparative Public Policy
Douglas E. Ashford, Editor

Homeward Bound: Explaining Changes in Congressional Behavior
Glenn Parker

How Does Social Science Work? Reflections on Practice
Paul Diesing

Imagery and Ideology in U.S. Policy Toward Libya, 1969–1982
Mahmoud G. ElWarfally

The Impact of Policy Analysis
James M. Rogers

Interests and Institutions: Substance and Structure in American Politics
Robert H. Salisbury

Iran and the United States: A Cold War Case Study
Richard W. Cottam

Japanese Prefectures and Policymaking
Steven R. Reed

Making Regulatory Policy
Keith Hawkins and John M. Thomas, Editors

Managing the Presidency: Carter, Reagan, and the Search for Executive Harmony
Colin Campbell, S.J.

The Moral Dimensions of Public Policy Choice: Beyond the Market Paradigm
John Martin Gillroy and Maurice Wade, Editors

Native Americans and Public Policy
Fremont J. Lyden and Lyman H. Legters, Editors

Organizing Governance, Governing Organizations
Colin Campbell, S.J., and B. Guy Peters, Editors

Party Organizations in American Politics
Cornelius P. Cotter et al.

Perceptions and Behavior in Soviet Foreign Policy
Richard K. Herrmann

Pesticides and Politics: The Life Cycle of a Public Issue
Christopher J. Bosso

Policy Analysis by Design
Davis B. Bobrow and John S. Dryzek

The Political Failure of Employment Policy, 1945–1982
Gary Mucciaroni

Political Leadership: A Source Book
Barbara Kellerman, Editor

The Politics of Public Utility Regulation
William T. Gormley, Jr.

The Politics of the U.S. Cabinet: Representation in the Executive Branch, 1789–1984
Jeffrey E. Cohen

Politics Within the State: Elite Bureaucrats and Industrial Policy in Authoritarian Brazil
Ben Ross Schneider

The Presidency and Public Policy Making
George C. Edwards III, Steven A. Shull, and Norman C. Thomas, Editors

Private Markets and Public Intervention: A Primer for Policy Designers
Harvey Averch

The Promise and Paradox of Civil Service Reform
Patricia W. Ingraham and David H. Rosenbloom, Editors

Public Policy in Latin America: A Comparative Survey
John W. Sloan

Reluctant Partners: Implementing Federal Policy
Robert P. Stoker

Roads to Reason: Transportation, Administration, and Rationality in Colombia
Richard E. Hartwig

The SEC and Capital Market Regulation: The Politics of Expertise
Ann M. Khademian

Site Unseen: The Politics of Siting a Nuclear Waste Repository
Gerald Jacob

The Speaker and the Budget: Leadership in the Post-Reform House of Representatives
Daniel J. Palazzolo

The Struggle for Social Security, 1900–1935
Roy Lubove

Tage Erlander: Serving the Welfare State, 1946–1969
Olof Ruin

Traffic Safety Reform in the United States and Great Britain
Jerome S. Legge, Jr.

Urban Alternatives: Public and Private Markets in the Provision of Local Services
Robert M. Stein

The U.S. Experiment in Social Medicine: The Community Health Center Program, 1965–1986
Alice Sardell